Management Information Systems

Management Information Systems

A Handbook for Modern Managers

DONALD W. KROEBER

THE FREE PRESS
A Division of Macmillan Publishing Co., Inc.
NEW YORK

Collier Macmillan Publishers
LONDON

The Free Press
A Division of Macmillan Publishing Co., Inc.
866 Third Avenue, New York, N.Y. 10022

Collier Macmillan Canada, Inc.

Library of Congress Catalog Card Number: 81–71954

Printed in the United States of America

printing number
1 2 3 4 5 6 7 8 9 10

Library of Congress Cataloging in Publication Data

Kroeber, Donald W.
  Management information systems.

  Includes index.
  1. Management information systems. I. Title.
T58.6.K76   658.4'038   81–71954
ISBN 0-02-917990-4   AACR2

To Jamie, with love

Contents

List of Figures   *ix*

List of Tables   *xiii*

Preface and Acknowledgments   *xv*

Part   I   The Foundations of MIS   **1**

    1. An Introduction to MIS   3

    2. Computer Hardware and Software   20

    3. Data Processing   46

    4. Decision Making   63

Part II   The Management of MIS   **95**

    5. MIS and Management   97

    6. MIS and Organizations   117

    7. The MIS Life Cycle   132

Part III   The Structure of MIS   **167**

    8. An Overview of MIS   169

    9. Data Base Management Systems   185

   10. MIS Activity Levels   206

   11. Functional Subsystems of MIS   222

Appendix

    A. Flowchart Symbols   *247*

    B. Glossary of Terms   *249*

Index   *259*

List of Figures

1-1   Diagram of a System   10

1-2   The Hierarchy of Systems   13

1-3   Control in a Heating System   13

1-4   Control in an MIS   14

2-1   Computer Hardware Components   22

2-2   Magnetic Tape   25

2-3   Magnetic Disk Pack   26

2-4   Preparation of Data for Card Input   28

2-5   Punched Cards   29

2-6   Distributed Systems   38

3-1   COBOL File Description   48

3-2   Sequential Files   50

3-3   Random File   51

3-4   Card System   52

3-5   Tape System   53

3-6   Disk System   55

3-7   Batch Processing   57

3-8   Transactional Processing   59

3-9   Real-time Processing   60

3-10 Data Processing and MIS   61

4-1   Decision Environments   64

4-2   Dimensions of the Decision Environment   67

4-3   Decision Tree with Simple Probabilities   73

4-4   Decision Tree with Revised Probabilities   75

4-5   Decision to Wait for Indicator   76

4-6   Linear Programming Graph   78

4-7   Minimizing Annual Inventory Costs   79

4-8   Optimum Order Size   80

4-9   Financial Decision without Discounting   81

4-10 Financial Decision with Discounting   83

4-11 Trend Analysis of Amusement Park Attendance   87

4-12 Trend Analysis of Polaroid's Annual Net Earnings   87

4-13 Regression Analysis of Hot Dog Sales   89

4-14 Process Generator for Demand on Inventory   91

5-1   The Management Cycle   98

5-2   The Hierarchy of Management   102

5-3   The Allocation of Managers' Time   103

5-4   Management Functions and MIS Activities   104

5-5   The Impact of Computers on Management   113

5-6   Management Levels and Decision Making   115

6-1   First Generation Computer Location   118

6-2   Second Generation Computer Location   119

6-3   Third Generation MIS Location   120

6-4a Current MIS Organization—Activity Orientation   122

6-4b Current MIS Organization—Project Orientation   122

6-4c Current MIS Organization—Life-cycle Orientation   122

6-5   MIS in a State Division of Motor Vehicles   127

6–6   MIS in a Multibranch Bank   128

6–7   MIS in a Multiplant Manufacturing Firm   129

7–1   MIS Project Life Cycle   133

7–2   MIS Project Management Team   138

7–3   Partial Gantt Chart for MIS Project   140

7–4   Partial PERT Network for MIS Project   141

7–5   Sample Systems Flowchart   147

7–6   Sample Programming Flowchart   148

8–1   A Classification of Models   170

8–2   The Processing Dimension of an MIS   172

8–3   The Processing and Activity Dimensions of an MIS   176

8–4   The Functional Dimension of an MIS at the Transaction-
      processing Activity Level   181

8–5   The Functional Dimension of an MIS at the Tactical Activ-
      ity Level   182

8–6   A Three-dimensional View of an MIS Model   183

9–1   An Expanded View of the Data Base Management
      System   187

9–2   Schema for a Data Base on Computer Customers   188

9–3   A City Map   189

9–4   Subschema for Leased Equipment Fees by State   190

9–5   Route Map from the High School to Northside Park   190

9–6   A Tree Data Structure   192

9–7   Inverted Trees   193

9–8   A Plex Data Structure   193

9–9   Relational View of a Data Base   194

9–10 Schema Description in Data Definition Language   195

9-11   Partial Logical Entry in a Computer Customer Data
       Base   197

9-12   Data Values for Computer Customer Schema   198

9-13   Data Entry Format for Loading the Data Base   199

10-1   Decision Processes at Different Activity Levels   208

10-2   Data Requirements at Different Activity Levels   211

10-3   Problem Identification at Different Activity Levels   212

10-4   Model Usage at Different Activity Levels   213

10-5   Choice Criteria at Different Activity Levels   215

10-6   Activity Levels in an Automobile Insurance Company
       MIS   217

11-1   Information Exchange among Functional Subsystems   223

11-2   Application Modules in Functional Subsystems   224

11-3   The Production Subsystem   225

11-4   The Marketing Subsystem   232

11-5   The Finance Subsystem   242

11-6   The Personnel Subsystem   244

List of Tables

2-1   Computer Input Devices   33

2-2   Computer Output Devices   36

2-3   Classification of Computers   44

4-1   Payoff Table for an Electronics Firm   68

4-2   Maximax View of Expected Profits   68

4-3   Maximin View of Expected Profits   69

4-4   Opportunity Loss for an Electronics Firm   70

4-5   Minimax View of Opportunity Loss   71

4-6   Payoff Table with Expected Values   72

4-7   A Product Mix Problem   77

4-8   Hot Dog Sales and Winning Percentages   88

7-1   Partial Milestone Schedule for an MIS Project   140

10-1 Representative Characteristics of Activity Levels   207

11-1 A Cash-flow Budget   240

Preface and Acknowledgments

Of all the buzzwords in the lexicon of business, few are used with less understanding than "MIS."

When management information systems became fashionable in the early 1960s, many organizations acquired MIS with the stroke of a pen by redesignating their data processing systems. In recent years, however, there has emerged among scholars and practitioners a clearer, if not yet precise, concept of just what constitutes an MIS. And the key word here is *concept*. Because an MIS is at least partially conceptual and partially physical.

This book addresses both aspects of MIS and attempts to tie them together in a unified model. The physical component—computer hardware—and the data processing function usually associated with it are discussed along with conceptual components of management, organizational structure, and decision making. Finally, an MIS is described in terms of the management structure it supports and the way it coordinates information flows among various functional departments.

This is a book for managers who can reason deductively—from the general to the specific. From a broad description of methods and capabilities to the much narrower application in one department of a given organization. It is not a cookbook. Not that there is anything wrong with cookbooks; they are wonderful aids in cooking—or in TV repair, or any other specific task. But there is no universal recipe for MIS because there is no universal formula for organizations. This book should serve equally well managers in service industries, manufacturing, government, education, and other areas.

Many debts of gratitude are incurred during the writing of a book, and this one is no exception. It is impossible to acknowledge everyone who contributed in some fashion—former teachers who stimulated the imagination, colleagues who offered suggestions, clients who provided examples (good and bad), and friends who gave encouragement—but some deserve special recognition: Hugh Watson who reviewed the entire manuscript and offered numerous suggestions for improvement; Lester Bittel who reviewed Chapters 5 and 6, similarly; Phyllis Price who typed the manuscript with her usual efficiency; my students at James Madison University who acted (unwittingly) as guinea pigs for many of the ideas presented here; and, most of all, my wife, Jamie, without whose patience, support, and encouragement this book could not be possible.

In spite of all the care on the part of the author, the typist, the reviewers, and the editors, errors invariably remain and, where they do, the responsibility is, of course, mine and errors called to my attention will be gratefully received.

DWK

Management Information Systems

PART I

The Foundations of MIS

This is a *practical* guide to management information systems. It is tempting, therefore, to launch into an immediate description of an operating MIS, to describe what it does and how it does it, and to tell managers exactly how to use it to their benefit.

Such an approach is not impossible and the reader who follows that description with care would undoubtedly learn a great deal about the MIS described. But how well that reader could apply his or her newly gained knowledge to a different MIS in a different environment is questionable. After all, tinkering with a Volkswagen may be informative, but it does not teach one all there is to know about automobiles.

A better preparation for the manager who would understand MIS more thoroughly is to first become familiar with certain theoretical building blocks. That is the approach followed in this book and the building blocks that form the foundation of MIS are discussed in the first four chapters.

Chapter 1 is an introduction that covers a number of relevant topics, but that focuses on one rather important foundation of MIS—the concept of a *system*. The systems view explains how the many, seemingly independent, parts of an MIS work together to improve operations and decision making in an organization.

1

Chapter 2 discusses computer hardware and software. It is sometimes tempting to view a computer as a "black box" that will tell managers anything they need to know. The truth of the matter is that computers have not progressed to that state—yet—and until they do it is helpful to know something about their capabilities and limitations.

Chapter 3 covers the subject of data processing. Although MIS are different from data processing, the two are closely related and MIS are very much dependent upon data processing systems. This chapter is not an exhaustive discourse on data processing, naturally, but touches on data processing principles of importance to MIS.

The fourth foundation chapter is devoted to decision making. It is the author's point of view that MIS exist to serve managers and that the most important thing managers do is make decisions. The subject of decision making is perhaps more appropriate for a *book,* and a *chapter* can only scratch the surface. Chapter 4 therefore describes only those decision tools and models most commonly incorporated into MIS.

Those who would still prefer to dispense with the foundations are reminded of the admonition of Euclid to King Ptolemy I of Egypt. When Ptolemy, who had sent for Euclid to teach him geometry, protested the length of the 13 volumes of *The Elements,* Euclid reportedly replied, "There is no royal road to geometry." Neither is there a royal, or even a managerial, road to MIS.

CHAPTER 1

An Introduction to MIS

Management Information Systems are not new. Managers have always had systems to provide themselves information. Some of the oldest known examples of written language are on clay tablets that preserve the transactions of ancient Mediterranean merchants. When deciphered by archaeologists, the similarity of these records to modern management reports is almost eerie: there are inventory records, accounting statements, receivables, and even what appear to be production records of piece-rate workers.

The need for management information has not been restricted to commerce and industry. In the public sector, governments have felt obliged to collect and maintain information on the number and wealth of their citizens for as long as there have been governments. And there is no sign that government's appetite for information will be diminished in the future.

Clearly, organizations in government and business have survived with traditional, even primitive, methods of gathering information. But recently, a great deal has been written and said on this apparently old subject of management information systems or MIS. What now makes MIS so important? Why are time-proven methods no longer adequate? In short, why all the fuss about MIS?

WHY MIS ARE IMPORTANT

Growth has a way of sneaking up on us. For hundreds of thousands of years, the earth accommodated its human tenants with ease. Now suddenly we seem to be taxing the resources of our planet to their very limits. So it has been with organizations. Changes that once took place at an evolutionary rate now seem more revolutionary in their impact on the way we conduct business. Specifically, the nature of modern organizations, the current legal and social environment, advancing technology, and the expanding role of management have created information needs that cannot be satisfied by traditional means. A closer examination of these four areas will underscore the demand for more sophisticated management information.

THE NATURE OF MODERN ORGANIZATIONS

Although only 5 percent of the ten million or so nonfarm businesses in the United States are classified as "large" (i.e., not small) by the Small Business Administration, that 5 percent accounts for over one-half of the national output of goods and services and employs over 40 percent of the labor force. We already have seen the first "one-million-employee firm" (AT&T) and rising oil prices will soon drive annual sales of the largest oil company (Exxon) over the $100-billion mark. When one envisions the volume of data associated with the operation of such firms, it is no surprise that the sheer size of many modern organizations led them to pioneer systems for the management of information. But while size motivated early development efforts, it is no longer a prerequisite for an MIS. Indeed, the most recent developments in computer technology have contributed more to the establishment of MIS in small organizations than in large ones. Minicomputers, data communications devices, microprocessors, and vendor-prepared software packages have all served to bring MIS within the budget of the small business.

Not only are many modern organizations large, they are also diverse—diverse in the variety of products or services they offer, in the number of subsidiary plants and offices they maintain, and in the number of other firms with which they deal. The larger retail corporations, particularly those with mail order operations, maintain inventories of several hundred thousand different items. When variations in size and color are considered, there can be millions of different items in inventory. If a computer were used to do nothing more than keep track of these items, it would be well worth the associated costs. But make those inventory records part of a management information system, and they also form the basis for decisions on pricing, ordering, advertising, and purging items.

The MIS is particularly useful when company operations are scattered geographically. Parts needed in one plant of a company may well be gathering dust on the shelves of another plant without an MIS to make managers aware of their whereabouts. Automobile dealers frequently make use of such systems to share their inventories of spare parts and, sometimes, whole automobiles.

It is a rare firm today that starts with only raw materials and manufactures a finished product for the consumer. As an extreme example, consider the automobile, which is *assembled* rather than fabricated in the plant from which it emerges in its final form. Hundreds of vendors supply components from tires to spark plugs to quartz clocks. The management of information on the specifications, price, availability, shipping time, and reliability of these components is even more critical and more difficult than maintaining records of in-house inventories. The modern production manager does not make decisions solely on the basis of internal information but relies heavily on the MIS to provide vendor-related data as well.

THE LEGAL AND SOCIAL ENVIRONMENT

The U.S. Government has over 60 agencies with the power to regulate, either directly or indirectly, business activities. The old, familiar ones such as the Interstate Commerce Commission, the International Trade Commission, the Federal Trade Commission, and the Federal Power Commission have been joined by a host of newcomers such as the Consumer Product Safety Commission, the Equal Employment Opportunity Commission, the Occupational Safety and Health Review Administration, and the Environmental Protection Agency. Although there are great jurisdictional differences among agencies, all have one common impact upon businesses: they require, explicitly or implicitly, the maintenance of records or the preparation of reports to show compliance with agency regulations. Whether the social benefit of these regulations is greater or less than the cost of monitoring compliance with them is moot. What is of immediate significance to managers is that much of the data required for these records and reports is routinely processed by the firm in other applications. For example, the reports for workmen's compensation insurance include all the data required for the OSHA log of occupational injuries and illnesses. If the data for one report are captured and stored in such a way to make them available for the second report, the additional cost of preparing the second report may be only a few seconds of computer time. One may still find fault with "Big Brother" trends in government, but the associated information processing costs can be minimized if the firm has considered regulatory requirements in the design of its MIS.

ADVANCING TECHNOLOGY

To a large extent, methods of collecting and analyzing management information are driven by the technological sophistication of the production process. In the preindustrial revolution cottage industries, handcrafted output was counted and perhaps inspected visually to satisfy management's need for quantity and quality data. For comparison, consider the high-technology industry that produces integrated circuit chips: in order to accommodate the 250,000 or so circuit elements represented on each chip, it must be laid out on a "blueprint" approximately 20,000 times full size; tolerances on the chip itself, which is only one-quarter-inch square, are measured in millionths of an inch; and, in spite of the sterile production environment, stray dust particles and other imperfections render about 10 percent of the chips useless. Clearly, this industry requires sophisticated information-gathering techniques to satisfy management that the process is under control. No human eye can detect flaws in chips nor can the human hand etch the delicate pattern on the surface of the semiconductor. Managers must rely on computers to control the production process as well as to furnish information on the quality of the final product.

The role of the computer is easily accepted in tasks that cannot be accomplished otherwise. The electronics firm is one example; the computation of mid-course corrections that guided astronauts safely to the moon and back is another. But managers have in the past been strangely reluctant to accept the help of computers in more common situations. It is one thing to entrust the lives of astronauts to a computer, but it is quite another matter to entrust the cash flow budget to one. Today, managers can no longer ignore advancing computer technology when it comes to the management of information. The competitive edge gained by the innovative firms that first developed computer-based information systems leaves little choice. To try to manage information without a computer today is about as practical as making integrated circuit chips with a soldering iron. Indeed, the computer is undoubtedly the single most compelling reason for the current level of interest in MIS.

THE EXPANDING ROLE OF MANAGEMENT

At one time, a thorough schooling in the fundamental operations of the firm was thought to be the best preparation for a management position. While the "office-boy-to-president" rise may not have been nearly so common as the Horatio Alger stories would lead us to believe, many senior executives in U.S. industry did in fact "rise from the ranks." Even more typical was the middle manager who, for example, started as a salesperson and rose to head of the marketing department after 15 or 20 years with the same firm.

Today we believe that the functions of management are, for the greater part, industry-independent (see Chap. 5). In other words, managers in the automobile industry have approximately the same duties and responsibilities as managers in, say, the office equipment industry. This has given a great deal of mobility to American managers, of course, but, more important, it lends a note of stability to the tasks of management and the information-producing processes that support those tasks. If managing an automobile manufacturing firm were totally unique, then so too would the automobile manufacturer's MIS be unique. And the office equipment manufacturer's MIS, and the catalog sales firm's MIS, and so on. Certainly under such conditions a book like this, which addresses MIS in generic terms, would not be possible. But happily (for the reader *and* the author), this is not the case. Just as management functions are transferable among industries within the private sector—and even between the private and public sector—so are the concepts that underlie management information systems.

Not only is it *possible* for a manager to attain a position of responsibility without having devoted his or her entire career to one specialized field, in many cases it is also *desirable* to follow some other route. No manager today operates in the vacuum of a single functional area. It is often helpful to have had experience (real or educational) in other functional areas. For example, a marketing decision may be based as much on production and financial information as on marketing information. Without some knowledge of how the production and finance departments operate, a manager cannot properly understand and use information from them. And if it is important for managers to be familiar with operations in other departments, it is doubly important for the information system to cut across departmental lines. The interdepartmental nature of MIS is a theme that recurs throughout this book.

Finally, just as modern production processes have become more complicated with advancing technology, so have the decision-making tools available to modern managers. Regression analysis, linear programming, Monte Carlo simulation, Performance Evaluation and Review Technique (PERT), and other management science/operations research methods are widely used throughout government and industry (see Chap. 4). While the mathematical and statistical processes involved in these methods have been known for years, practical applications in management are fairly recent developments. Once again, it is the computer that has facilitated the application of the technology. The sheer computational complexity of a realistic problem in, say, linear programming is so great and so error-prone as to preclude manual solution. The speed and accuracy of the computer, along with modern collegiate business school curricula which stress such subjects, have turned the mathematician's toys into everyday management tools.

WHAT IS AN MIS?

The case for studying MIS has been stated. Those in agreement, and perhaps some who do not agree, are now entitled to a preview of what they are about to examine. There is no generally accepted definition of an MIS, but we can synthesize one from the works of scholars in the field:

> *A management information system is an organized set of processes that provides information to managers to support the operations and decision making within an organization.*

Most of the terms in this definition are used in their normal context and need little further explanation, although much more is said on *decision making, management,* and *organizations* in Chapters 4, 5, and 6. The term *information* is commonly defined as "processed data" in an MIS or data processing context. This definition emphasizes the fact that an MIS is more than just a data collection network; data is refined and transformed for specific management purposes in an MIS.

SYSTEMS

The one term in the definition of an MIS that is used in a rather special, rigidly defined sense is *system.* Systems concepts are extremely important to the understanding of MIS and will be discussed in some detail here.

GENERAL SYSTEMS THEORY

In the 1950s, a group of scientists led by Kenneth Boulding and Ludwig von Bertalanffy founded the Society for General Systems Research to further a "systems approach" to traditional fields of study. The principles involved in this approach are known collectively as General Systems Theory or GST. It must be pointed out that GST has its detractors, and there certainly are practical limits to the application of GST. But the fact remains that GST had a great impact on early MIS research and is still useful in explaining certain MIS characteristics even when the designers do not consciously follow GST principles. Some of the tenets of GST that are particularly helpful in understanding the systems nature of an MIS are explained briefly.

Systems transform inputs into outputs. All but the lowest level of systems involve some sort of transformation process.[1] It has become conventional to illustrate the transformation process by the symbols shown in Figure 1–1. This figure also illustrates a point made earlier—that information is processed data.

FIGURE 1-1.   Diagram of a system.

Systems are interdisciplinary.   One of the main concerns of the founders of the Society for General Systems Research was the tendency of scientists to overspecialize, thus isolating themselves from developments in other fields that might apply to their own. The use of exotic materials developed for spacecraft in the fabrication of prosthetic devices illustrates this kind of transference between aerospace science and medical technology.

The fact that managers in one industry could benefit from the experiences of managers in another industry had been recognized for some time when GST was first advocated, but there are even greater interdisciplinary implications in MIS. First, the physical components of the MIS are products of disciplines far removed from management. It is doubtful that computers, telecommunications devices, and other peripherals would have been developed solely to meet the information-processing needs of managers. Second, many of the modern management tools facilitated by these physical components were also developed without management applications in mind. Linear programming, regression analysis, and other operations research methods are mathematical in origin but have been adapted to management purposes. The modern MIS not only borrows these tools from other disciplines, it also shares them among branches of its own discipline. Thus, we may find marketing managers using the same linear regression model to forecast sales that financial managers use to predict the availability of capital funds.

Systems are holistic.   The proper functioning of a system is a result of the interdependence of its parts. Therefore, the system must be viewed as a whole, considering all parts, even though only one may be of immediate concern. The value of a holistic approach is quite evident in environmental matters. The entomologist, for example, must consider the whole ecosystem when developing a pesticide. There is little point in wiping out potato bugs if the potatoes are also destroyed in the process. Interdependencies in MIS are less dramatic, but still important enough to warrant a holistic view. Market research information influences product design and production scheduling, production volumes determine personnel requirements, the hiring of personnel creates financial obligations, and so on. Only if the MIS is viewed in its entirety can these relationships be incorporated into the information flow. We now routinely design MIS from a holistic point of view; it has not always been so and, directly or indirectly, we have GST to thank for it.

Systems are differentiated. Although it is important to view a system holistically, one must not lose sight of the fact that systems consist of a number of different parts. In fact, one of the simpler definitions of a system is that it is a "set of related parts." It almost goes without saying that an MIS has many parts. At a minimum, the kind of MIS addressed here will have a computer, input and output devices, storage facilities, personnel to manage and operate the computer and associated equipment, procedures for the collection of data, programs to analyze data and produce output, instructions for the interpretation of output, and, of course, managers to use the output.

Systems are synergistic. Synergism is sometimes defined as the quality of the "whole exceeding the sum of its parts." This should not be taken literally, of course, but in the figurative sense that the system is capable of results not possible from the individual efforts of its parts. Suppose an automobile stalls at a railroad crossing a few minutes before a fast freight train is due. The four occupants might choose to push the car for one minute each, or to push all together for 60 seconds. The latter approach is synergistic in that the four pushing in concert will undoubtedly move the car farther and faster than the sum of the four individual efforts. In an MIS, it is possible to have one part of the system serve the accounting department and none other while another part serves only the marketing department. The total benefits to the organization from such a system are far less than they would be if the parts were integrated. In particular, top management suffers when the parts of an MIS do not combine synergistically. The fact that MIS in the past have not satisfied top management's information needs especially well is partially a reflection on MIS designers' inability to achieve synergism.

Systems are hierarchical.   When a part of a system is itself a system, we call it a *subsystem* to avoid confusion in terminology. Similarly, the system may be part of a larger system, which is then referred to as a *suprasystem.* This hierarchy of nested systems is useful in examining MIS and their role in the organization. MIS have subsystems. In this book, subsystems are defined according to function—accounting, finance, marketing, production, and so on. MIS are also part of a suprasystem—the organization. Labor, management, and the physical plant may be thought of as additional systems in the organization. As parts of a suprasystem, they bear the same relationship to each other and the MIS as the parts of the MIS do to each other. In both cases, differentiated parts must work together to achieve a synergistic effect. The MIS designer must not only integrate parts of the MIS, he or she must also integrate the MIS into other parts of the organization.

Beyond the suprasystem lies the environment. In a sense, the environment is like a suprasuprasystem in that it contains other systems and/or suprasystems. Environmental systems that are of particular significance include the government, the community, customers, and competitors.

The terminology of hierarchical systems can be confusing. Often times the hierarchical term used is dependent on one's point of view. When examining the MIS, we refer to the organization as the suprasystem. If organizations were our major concern, we might consider a single organization to be a system, its MIS to be a *sub*system, and the business community to be the suprasystem. Figure 1–2 illustrates the hierarchy and terminology used in this book.

Systems must be regulated.   In keeping with the interdisciplinary nature of systems and GST, we justify this statement with a concept borrowed from physics—entropy. Entropy is the state of maximum disorder in which the parts of the system have only random relationships with one another. Closed systems, those that do not interface with their environment, constantly tend toward entropy. MIS are no exception to this rule. An MIS left untended will quickly break down. As information needs change, as government regulations are created, as competition increases, and as the organization itself changes, an unregulated MIS will become less and less efficient in its purpose.

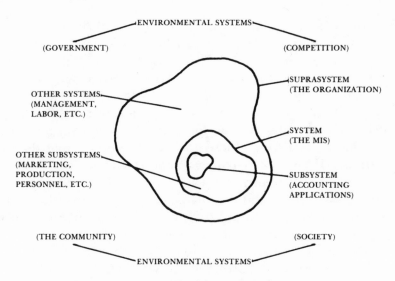

FIGURE 1-2.   The hierarchy of systems.

Regulation is achieved by a control subsystem. Inputs to this subsystem may be from the environment or *feedback* from the output of the system itself. Outputs of the control subsystem in turn regulate system inputs. These concepts are illustrated in Figure 1-3 for the familiar home heating system in which fuel is converted into heat through a burning process under the control of a thermostat.

Systems are goal-oriented.   The earlier, simple definition of a system should now be amended to read, "A system is a set of related parts that work together to achieve a goal." The impor-

FIGURE 1-3.   Control in a heating system.

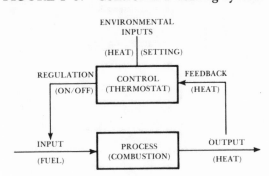

tance of goals and objectives to the successful operation of an organization needs little repetition here. What may need some comment, however, is the fact that those organizational goals and objectives also guide the MIS. To be sure, MIS managers will have certain unique goals pertaining to the MIS—goals that set standards for accuracy of information, timeliness of reports, physical security, and the like. It is all too easy for MIS managers to become totally absorbed in these goals and to forget that the purpose of the MIS is to serve management. If a mail-order house has an objective to fill all orders within 48 hours of receipt, then the efforts of the MIS and its managers, as well as the order-processing department and its managers, should be directed toward the accomplishment of that objective. Unfortunately, many managers in the past were made to feel that they were supporting the data processing department, rather than the reverse. MIS personnel are *still* trying to convert those turned-off managers.

Goals and objectives are also inputs to the control subsystem in an MIS. MIS managers evaluate output from the information processor in light of organizational goals and objectives and, if necessary, direct changes to maintain the system. The control subsystem as it applies to an MIS is illustrated in Figure 1–4.

MANAGEMENT INFORMATION SYSTEMS

The theoretical picture of an MIS now becomes somewhat clearer. MIS transform data into information that managers use to control, and make decisions concerning, the operation of an organization. The system consists of hardware (computer equip-

FIGURE 1–4.   Control in an MIS.

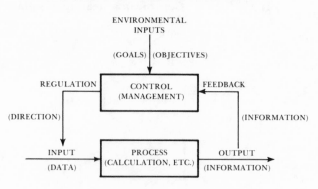

ment), software (computer programs), procedures, and people. The use of these parts in functionally defined applications, such as marketing,. production, and so on, forms the basis for a set of subsystems within the MIS. The sharing of data and software between subsystems increases the total benefit of the system to the organization and its management. The MIS is management-oriented but also draws on computer science for its hardware components, on mathematics and operations research for some of its software, and on psychology and sociology to make its human component more effective. The MIS supports the goals and objectives of the organization and MIS managers exercise control over the MIS to ensure that MIS efforts are directed toward this end.

Theory helps one *understand;* it is not particularly useful as a guide for day-to-day operation. The specifics of how an MIS operates in a typical business firm are described in Part III.

THE ROLE OF COMPUTERS IN MIS

There certainly was no computer in the information systems of ancient Mediterranean merchants, nor, for that matter, in any information system before the mid-1950s. Yet now there is reference to computers in almost every mention of MIS. Is a computer an indispensable part of an MIS? If so, were there really MIS before the introduction of computers?

The answer to both questions is an unequivocal "yes." If this seems to be a contradiction, it is one that is easily resolved: like many things that have existed for a long time, information systems have evolved and are similar to their forerunners only in the abstract. In the 1980s, and presumably for a long time to come, when one addresses MIS in specific terms, there is an implicit assumption that the processing of data into information is accomplished by means of a computer.

To many managers, this is not particularly welcome news. Early business computers were limited in computational power and storage capacity, they were subject to frequent malfunctions and extensive maintenance, benefits were primarily operational rather than managerial, and many employees viewed them as job threats. As a result, there is still a great deal of suspicion concerning the computer component of MIS. But computers have also evolved. To illustrate the improvement in computer reliability and efficiency, one might compare first generation computers, (1954 to 1958) to the Ford Tri-motor passenger plane, the second generation (1958 to 1968) to the DC-3, and the third generation (1964 to the present) to the Boeing 747. The fourth generation of computers, which is just emerging, as yet has no counterpart in commercial aviation, although a perfected supersonic transport might come close.

The aviation analogy goes on. Just as aviation support facilities—airports, passenger terminals, air traffic control procedures, and ground controlled landing systems—have improved, so have computer support facilities. Computer users today can choose from a wide variety of hardware components, management-oriented programming languages, manufacturer-prepared software packages, alternative means of data communications, and expert advice from computer consultants.

Computer people themselves must accept a large share of the blame for the early alienation of management. Computer experts, perhaps overly impressed with their special skills, did little to make computer operations understandable to managers. Those few conscientious managers who tried to gain an insight into computers and data processing were scared off by the complexity and strange jargon that accompanied them. It is ironic that advancing computer technology makes the understanding of internal computer operations *less* important than before. Middle and top managers who use information systems today need to know no more about how to program and operate a computer than how to fly the jet aircraft that takes them to a business conference. Both the computer and the jet are modern marvels that ease business problems; the manager today who is apprehensive of a computer-based information system is as handicapped as the one who fears to fly.

THE DIFFERENCE BETWEEN
DATA PROCESSING AND MIS

With the emphasis on computers and the repeated reference to the processing of data, many readers will say to themselves, "That's just a fancy name for a data processing system; my company has been doing that for 20 years."

It is true that many established data processing (DP) systems have in fact been upgraded to MIS. An even greater number were simply redesignated MIS by a buzzword-conscious management. This has not helped to resolve the confusion that exists over the difference between data processing systems and MIS.

The differences, some of which are quite subtle, center about the kinds of processes involved, the use made of the output, and the extent of interface with management. More is said on data processing activities in Chapter 3, but it is appropriate to expand somewhat on the differences between MIS and data processing before we conclude this introduction.

PROCESSING DIFFERENCES

At least one MIS scholar distinguishes MIS from data processing by the result of the transformation process. According to Raymond McLeod, data processing systems output data while MIS output information.[2] Why one system produces information and the other produces data can be explained best by differences in the processes involved.

Processes such as storing, retrieving, sorting, duplicating, and classifying data, which are typical of DP systems, do not really convert data into information. The data are unchanged except for location, position, quantity, and perhaps the addition of an identifying code. This is not to say that these are unimportant processes or that they underutilize the computer. Nor does it imply that these are the *only* processes carried out by a data processing system. They merely serve to illustrate the kind of process associated with DP systems.

By contrast, MIS tend to change the form and content of data by processes such as calculation, summarization, and combination. According to this method of distinguishing the two kinds of systems, we would consider a report that lists all items in inventory, ordered by stock number and coded to identify the vendor, to be the output of a data processing system. Another report, based on exactly the same input data, but which shows the average daily balance of high-demand items and the names of vendors with whom items are backordered, would be considered management information.

THE USE OF SYSTEM OUTPUT

The complexity of the transformation process is only a rough guide to the difference between a DP system and an MIS. A more critical test lies in how the output is used.

Data processing output is primarily designed for recordkeeping and operational uses. Automobile sales records maintained in computer-readable form to facilitate the notification of owners in the event of a recall or to satisfy product liability laws fall into this category.

The output of an MIS is intended for management use—planning, controlling, decision making, and similar activities. When the automobile sales records are analyzed to identify concentrations of owners in order to find the most convenient location for a new service facility, there is a clear-cut management use involved.

It is interesting to note that usage may be independent of output design. A report may contain *potential* management information but not be used for that purpose. This merely emphasizes the importance of one MIS element identified earlier—the managers themselves. It is possible that an unenlightened or indifferent management can keep a system from being a true MIS by its failure to use the output properly.

INTERFACE WITH MANAGEMENT

The last point made suggests the final area of difference between DP systems and MIS—the interface with management. "Interface" has become something of a buzzword itself, and we constantly hear of "man-machine interfaces," "interfacing systems," and other terms that suggest cooperation or good working relationships. In an MIS context, interface implies an exchange of inputs and/or outputs. The interface is most complete, of course, when the exchange is two-way. Managers who read computer-generated reports interface with the MIS after a fashion, but not nearly as well as those who both receive output and furnish input. MIS that incorporate data base management systems (DBMS) facilitate this kind of two-way interface especially well; but it is extremely unusual for managers, except data processing managers, to interface with a DP system in such a way. More is said on DBMS and the way managers use them in Chapter 9.

THE RELATIONSHIP BETWEEN
DATA PROCESSING AND MIS

A final word is necessary to dispel any notion that data processing and MIS might be totally different, incompatible systems. Quite to the contrary, as some of the illustrations above have suggested, data processing plays an indispensable role in MIS. MIS evolved from data processing systems and could not now exist without the base of transactional data supplied by data processing. In later discussions of MIS, there is always an assumption of an underlying data processing system which provides the bulk of input required by the MIS.

As in many other evolutionary processes, the newly emerged system exists side-by-side with the old system—for a while. At the moment, MIS and DP systems coexist in a symbiotic fashion: MIS are dependent upon operational data processed in DP systems, and DP systems require the workload imposed upon them by the MIS.

It may be that MIS will someday absorb the DP function and totally replace DP systems. Higher species on the evolutionary ladder sometimes do that. Whether or not that happens is of little consequence, for the function will continue to exist under either name. For now, we will still treat data processing as a separate, but closely related to MIS, system.

NOTES

1. In his article "General Systems Theory—The Skeleton of Science," Kenneth Boulding describes an ordering of systems by complexity— the first level of which is a static system called a "framework" and which involves no transformation process. A system of highways is an example of such a framework. All other levels of systems are dynamic and transform inputs into outputs. *Management Systems,* ed. Peter P. Schoderbek, 2nd ed. (New York: Wiley, 1971).
2. Raymond McLeod, Jr., *Management Information Systems* (Chicago and Palo Alto, Calif.: Science Research Associates, 1979), p. 18.

CHAPTER 2

Computer Hardware and Software

The first electronic computer was constructed only 35 years ago. ENIAC (for Electronic Numerical Integrator and Calculator) covered 1,500 square feet and weighed over 30 tons. At the time, one expert felt that six or seven such machines would satisfy the entire U.S. computer market. Ten years later, there were over 3,000 installed computers in the U.S. In another ten years, that number had grown to 30,000; and in still another ten years, to 100,000. Today there are over 5 million computers worldwide, and the computational power of ENIAC can be duplicated in an integrated circuit chip one-quarter-inch square weighing less than one one-hundredth of an ounce. It is no wonder that people speak of the "computer revolution."

Computers today range from single-chip microprocessors in home appliances to "supercomputers" that can perform several hundred million operations per second, store 16 million characters in internal storage with billions more available in microseconds, and cost several million dollars.

They are used to route telephone traffic, maintain banking records, simulate automobile designs, process tax returns, regulate heating and cooling systems, provide home entertainment, and perform thousands of other tasks from the mundane to the fantastic. It is difficult to imagine any aspect of government, business, or personal life that somehow has escaped the influence of this computer revolution.

In addition to being part of a management information system, computers are themselves systems. A computer system consists of *hardware* and *software*. Computer hardware includes the physical components of the system—the mechanical and electronic parts. It is the image of hardware, flashing lights and spinning tape reels, that is evoked when the average person thinks "computer." Computer software is less spectacular than hardware but equally important. Software consists of the coded instructions that direct the operation of hardware. In true systems fashion, one is worthless without the other.

COMPUTER HARDWARE

Given the number of computers in operation and their broad range of size and application, it is not surprising that there is no such thing as a typical computer hardware configuration. Nonetheless, for MIS purposes, some extreme configurations can be eliminated and we can describe the kind of computer hardware that managers are likely to encounter in MIS.

A typical MIS computer will have a CPU (for Central Processing Unit) and one or more devices each for the external storage, input, and output of data.[1] These hardware components, shown schematically in Figure 2-1, play an important role in determining MIS capabilities. Functional managers will find some knowledge of hardware useful in communicating their future information needs to computer specialists as well as helping them gain the maximum benefit from their organization's information system.

THE CENTRAL PROCESSING UNIT

The CPU is the heart of any computer. The characteristics of the CPU—storage capacity, speed of operation, the number of peripheral devices it can accommodate, and so on—establish the limits of the computational power available in the computer. It is convenient to view the CPU as having three parts: storage, an arithmetic and logic unit, and a controller—although these parts

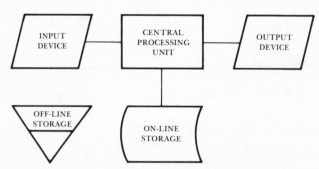

FIGURE 2–1. Computer hardware components. NOTE: *See Appendix A for a complete listing of symbols used to represent computer hardware and functions.*

may not occupy distinctly separate physical locations in a contemporary computer.

STORAGE

Data are stored in a computer in a binary code; that is, words and numbers are expressed in combinations of electrical pulses instead of letters and digits. In writing, we usually express the presence of a pulse with a "1" and the absence of a pulse with a "0." Any letter or number can be coded using these two characters. For example, the Extended Binary Coded Decimal Interchange Code (EBCDIC) for the letter "A" is 1100 0001 and 1111 0101 for the digit "5." These 1's and 0's are called *bits* (for binary digits). It is possible to code 256 different characters using eight bits; a ninth bit is usually added to facilitate an internal computer check for errors during data transfer. The grouping of eight bits is called a *byte*. Since one byte is normally used to code one character, we will use the two terms interchangeably.

The use of a binary code greatly simplifies storage in the CPU. The two binary characters can be represented by the presence or absence of a magnetic field, the off-on positions of a switch, or any other two-state condition. Until recently, most CPU storage consisted of a three-dimensional grid of tiny ferrite rings, or *cores*, strung on a network of wires. Magnetic fields were induced in the cores by passing an electric current through a certain wire. Each core represented a bit. More recently, integrated circuit chips have been used for CPU storage. A single chip may contain circuitry to represent 16,000 bits and a 256,000-bit chip has already been tested. Some advanced computers represent bits with magnetic "bubbles," and still more exotic devices are under development.

$\rightarrow 1024 = 2^{10} = 16^{2.5}$ $\rightarrow 1,048,576 = 2^{20} = 16^5$

In the jargon of computer technology, CPU storage capacity is measured in either K (for kilo or thousand) or M (for mega or million) bytes. Thus, a 4K microcomputer can accommodate 4,000 bytes or characters in CPU storage and a 16M supercomputer can accommodate 16 million bytes. Storage capacity is important because certain data processing and MIS applications require very large amounts of storage. Data base management systems in particular place heavy demands on CPU storage.

Access time, the time it takes to retrieve data from storage and make them available for processing, is also a key characteristic of storage. Access time varies with the storage medium—core, integrated circuit, bubble, etc.—but a typical late-model CPU will have access times on the order of 50 billionths of a second or so. Again, to use computer jargon, a billionth of a second is called a *nanosecond* and a millionth of a second, abbreviated μsec, is called a microsecond. Current access times then are around .05 μsec or 50 nanoseconds.

The Arithmetic and Logic Unit

The arithmetic and logic unit (ALU) contains the electronic circuitry to perform the data transformation operations conducted in the CPU. It also contains a few storage locations, called *registers,* to which data are moved for the actual operation. As suggested by "arithmetic," many of the operations are purely mathematical—adding, subtracting, multiplying, dividing, finding logarithms, and the like. These operations are carried out in binary numbers, of course, which is quite cumbersome for hand manipulation but extremely efficient in computers.

The "logic" part of the ALU is based on the comparison of one data element to another and circuitry that initiates one operation if they are the same and another if they are different. This seemingly simple operation is a very powerful tool that facilitates much of what computers are able to do. Logical comparisons ensure that your bank deposit is credited to your account instead of someone else's, that credit purchases are charged to the proper account, that sales are analyzed by product line, and so forth.

THE CONTROLLER

The controller contains electronic circuitry that reads coded instructions in software and initiates appropriate activity in other hardware components of the computer. The controller brings programs and data into CPU storage from an input device or an external storage device, routes data to the ALU for transformation, restores the transformed data, and finally sends the transformed data to an output device or back to external storage.

The electronic circuitry to carry out these operations is usually built into the controller, which somewhat restricts the choice of compatible software. Recently, some additional software flexibility has been gained by incorporating controller-like instructions in small storage facilities within the CPU. The technique of substituting coded instructions—software—for electronic circuitry—hardware—is called *microprogramming*. The microprogrammed instructions are frequently stored on interchangeable circuit boards that permit the computer to accommodate different programming languages, interface with different peripheral devices, or even act as a different model computer. This blurring of the traditional lines between software and hardware has given rise to the term *firmware* to describe microprograms fixed on circuit boards.

EXTERNAL STORAGE DEVICES

CPU storage, even in supercomputers with megabyte capacities, is rarely adequate to store all the programs and data associated with an MIS. When they are not actually required by the CPU, additional programs and data are maintained in external storage devices. External storage devices are said to be *on-line* when they have an electronic data linkage to the CPU; otherwise, they are *off-line*. Some storage media are always off-line. Card decks, optically scanned documents, and similar media require human intervention to make them available to the CPU. Other media, such as magnetic tape and magnetic disks, are on-line when mounted on storage devices connected to the CPU but off-line when stored in the data processing library.

External storage devices can also be classified by the mode of access—either *sequential* or *direct*. Two of the media suggested previously, tape and disk, will serve to illustrate these two modes of access.

SEQUENTIAL ACCESS STORAGE DEVICES

A sequential access storage device (SASD) is one in which data can be accessed only in the sequence in which they are stored. It is somewhat analogous to a dial telephone: to dial the number 9, the dial must rotate through the numbers 1, 2, 3, and so on until 9 is reached. It takes longer to dial 9 than, say, 5.

If your bank records are stored on an SASD, they can be accessed only by "rotating" through the device until your account number is reached. Of course, there are many more accounts than there are digits on a telephone dial and the search will be correspondingly longer.

The most common SASD is the *magnetic tape drive.* Computer magnetic tape is similar to audio recording tape. Most computers use 2,400-foot reels of tape, although some input terminals and many microcomputers are designed to use audio-style tape cassettes.

Data are recorded on magnetic tape in binary code, with a magnetized area corresponding to a "1" and an unmagnetized area corresponding to a "0." Heads positioned over the tape "write" by inducing magnetic fields in the magnetic oxide coating on the tape. Other heads "read" the tape by sensing these areas. There are usually nine read and nine write heads on a tape drive to accommodate an eight-bit byte and one check or *parity* bit. Figure 2–2 shows how data are represented on a nine-track tape.

The storage capacity of a tape is a function of its length and the recording density. One common recording density is 800 characters per inch (CPI), which gives a 2,400-foot reel a capacity of over 20 million characters—the equivalent of about 20 books the length of this one.

$$\frac{10^6 \ char/bк}{250 \ page/bк} = 4000 \ char/page$$

FIGURE 2–2. Magnetic tape. NOTE: *Characters are shown in EBCDIC with* even *parity; that is, a parity bit is added, if necessary, to give each character an even number of bits. An odd number therefore indicates a data transmission error.*

1 1 1 1 1 1 1 1 1 1	1 1 1 1 1 1 1 1 1 1	1 1 1 1 1 1	0 1 1 1 0
1 0 0 0 0 0 0 0 0 0	1 0 0 0 0 0 0 0 0 0	1 0 0 0 0 0	1 1 1 1 1
0 0 0 0 0 0 0 0 0 1	0 0 0 0 0 0 0 1 0 0 0	1 1 1 1 0 0 1	0 0 0 1 0
1 0 1 0 0 0 1 0 1 0	0 1 0 1 1 1 0 0 0 1 1	0 0 0 0 0 1 0	0 1 0 0 1
0 0 0 0 0 0 0 0 0 0	1 0 0 0 1 0 0 0 1 0 0	0 1 0 0 0 0 0	1 0 1 0 1
1 0 1 0 1 1 1 1 1 0	0 1 1 1 0 1 0 0 0 1 1	0 0 0 0 1 1 0	1 1 0 0 1
0 0 0 0 1 0 0 0 0 1	0 0 1 1 0 0 0 0 1 0 1 0	1 0 1 1 0 0 1	0 0 0 1 0
0 1 1 1 1 1 0 1 1 1	1 1 0 0 1 0 1 1 1 0 1	0 0 0 1 1 0 0	1 0 1 0 1
0 0 0 0 0 1 1 1 0 0	0 0 1 0 0 1 0 0 1 0 0	0 1 1 0 1 1 1	0 0 0 0 1

8-BIT BYTE (brace on left spanning rows)

PARITY BIT— (bottom left)

Management Information Systems (MIS)

DIRECT ACCESS STORAGE DEVICES

A *direct access storage device (DASD)* is one in which data can be accessed directly without regard to the sequence or order in which they are stored. To continue the telephone analogy, a DASD is similar to a push-button telephone: any digit can be "dialed" directly with one touch of the proper button. The total "dialing" time is reduced and the telephone company imposes a slightly higher service charge for this convenience.

If your bank records are on a DASD, they can be accessed with equal ease—perhaps even by a clerk who keys in your account number in much the same fashion as one keys in a telephone number on a push-button telephone. And the bank pays the computer hardware vendor more for a DASD than for a SASD.

The most common DASD is the *magnetic disk drive*. Magnetic disks are similar in appearance to phonograph records, but are more like magnetic tape in the way in which data are recorded on them. Disks do differ from tape, however, in the number of tracks used to record data. Instead of recording a byte *across* parallel tracks, bits are recorded *along* the tracks on a disk. The method of recording data on disks is shown in Figure 2–3.

There is a great variety in the way different manufacturers design disk drives. The disks may be used singly, as they frequently are in minicomputers and microcomputers, or be arranged in *disk packs* of 6 to 20 disks. Disks in packs also may vary in

FIGURE 2–3. Magnetic disk pack.

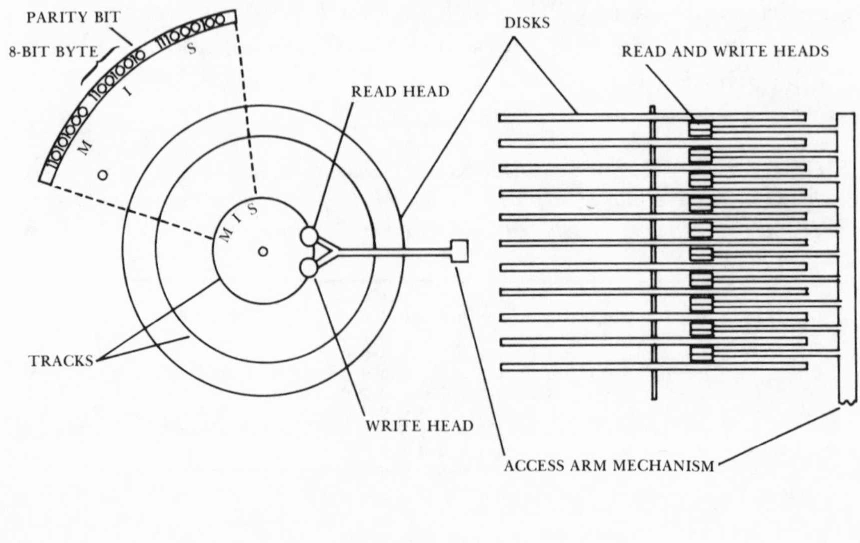

diameter (from 12 to 18 inches), the number of tracks per disk (from 100 to over 500), the speed at which they rotate (from 800 to 2000 rpm), and recording densities. All of these factors combine to give disk packs storage capacities that range from 1 million bytes to over 100 million bytes.

The single disks used on small computers look more like 45 rpm records. They are flexible, either 5½ or 8 inches in diameter, and hold approximately one-half million bytes. These smaller disks are called *diskettes* or, because they are flexible, "*floppy*" *disks*.

Direct access to storage locations on a disk pack is achieved by a combination of electronic and electromechanical action. Read and write heads mounted on movable arms float a few millionths of an inch above and below the disks as shown in Figure 2-3. An address code identifies the surface of the pack on which the data are stored as well as the track on which they are located. The surface is selected by completing the electronic circuit to the appropriate head and the arm is moved by electomechanical action to position the head over the appropriate track. The head then senses the magnetized areas on the disk in the same manner in which magnetized tape areas are sensed.

Although there are other external storage media and devices—magnetic drums, magnetic cards, and magnetic tape cartridges, to name the most popular ones—punched cards, magnetic tape, and magnetic disks are the most representative of off-line, on-line sequential, and on-line direct access devices, respectively, now in use. Some familiarity with these media and devices will equip the reader to understand other similarly classified external storage systems.

INPUT DEVICES

An input device is a computer hardware component that converts input data into a machine-readable binary code and transmits them to the CPU where they may be used in processing or be sent to storage for later use. In a sense, input devices "digest" data for the computer. But input devices have very restrictive diets. In most cases, there first must be an off-line auxiliary operation to convert source data (documents, transactions, etc.) into a form or medium that is acceptable to the input device. This process is shown for punched cards in Figure 2-4 and is explained in the following discussion of the card reader. Other media and data

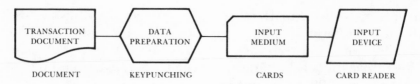

FIGURE 2–4.   **Preparation of data for card input.**

preparation devices are included in the discussions of their respective input devices.

CARD READER

A card reader is used to input data recorded on punched cards. Punched cards were one of the first computer input and storage media and remain an important one still. The most common cards have 80 columns and 12 rows. Each column represents a character or space according to a code of rectangular holes punched in the various row positions. These cards are called *Hollerith* cards after Herman Hollerith who invented punched-card machines and developed the coding system. A smaller card, used with the IBM System 3 minicomputer, has only 32 columns, but uses a smaller, round hole and only 6 rows to define a character. Three sets of rows give the card a potential of 96 characters or spaces. Examples of the Hollerith and System 3 cards are shown in Figure 2–5.

Punched cards are prepared off-line on a device called a *keypunch* machine. In addition to punching holes in cards when keys on the typewriter-like keyboard are struck, a keypunch machine also prints the characters across the top of the card. The process of printing characters, called *interpretation,* aids in visual verification of the data punched on cards. Cards may also be verified mechanically on a machine called a *verifier.* A verifier is similar to a keypunch machine in appearance, but it does not actually punch holes. Instead, it compares keystrokes with holes already punched. Any difference is signalled to the operator who must then make a visual comparison of the card to the source document and repunch the card, if necessary.

The card reader converts the holes in the cards to electrical pulses. Early card readers used a series of metal brushes which completed an electrical circuit when they passed over a hole, but kept the circuit open when no hole was present. Current card readers use photocells to detect the presence of holes. A card

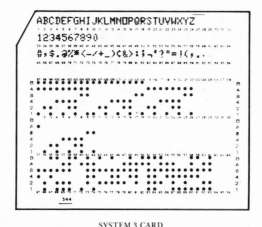

HOLLERITH CARD

SYSTEM 3 CARD

FIGURE 2-5.   Punched cards.

reader using the photocell method can read as many as 2,000 cards per minute. Although the potential of 160,000 characters per minute (2,000 cards times 80 columns) may seem impressive, card readers are among the very slowest of data input devices.

Tape Drives

Although magnetic tape is ordinarily considered to be a storage medium, it plays an important role in data entry. CPU operations are invariably faster than input operations. This results in a "bottleneck" in which the CPU must wait for input. One solution to this problem is to speed up input. As an input device, a magnetic tape drive is about 60 times faster than a card reader. In other words, the 20 million characters on a magnetic tape can be read into the CPU in about two minutes—a rate of over 165,000 characters per second.

Magnetic tape can be prepared off-line on a *key-to-tape* machine. A key-to-tape machine also has a typewriter-like keyboard, but keystrokes result in magnetic impressions on the tape instead of holes. Keystroked data are temporarily held in a small buffer storage area and written onto the tape in short bursts. This procedure is followed to simplify the problem of matching tape speed to keystroking speed as the tape passes through the machine.

Magnetic tape can also be prepared on-line. Many card-oriented systems use tape as an input device but retain cards for their convenience as documents in payroll, inventory, billing, and similar applications. In these systems, it is more efficient to convert cards to tape in a separate computer operation and then conduct processing using taped input. In large-scale operations, a small computer may be dedicated to tape preparation while the larger computer performs the actual processing tasks.

DISK DRIVES

The use of disks as an input medium is exactly parallel to the use of magnetic tape in that role, even to the use of a *key-to-disk* device for off-line data preparation. Disk input is particularly popular in small computers using diskettes or floppy disks.

Disks have several advantages over tape in an input role. First, because the disk drive is a direct access device, input can be selective, that is, only that input actually required for an operation need be input. (Theoretically, this can also be done with tape, but it would be very inefficient.) Second, disk drives are usually faster than tape in an input role, further alleviating the input bottleneck. Because of the variety in disk-drive design mentioned earlier, there is no fixed rate of input for disk drives, but the range is from 80,000 characters per second to over 650,000 characters per second. The smaller floppy disks have an input rate of about 8,000 characters per second.

TERMINALS

Terminals are sometimes referred to as *direct* input devices because they do not require off-line data preparation nor do they use an intermediate data medium. Instead, terminals generate machine-readable electrical pulses directly from keystrokes or other operator actions and transmit them to the CPU. *General purpose* terminals usually have a typewriter-like keyboard on which the operator types data or program statements. *Special purpose* terminals are designed to collect data from a specific activity, such as a manufacturing process, a retail-store sale, or a hospital patient's vital life functions. Special purpose terminals capture data via sensors or special, application-oriented keyboards.

When terminals have a limited processing capability, they are referred to as *intelligent* or *smart* terminals. Processing at a smart terminal is usually restricted to editing input and performing simple arithmetic operations prior to input. Many computer personnel include minicomputers or microcomputers in the definition of smart terminals, in which case much more extensive processing is possible.

Keyboard terminals are limited in input speed to the rate at which the operator can type—perhaps 7 or 8 characters per second. Why then would anyone choose a terminal over, say, a disk drive, which can input as much as 100,000 times faster? One reason is the lack of any requirement for off-line preparation, but a more important reason lies in the fact that most terminals are also *output* devices. The capability to act as both an input and an output device, on-line, permits the terminal user to operate *interactively* with the computer. In other words, input can be processed and the output returned to the user in time to be considered before the next input. This makes the terminal particularly useful in the management decision-making process where data recovery and analysis might otherwise be prohibitively time consuming.

OTHER INPUT DEVICES

The input devices, media, and data preparation devices described above are those most commonly used in MIS applications. Other input devices have limited MIS usage but are important in scientific or straight data processing applications.

Paper tape is an input medium that combines some features of punched cards and magnetic tape. Like magnetic tape, paper tape is rolled onto reels and, like punched cards, binary code is represented by holes. Paper tape is prepared off-line on a *paper tape punch* and read into the CPU by means of a *paper tape reader*. Input speeds are about 1,600 characters per second.

Magnetic ink characters are used almost exclusively by the banking industry. The stylized type font is limited to ten digits (0 to 9) and four special characters that identify routing through the Federal Reserve system, banks, account numbers, and the number and amount of each check. Characters are printed in magnetic ink when the checks are produced, except for the amount of the check which is added by a *magnetic ink character recognition (MICR) encoder* at the bank when the check is returned for processing. An *MICR reader-sorter* arranges the checks in numerical sequence by account number and transfers data to the CPU at about 3,000 characters per second.

Remote job entry terminals (RJET) differ from the terminals described earlier in that they *do* require off-line data preparation. A typical RJET may incorporate a card reader for input and a line printer for output. This combination permits much higher volumes of input and output than a keyboard terminal, but it also precludes interactive use in most instances.

Some data input devices read directly from source documents. A *mark-sense reader* picks up electrographic pencil marks on a Hollerith-type card. *Optical scanners* detect similar marks made with ordinary pencils on carefully formatted forms. Both mark-sense cards and optically scanned forms can be used to collect limited responses (true-false, multiple choice) in customer surveys, student testing, and similar applications. Where a greater variety of data is needed, an *optical character reader* may be more appropriate. One form of optical character reader, commonly incorporated into *point-of-sale terminals* in large retailing operations, reads the 26 capital letters of the alphabet, the 10 digits, and 6 special characters—provided they are printed in a special type font called OCR-A. Another type of optical character reader can read hand-printed characters—if they are printed neatly and according to specified rules, such as crossing a "z" to distinguish it from a "2," and so on.

CONSIDERATIONS IN CHOOSING AN INPUT DEVICE

Most computer installations, particularly those that serve an MIS, will have a variety of input devices. The considerations in selecting one or more such devices include input speed, cost, convenience, and the nature of the applications. These considerations are summarized for various input devices in Table 2-1.

OUTPUT DEVICES

Output devices accept processed data in binary coded form and record them on various output media. Some output is stored

TABLE 2-1. Computer Input Devices

DEVICE	CHARACTERISTICS	APPLICATIONS
Card reader	Low cost, slow speed, inconvenient medium	Inventory, billing, payroll where card doubles as document
Tape drive	Moderate cost, high speed, sequential access	High volume, periodic processing such as payroll or billing
Disk drive	High cost, high speed, direct access	High volume, continuous processing such as airline reservation or data base management
Terminals	Low cost, very slow speed, interactive access	Remote data entry, management queries
Paper tape	Low cost, very slow speed, fragile medium	Scientific data input
MICR reader	Moderate cost, slow speed	Check processing
Mark-sense reader	Low cost, slow speed	Student testing, customer surveys
Optical character reader	Moderate cost, slow speed	Retail store sales, credit card billing
Remote job entry terminal	Moderate cost, speed varys with medium	High volume remote processing, such as branch office payroll

externally for additional processing at a later date or for record-keeping purposes. Such output is most conveniently stored on a machine-readable medium such as tape, disks, or even cards. Other output, particularly in an MIS, is used to provide information to humans and must be recorded or displayed in letters, numbers, and other easily recognized characters. Paper and video displays are the best media for this purpose. Printed output on paper can be produced either by a printer or a typewriter terminal, while CRT (for Cathode Ray Tube) terminals are used for video displays. Each device has distinguishing characteristics that makes it suitable for certain applications.

PRINTERS

There are perhaps more approaches to the design of printers than to any other computer peripheral device. These design differences result in printing speeds that vary from 10 characters per second to over 10,000 characters per second.

The lower speeds (10 to 100 characters per second) are representative of *character printers* that are similar to electric typewriters and are used primarily with microcomputers. Character printers typically use narrow paper and print 32 to 80 characters per line.

Higher speeds (200 to 2,000 lines per minute) are achieved by *impact printers.* As the name implies, impact printers strike through a ribbon to leave an impression on paper. Some impact printers align print wheels in each position and print an entire line at once; others strike through rotating bands or chains of characters to achieve almost the same effect.

Nonimpact printers avoid the mechanical action that limits (and sometimes plagues) impact printers and use ink jet, laser, or electrostatic processes to achieve very high speeds (500 to 5,000 lines per minute). These speeds are necessary in high volume operations where output bottlenecks may be just as troublesome as the input bottlenecks discussed earlier.

The higher speed printers use wider paper with standard widths of 120, 132, or 144 characters per line.

TERMINALS

It was noted earlier that many terminals are also output devices. Typewriter terminals may use an electric typewriter-style ball or a wire-dot matrix to strike through a ribbon. A typical matrix design uses 35 wires grouped in a 5 by 7 matrix. Different combinations of wires are extended to print different characters in patterns not unlike those formed by light bulbs in many outdoor signs. Some ribbonless typewriter terminals heat the wires in the matrix to form characters on special heat-sensitive paper. Typewriter terminals print one character at a time and have print speeds similar to character printers.

CRT terminals have small television-like screens instead of typewriter mechanisms. CRT terminals are faster (250 to 5,000 characters per second) but do not leave the user with a hard copy of the output. CRT terminals are also better than typewriter terminals for graphic displays. Graphics can even be modified on some CRT terminals through the use of a *light pen* which can "erase" and originate lines on the CRT display surface.

Even though the upper limits of output speeds on a CRT terminal are quite high, terminals should be used only for limited volumes of input and/or output. There are more efficient devices for high volumes and in many systems these other devices can be activated from a terminal.

CARDPUNCH

There are not many card-oriented applications in an MIS, but when they do occur there may also be a requirement to produce output in the form of punched cards. The device to produce this output is called a *cardpunch* (not to be confused with the *keypunch*, an off-line data preparation device). A cardpunch can turn out between 80 and 650 cards per minute, depending on the model and the number of columns used per card.

OTHER OUTPUT DEVICES

The focus on output devices thus far has been on those that produce documents or other human-readable output. A great deal of computer output goes directly into storage and is never seen by humans. For example, master files and databases are almost never printed in their entirety but are maintained in external storage as the basis for further processing. When output goes directly to storage, the storage device itself is also the output device. Any on-line storage device, such as the tape drive or the disk drive described earlier, can serve as an output device. Output speeds for these external storage devices are approximately the same as their respective input speeds.

CONSIDERATIONS IN SELECTING AN OUTPUT DEVICE

The computer system serving an MIS will have a variety of output devices to satisfy various requirements. The characteristics to be considered in selecting an appropriate mix of such devices—cost, speed, and the nature of the application—are summarized for the most common output devices in Table 2–2.

DATA COMMUNICATIONS

One of the more interesting recent trends in computer hardware is the increased use of data communications to link widely separated hardware components. It is now quite common for input and output devices, particularly terminals, to be located some distance from the CPU. For short distances, say, within the same building, terminals may be connected directly to the CPU simply by using longer cabling. In this case, data to and from the terminal are transmitted in digital form as they are used in the CPU.

TABLE 2–2. Computer Output Devices

DEVICE	CHARACTERISTICS	APPLICATIONS
Character printer	Low cost, slow speed, limited capabilities	Small business, microcomputers
Inpact printer	Moderate cost, high speed, very versatile	High volume, hard copy output; report generation
Nonimpact printer	High cost, very high speed, very high quality output	Very high volume; personalized documents to customers, stockholders, etc.
Terminals	Low cost, very slow speed, limited volume	Real-time processing, management queries
Cardpunch	Low cost, slow speed, inconvenient medium	Card-only systems such as payroll or billing

For greater distances, it is usually better to convert digital data to another form for ease of transmission. When the communications channel is a telephone line, a *modem* (for modulator/demodulator) at the terminal converts the binary pulses of the digital code to an audio frequency which can be transmitted over telephone lines. A standard telephone handset may be fitted into the modem for this purpose. Since only a narrow frequency band is needed to code a binary signal, there is sufficient space in the telephone frequency range to accommodate a number of channels on one line. At the CPU end of the channel, a second modem converts the audio signal back to binary pulses and the communications link is completed.

The audio signal produced by a modem is an *analog* of digital data; that is, it is analogous to, but not exactly the same as digital data. A system developed by Bell Telephone, DDS (for Dataphone Digital Service), permits direct transmission of digital data, without the use of modems, between selected cities in the United States. Maximum transmission rates over DDS are about six times faster than regular telephone lines (56,000 bits per second compared to 9,600 bits per second), but DDS is somewhat limited in scope and is more expensive.

Data can also be communicated over other channels. Microwave transmission uses a radio frequency analog of digital data. Microwaves are "line-of-sight" and require frequent relay stations to follow the curvature of the earth. The use of satellites to relay microwaves requires only a few retransmissions to achieve intercontinental distances.

Even more promising than microwave transmission are the experiments using light analogs of digital data. Both visible and infrared light can be used as communications channels. While light has great speed, it too is line-of-sight and is subject to weather conditions.

DISTRIBUTED SYSTEMS

Input and output devices are not the only computer hardware with data communications capabilities. CPUs can also be linked together. Two or more CPUs joined by data communications networks form what is called a *distributed system.* Figure 2–6 shows two different types of distributed systems.

A *star system* has a large *host computer* with smaller computers as

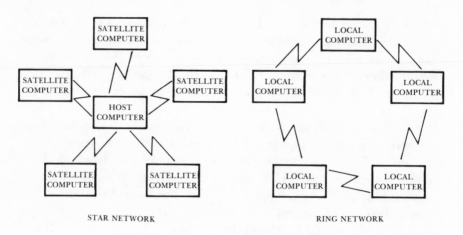

STAR NETWORK   RING NETWORK

FIGURE 2-6.   Distributed systems.

satellites. Data communication is possible between any two computers by going through the host computer, but the communications network is predicated on the assumption that most communication will be between the host and its satellites.

Star systems often reflect organizational structure, with the host at company headquarters and satellites at branch locations. Centralized applications, such as financial planning and market analysis, are performed on the host computer, but the satellites can draw on the programs and files for local applications in those areas. Similarly, the files of branch applications in production scheduling, inventory management, or other local concerns can be tapped by the host computer for organization-wide analyses.

A *ring system* has no host computer. Instead, each CPU in the system is linked to its neighbors. Ring systems are common in very homogeneous organizations, such as banks where a number of branches have identical computing requirements. In a ring system, each computer maintains a share of the files and programs which can be made available to any other computer. In the banking example, each branch maintains files for its own customers, but a customer can initiate a transaction from any branch. Some ring systems can also link CPUs to create the effect of a single larger computer for certain applications. This process is known as *multiprocessing.*

COMPUTER SOFTWARE

As noted previously, software consists of the coded instructions that direct the operation of computer hardware. Software can be divided into two broad categories: *application software* and *system software*. Application software contains specific instructions for the transformation of data while system software is oriented to the general control of computer hardware devices.

APPLICATION SOFTWARE

Application software is usually referred to simply as *programs*. An MIS may use hundreds of different programs to process pay, maintain inventory records, schedule production, generate reports, analyze sales, and otherwise support the managerial and operational activities in an organization.

Application software is written in a *programming* language—a systematic set of procedures and codes that enables the programmer to describe the transformation process. Programming languages are classified as *machine, assembler,* or *compiler languages.*

MACHINE LANGUAGES

Machine language instructions are in binary code—1's and 0's. The instructions are typically in two 4- or 5-bit parts: an *operation code* which tells what is to be done and an *operand* which tells where to store the results. For example, a machine language code to "store a value called X in register 11011" might be written 1100 11011.

Every computer has its own more or less unique machine language which is determined by the ALU circuitry. All computers ultimately operate in machine language, but almost none still require the programmer to use one. Instead, system software translates other, easier to use languages into machine language.

ASSEMBLER LANGUAGES

Assembler languages, sometimes called *symbolic* languages, substitute short alphabetic expressions for the operation code. For example, ADD x means "add the variable previously identified as x to the value currently in an accumulator register." While not strictly machine languages, assembler languages are nonetheless machine-oriented; that is, each computer has unique assembler language symbolic expressions that correspond to machine language instructions on a one-to-one basis. A type of system software known as a *language translator* performs the conversion of symbolic instructions into machine language instructions.

Some assembler languages now use *macro instructions* which generate two or more machine language instructions. For example, the macro instruction ADD A, B, C (add the variable A to the variable B and call the result C) replaces three simple instructions to load A into a register, add B to it, and store the result.

COMPILER LANGUAGES

Compiler languages, sometimes called "high-level" languages, use English-like statements to code instructions. Each statement requires many, possibly hundreds of machine language instructions. A statement such as IF (HOURS.GT.40.0) GO TO 180, which means "if the value of a variable called HOURS is greater than 40, program statement number 180 should be executed next," involves the evaluation of a variable, a logical comparison, a move within the program, and the execution of statement number 180 and all those that follow until control is returned to the original statement. The conversion of this program statement into the appropriate machine language instructions is accomplished by a type of system software called a *compiler*.

Compiler languages are machine-independent; that is, only minor differences in programming procedures occur among the various makes and models of computers. Of course, this means that the compiler itself must be unique in order to convert standard programming statements into unique machine language instructions.

The most common compiler languages in use are COBOL (for Common Business-Oriented Language), FORTRAN (for Formula Translation) and BASIC (for Beginners All-purpose Symbolic Instruction Code). COBOL is especially good for creating and maintaining files; FORTRAN has exceptional mathematical capabilities; and BASIC is a simple language well suited to interactive or terminal use. These languages are sometimes called

procedure-oriented languages because they describe the data transformation procedures in some detail. Other languages, somewhat
less versatile, are called *problem-oriented languages* because the procedures are fixed—only the input/output instructions need be
programmed. RPG (for Report Program Generation), a popular
minicomputer language for the updating of files and generation
of business reports, and GPSS (for General-Purpose Systems
Simulation), a language designed to facilitate the simulation of
business or scientific activities, are examples of this second category.

SYSTEMS SOFTWARE

The purpose of system software is to make the job of the
application software programmer easier. This is especially evident
in the one function of system software discussed above—that of
translating or compiling application programs into machine language. The system software, sometimes called the *operating system* of a computer, also includes programs that relieve the application programmer of responsibility to include routine, repetitive,
or purely "housekeeping" functions in the application programs.
Control programs and *service programs* are two types of such system
software.

CONTROL PROGRAMS

Control programs manage the input, output, and storage of
data required by application programs. These programs are concerned with the actual physical location of data as well as with the
logical relationships (processing sequence) that determine the organization of data in storage. Control programs schedule input
and output according to assigned priorities or standing instructions. They also maintain logs on machine and peripheral time
required for various applications and/or accounts. This latter
function is especially important where the data processing center
is operated as a profit center and must "bill" other departments
for services rendered.

SERVICE PROGRAMS

Service programs provide commonly used routines that might
otherwise have to be included in the application software. For

example, it is often necessary to sort data according to alphabetical or numerical sequence or to merge two sorted data sets into a single sequential list. Many operating systems permit the application programmer to call up a service program to perform these tasks with only one or two statements.

There are also service programs in operating systems to reformat data for a different medium (e.g., from tape to disk) and to detect errors in application programs. System software can only detect *syntax* errors—misspellings, incomplete statements, and other violations of programming rules. It cannot detect *logical* errors—programming statements that follow all the rules but have not been used in a manner to produce the desired output.

OTHER CAPABILITIES

System software can aid application programming in other ways. *Job processing* schedules application programs and the input/output devices to be used with each job. The application programmer provides input through statements in a special programming language called JCL (for Job Control Language). The operating system converts these statements to machine language for actual execution. JCL is also used to initiate and terminate processing, specify the application language, and identify the user for accounting purposes.

System software can also be used to achieve *timesharing*—the processing of two or more programs concurrently. There are many ways of sharing time in the CPU. Statements in several programs can be run alternately, small increments of time can be allotted to programs on an alternating basis, programs can be assigned processing priorities, storage space can be partitioned to accommodate several programs, or some combination of these methods can be employed. Timesharing is desirable because the CPU is so much faster than input or output devices and the CPU is often idle during input and output. Timesharing converts time idle with respect to one program into productive time for other programs. Timesharing through software is often called *multiprogramming* and should not be confused with the hardware technique of *multiprocessing* used to describe distributed systems earlier.

Another powerful capability of system software is *virtual storage*. This term refers to the ability of an operating system to make CPU storage appear virtually unlimited by moving data back and forth between CPU storage and external storage. Virtual storage permits the use, on small or medium-sized computers, of programs that ordinarily would require a very large computer.

SOFTWARE PHILOSOPHIES

There is a trade-off between application programming and system programming and, to a lesser extent, hardware. System programming and hardware circuitry can be minimized if one is willing to place the full software burden on the application programmer. Early computers did just that. Programmers worked directly in binary coded machine languages without the benefit of system software. Whatever control, service, or JCL program requirements existed were incorporated directly into the application program. Needless to say, application programmers had to be highly skilled and intimately familiar with the computers they programmed. They were also hard to find, but, since there were not many computers about, this did not present much of a problem.

As computers proliferated, it became apparent that programming had to be simplified. Assembler languages satisfied this requirement, but their machine orientation still presented problems in training and retraining programmers as hardware was upgraded or programmers changed jobs.

The adoption of standardized compiler languages seemed to solve the programming problem, but it placed a strain on CPU storage with the need for more complex system software. Today, CPU storage is no longer a technological problem—computers can be made about as large as one wants. What seems to be a problem now is the continued use of 20-year-old programming languages. The standardization of the sixties effectively froze language development. Hardware has now advanced well beyond software and, as computer usage continues to expand, there seems to be a need for even higher level languages to make full utilization of hardware and to bring programming down to the level of the layperson in the home or office.

COMPUTER CLASSIFICATION

No discussion of computers is complete without some comment on the classification of computers according to their cost and

TABLE 2-3. Classification of Computers

COMMON NAME	CPU STORAGE (BYTES)	COST	CHARACTERISTICS	EXAMPLES
Microcomputer	4K to 128K	$500 to $5,000	Desk-top size, slow operating speeds, limited peripherals and applications, BASIC programming, home and small business use	Apple II IBM personal computer TRS 80
Minicomputer	64K to 512K	$5,000 to $250,000	Desk-size; medium operating speeds; broad range of peripherals, applications, and programming languages; data processing small businesses; ring distributed processing.	HP 3000 IBM 34 TI 990 Wang 2200
Mainframe	512K to 4M	$250,000 to $5,000,000	Room-size; high operating speeds; full range of peripherals, applications, and programming languages; multiprogramming; multiprocessing; data base manage-	Amdahl 470 IBM Series 30 IBM Series 4300 UNIVAC 1100

COMMON NAME	CPU STORAGE (BYTES)	COST	CHARACTERISTICS	EXAMPLES
			ment systems; host computer in star distributed systems; government and large business use.	
Supercomputer	4M to 16M	$5,000,000 to $25,000,000	Similar to mainframe, but with extremely high operating speeds.	Burroughs ILLIAC IV CDC Cyber 205 Cray 1-S

capabilities. At one time, computers were classified by scale—large, medium, and small. The lines between classes never were very distinct and they are less so now. Today, it is more common to speak of *microcomputers, minicomputers, mainframes,* and *supercomputers.* The lines between these classes are also somewhat blurred and change constantly as computer manufacturers package more and more computational power into smaller and smaller machines. Nonetheless, because MIS users and other managers frequently encounter computer classification terms, a rough classification guide is presented in Table 2–3. The reader should understand that there is a great deal of overlap in these classes and that, as a general rule, costs will decrease and capacities will increase in each class over time.

NOTE

1. Many smaller computers, not capable of MIS support, incorporate all of these hardware functions into a single desktop-size device.

CHAPTER 3
Data Processing

Twenty years ago, this would have been a book on data processing instead of MIS. As MIS evolved, they assumed many of the roles, responsibilities, and concerns of their DP predecessors. Hardware, software, personnel, and procedures that now are considered part of MIS were once described as parts of a DP system. These components, along with management, organization, decision making, and other topics that make MIS different from data processing, are discussed elsewhere. But there is still a data processing function in MIS and there are still concepts and principles unique to this function. That is what this chapter is about.

There are three concepts of data processing that are particularly important in determining the kind of support furnished by an MIS. One is the manner in which data are organized for processing, a second concerns the medium used in processing, and the third deals with the mode or timing of processing. All three are very closely related characteristics of external storage devices described in the previous chapter.

THE ORGANIZATION OF DATA

Data processing requires the structuring of data according to very precise rules. Data must be in specified formats, with the right number and kind of characters, and in the proper storage location; if not, the transformation process will not yield the correct output or may not take place at all. Data organization is initiated by a systems programmer who follows certain programming language procedures to organize data into a *hierarchy*.

THE HIERARCHY OF DATA

The collection of bits into bytes to represent characters was described in Chapter 2. When a number of characters are grouped together, the result is a *data element*. Data elements represent basic facts that describe some entity involved in processing. An employee's name, social security number, address, and job code are all data elements that might be used in a personnel administration application. The number and type (numeric or alphabetic) of characters in a data element can vary, although there are upper limits to the length based on the programming language and the type of computer used.

A group of related data elements is called a *data record*. Data records also vary, within limits, in the number of data elements they contain. In order to distinguish among similar records, one element is usually designated the *key element* or *record key*. In a personnel record consisting of elements all related to one employee, the element for the social security number would probably be the record key. Numerical elements are generally preferred as record keys because they are less subject to duplication and quirks of spelling. If the employee's name were used as the record key, there could be several employees with the same name or the omission of a middle initial might prevent the proper identification of a record.

Finally, related records may be grouped to form a *data file*. The personnel records of all employees in an organization constitute the personnel file. Files, too, vary in length with the maximum number of records dependent on record length and available storage space.

Files are usually classified according to their use. A *master file* contains complete records and is the basic source of data in any DP application. *Transaction files* may contain only partial records of those data elements necessary to identify and update a record on the master file. For example, a transaction to change an employee's address needs only the social security number (the key element for record identification) and the new address. Of course, if the nature of the transaction is to add a new employee, there will be no existing record on the master file and the transaction file must contain all the data elements necessary to establish a record.

The way in which a programmer defines a hierarchy is prescribed by the rules of the programming language used. In most cases, short names are assigned to the file, record, and each data element. Data elements are also formatted for length and character composition. The file-record-element hierarchy is established by the order in which names are listed in the program, the use of alphabetic or numeric codes, and indentation. An example of the

FIGURE 3-1.   COBOL file description.

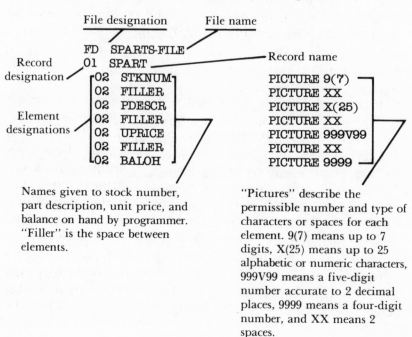

Names given to stock number, part description, unit price, and balance on hand by programmer. "Filler" is the space between elements.

"Pictures" describe the permissible number and type of characters or spaces for each element. 9(7) means up to 7 digits, X(25) means up to 25 alphabetic or numeric characters, 999V99 means a five-digit number accurate to 2 decimal places, 9999 means a four-digit number, and XX means 2 spaces.

file description for a spare parts inventory, using the COBOL programming language, is shown in Figure 3-1.

FILE ORGANIZATION

File organization refers to the *physical* order of records on the storage medium. Records also have a *logical* order—the order in which they are normally processed—which may or may not be the same as the physical order. File organization is described as being *sequential, random,* or *serial.*

SEQUENTIAL FILES

A sequential file is one in which the physical order and logical order are the same. In a billing application, the logical order might be by account number, in which case a sequential billing file would also be arranged in account number sequence.

Files are always sequential when using a sequential access storage device such as a tape drive. Files may also be organized sequentially on a direct access storage device, such as a disk drive, if other factors so dictate. When sequential files are stored on disks, data can be "packed" into every available storage location. This is in marked contrast to the storage of random files on disks. Sequential files on tape and disk are shown in Figure 3-2.

RANDOM FILES

Records in a random file are distributed about the storage medium according to a process that selects storage locations randomly. Often, some data element in the record itself, usually the record key if it is numerical, is used to determine the storage location. This process is known as *hashing* or *key transformation.*

There are many ways to transform a key element into a storage location; one example will serve to illustrate the kinds of processes involved. Suppose a billing file is to be stored randomly and there are 1,268 storage locations available. The key element in each record is a seven-digit account number. Each account number is divided by 1,268 and the remainder determines the storage location (using a divisor equal to the number of storage locations insures maximum utilization of storage space). Thus, the record for account number 2649371 would be stored in location

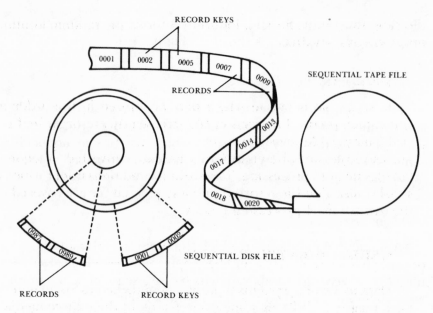

RECORD KEYS

0001   0002   0005   0007   0009

RECORDS

SEQUENTIAL TAPE FILE

0013

0014

0017

0018   0020

SEQUENTIAL DISK FILE

RECORDS   RECORD KEYS

FIGURE 3-2.   Sequential files.

519, because 2,649,371 divided by 1,268 equals 2,089, remainder 519.

It is possible that key transformation will produce the same storage location for more than one record. In the example above, key transformation would also direct account number 1069443 to location 519, since 1,069,443 divided by 1,268 equals 843, remainder 519. Records with the same storage location are called *synonyms*. When key transformation produces synonyms, they are placed in an overflow area called a *bucket*. Any process that tries to locate a record in a random file must include a check for the correct record key; if the key is not the one desired, the process must be diverted to the overflow area to search for the correct record.

As more and more records are added to a random file, the probability of synonyms increases. It has been found that when the storage medium for a random file is filled to more than 50 percent of capacity, the time spent searching for synonyms is more costly than introducing additional storage space—another disk, for example. For this reason, random files seldom occupy more than half of the possible storage space.

Although sequential files can be sorted on either direct or sequential access devices, random files can be placed only on direct access storage devices. Figure 3-3 shows the random location of records on a disk.

SERIAL FILES

A serial file is one in which data are stored in the order in which they occur. Transaction files frequently are organized serially, master files never are.

Serial files are often temporary and are converted to sequential files prior to processing. The various conditions under which a serial transaction file is sorted into a sequential file are covered in the discussion of processing modes.

MEDIA-ORIENTED SYSTEMS

Data processing systems typically use punched cards, magnetic tape, magnetic disks, or some combination of these three media.[1]

FIGURE 3-3.   Random file.

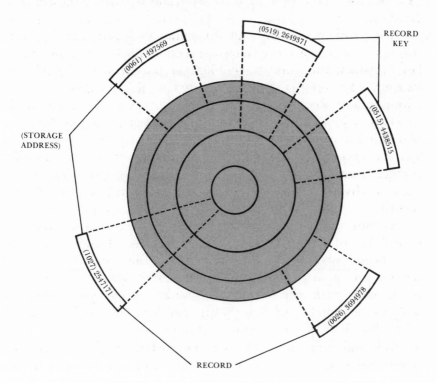

Combinations can occur when different media are used for transaction and master files. For example, a billing application could use punched cards as transaction documents, transfer data on the cards to tape, and then use the tape to update a master file on disk. This is a rather extreme example, however, and in those that follow it will be assumed that transaction and master files are on similar media.

Even if a single medium were always used throughout an application, differences among applications would necessitate a combination of media within the DP installation. Most DP systems that serve MIS have facilities for cards, tape, disks, and perhaps other media. The exact proportion of work carried out on the various media is dictated by the mix of applications.

CARD SYSTEMS

A system that uses only cards, such as the one shown in Figure 3-4, does not use files in external storage. Instead, all of the data required for processing—the program, the transaction file, and the master file—must be input through a card reader. Part of the output, in addition to any reports generated, will be a new master file. In the next processing cycle, this file, along with the program deck and a new deck of transactions, will be input. The old transaction and master file decks may be saved as historical records or as back-up material to re-create a new master file should something happen to the current one.

Card systems are simple and somewhat reassuring to laypeople because of the built-in back-up capability and the fact that cards can be read visually as well as by machine. These were distinct advantages in early data processing applications, particularly in finance and accounting, when computers were less reliable and auditors were inexperienced in computer operations. It is still

FIGURE 3-4.   Card system.

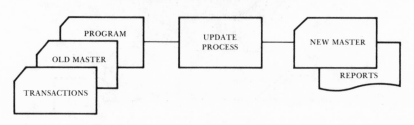

common to use card systems in payroll and billing applications (look at your last paycheck or utility bill), but cards are slowly and surely being replaced by other media.

One reason for the decline of card systems is, of course, the slow speed of card readers and card punches and the consequential underutilization of the CPU. But cards are also bulky and difficult to use when damp (from humidity, for example) or dog-eared. Cards also require extensive off-line operations in the form of keypunching, verifying, sorting, collating, duplicating, and the like—most of which can be done in the CPU or are unnecessary with other media. These off-line operations also involve special pieces of equipment that are increasingly idle as card usage declines, thereby creating further pressure to eliminate cards and their associated equipment.

TAPE SYSTEMS

Tape systems differ radically from card systems not only in the file·medium but also in the basic approach to file maintenance. Tape systems, as shown in Figure 3–5, keep the program, transaction file, and master file in external storage, calling data into the CPU only when needed. In a typical tape operation, files are organized sequentially with the program, which is relatively short in comparison to file length, stored at the beginning of the master file. After the program is read, the first transaction is compared to the first record on the master file. If the record keys are the same, transaction data and master file data are combined to create a new

FIGURE 3–5. Tape system.

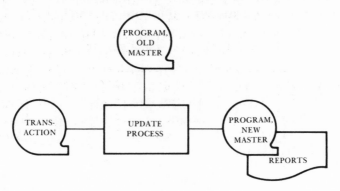

record which is written onto another tape. If the transaction record key is *greater* than the master file record key, it is an indication that one or more master records are not to be updated and
the master file tape is advanced until the record keys match. If the
transaction record key is *less* than the master file record key, it is
an indication that no master file record with that key exists and a
new record is to be created from the transaction file. These rules
are dependent upon accurate sequencing of records in both files
and the absence of errors. In practice, additional steps, such as
editing the transaction file and grouping the transactions by the
kind of updating process (to add, delete, or change a master file
record), are taken to insure accuracy.

At the conclusion of processing, there are three tapes—the
transaction file, the old master file, and a new master file—where
there previously had been two. At this time, any printed output is
prepared from the new master tape according to program instructions. The new master file becomes the basic source of data
for the application and the old master file and transaction file are
usually stored, off-line, for a few cycles as a back-up in the event
of loss or damage to the new master file.

Tape systems have several distinct advantages over card systems. Not only is tape faster, but the technique of reading one
transaction and one master record at a time uses very little CPU
storage. This is particularly advantageous when files are extremely large or when other programs are being processed concurrently under timesharing. The creation of a completely new
master file, with the old master file and transaction file intact for
back-up purposes, is also an advantage over the disk system described in the following section.

The biggest disadvantage of tape systems is that they are limited to sequential files. When many transactions are to be processed at once, as in the case of a monthly billing system or a
payroll system, transactions can be sequenced as in the master file
and processing with tape is quite efficient. However, if transactions must be processed serially, as they occur, tape systems are
prohibitively slow. A lesser disadvantage is that tape systems tie up
a lot of equipment. In order to update a master file on tape with a
taped transaction file, a minimum of three tape drives are
required—one each for the transaction file, the old master file,
and the new master file.

DISK SYSTEMS

Files in disk systems can be organized either sequentially or randomly. When disk files are sequential, processing is conducted almost exactly as in a tape system with the obvious exception that disk drives are substituted for tape drives. There are several reasons for using disks in sequential processing: disk drives are faster (although somewhat more expensive) than tape drives and there is a limited capability to update a sequential master file on disk with a serial transaction file. But the most common use of disk systems, and the one that best utilizes the direct access capability of disk drives, is with randomly organized master files. A disk system with a random master file is shown in Figure 3–6.

When the master file is organized randomly, the sequence of transactions is unimportant. When a transaction is read, the master file record can be found by the key transformation process described earlier, or in an index located at the beginning of the master file, and brought into the CPU for update. In marked contrast to the tape system in which the updated record is stored on another tape, the disk system returns the updated record to its original storage location. The process of rewriting the new record over the old record effectively erases the old record, although it does cut down on the number of storage devices needed to hold the old and new master files.

Disk systems are popular because of their high speed, direct access capabilities, and large on-line storage capacities. They also permit considerable flexibility in the choice of file organization and processing mode, although it would be inefficient to use se-

FIGURE 3–6.   Disk system.

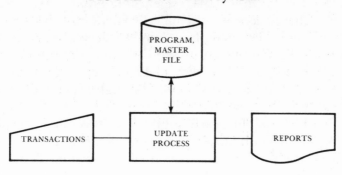

quential files exclusively and simply imitate a tape system with disks.

The one major drawback of a disk system is the erasing of the old master file during the updating process. Although it is now rare, disk drives are susceptible to "head crashes" in which a read or write head makes contact with the magnetized surface of the disk, scoring it and destroying any data recorded there. In such cases it is difficult to reconstruct a new master file without the old one. Also, certain financial and other applications have auditing requirements that are difficult to carry out without historical files. In these cases the master and transaction files are periodically transferred onto tape and held in the data processing library.

PROCESSING MODES

The *mode* of processing refers to the timing of the updating process with respect to the occurrence of transactions. Transactions may be processed periodically, say, at the end of each day, or as they occur. In the first case, the mode is said to be *batch* while in the second it is called *transactional* or *on-line*. In the special case in which a transactional system processes some data and returns output in time to influence the remainder of the transaction, it is further identified as being *real-time*. A few examples will illustrate the several processing modes.

BATCH PROCESSING

In many applications, output is needed only infrequently. A payroll is produced perhaps weekly or at even greater intervals although payroll transactions (the earning of pay) take place continuously. Charge accounts are billed on a monthly basis although credit purchases may take place daily. In these and similar cases, transactions are stored until processing time and then processed in a batch. Figure 3–7 illustrates a batch processing system, which also happens to be a card system, although any medium can be used to process in a batch mode.

Batch processing in a card or tape system is simply a matter of collecting transaction documents—time cards, charge slips, or whatever—and preparing a sequential transaction file to update the master file.

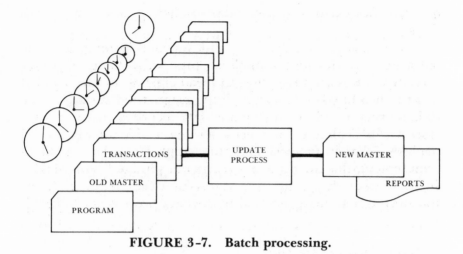

FIGURE 3-7. Batch processing.

Batch processing techniques in a disk system vary according to the organization of the master file.

WITH SEQUENTIAL MASTER FILES

If the disk master file is organized sequentially, batch processing proceeds as if on tape: the transactions are sorted into the proper sequence and records are updated in their physical order on the disk. The disk drive cannot access a record directly since there is no relationship between record keys and storage locations, so record identification is dependent upon comparisons of transactions and record keys as in a tape system.

WITH RANDOM MASTER FILES

If the disk file is organized randomly, there are two methods of batch processing. For small numbers of transactions—fewer than one-half of the number of records—the record location can be determined from an index or a key transformation process and updating can occur in the order in which the transactions are stored. If one-half or more of the records are involved in updating, it is best to sort the transactions into logical order and process them sequentially.

Sequential processing in a randomly organized master file is aided by the use of *pointers*. A pointer is a data element that gives the storage location of the next record in logical order. An *external access pointer* at the beginning of the file tells where the first logical record, i.e., the one with the lowest numerical record key, is stored. A pointer in that record gives the storage location of the second logical record, and so on. The disadvantage of adding an extra data element to each record for the pointer is offset by the efficiency of batch processing in sequence.

TRANSACTIONAL PROCESSING

When output is required for each transaction, say, to give a receipt to a customer, or when the data collection process is on-line, it is more efficient to process transactions as they occur. Many retail sales applications now operate in a transactional mode. Instead of punching sales data on cards or keying them onto tape or disk at the end of the day, transactions are recorded on *point-of-sale terminals* which double as cash registers. The operator may key in data such as the price, quantity, stock number, department, clerk identification, and sales tax, or some of these data may be read optically from the sales tag by a *wand*. The customer sees only limited output from the transaction in the form of a sales receipt. Unseen processes also post the sale to department accounts, deduct the quantity sold from inventory, debit charge accounts, and maintain records for sales and marketing analyses.

Transactional processing requires a direct access storage device such as a disk drive. Figure 3–8 illustrates a transactional system using terminals for input and a disk drive for master file storage. Once again, the exact processing techniques are dictated by file organization.

WITH SEQUENTIAL MASTER FILES

It is possible to process transactionally when the master file is sequential. As noted earlier, a disk drive cannot locate a record in a sequential file directly, but a disk drive *can* go directly to any given storage location. If a particular record in a sequential file is desired, it can be found by systematically halving the file in what is called a *binary search*. For example, if account number 353-62-4155 is needed for update and there are 2,000 accounts in the file, a check will be made of the 1,000th storage location. If the ac-

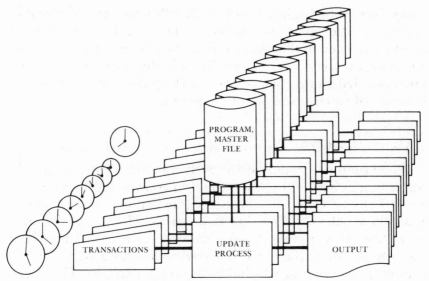

FIGURE 3-8. Transactional processing.

count number there is greater than 353-62-4155, that account must be somewhere among the first 1,000 locations. Next, location 500 is checked. If the account number there is less than 353-62-4155, then that account is somewhere between location 500 and location 1,000, so a check is made of location 750. Eventually, although not as long as it might seem, this process will find the desired record. It can be shown that the maximum number of steps needed to find any record by binary search is n where 2^n is greater than or equal to the number of records. Since 2^{10} is 1,024 and 2^{11} is 2,048, it will not take more than 11 steps to find any given record in a sequential file of 2,000 records. Of course, one might get lucky and find it much earlier—perhaps even on the first step.

WITH RANDOM MASTER FILES

The ability to process transactionally with a sequential disk file is merely a fringe benefit of disk drives. When the dominant processing mode is transactional, it is best to use a random file organization. The process of finding a record for update on a random master file has already been discussed—the storage location is determined from an index or by key transformation. In a sense, transactional processing with a random master file can be thought of as a special case of batch processing in which the batch is very small—only one transaction!

REAL-TIME PROCESSING

Real-time processing, the ability to influence a transaction while it is taking place, is one of the most powerful capabilities of data processing. The first real-time systems were developed by the U.S. Air Force for air defense missile control, where only fractions of a second could be tolerated between the detection of an approaching aircraft and the decision to launch a missile at it. This application led many to equate "real-time" with "instantaneous." This is not a bad interpretation for the air defense application, but, in an MIS, a much slower system can still be considered real-time.

Real-time processing is interactive; that is, there is an exchange of inputs and outputs at the source of the transaction. Real-time applications in business typically use a CRT or typewriter terminal to gain interactive access to a processor and master file as shown in Figure 3-9.

Real-time systems are of necessity transactional or on-line. Indeed, such systems are often described as on-line/real-time, although that terminology is somewhat redundant. Airline ticket reservation systems are excellent examples that demonstrate both real-time and transactional capabilities in a business application.

The ticket reservation system is real-time because the initial processing of a request for an airline ticket influences the outcome of the transaction—whether a ticket is sold or not. When a

FIGURE 3-9.   Real-time processing.

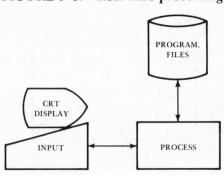

ticket request is keyed into a terminal at the reservation counter, the master file record for that flight is checked for the availability of a seat. If a seat is available, it is temporarily "booked" to prevent its commitment to another reservation office and that information is displayed on the CRT screen. A second input at the reservation terminal confirms the sale and makes the booking permanent. The entire process may take a few minutes, but that is real-time in ticket reservation if not in air defense!

The ticket reservation system is obviously transactional since requests for tickets are processed individually, as they occur, instead of periodically in a batch. Different versions of this system can also print tickets, bill customers for tickets purchased on credit, and provide data for scheduling and route optimization models.

Computer booking on airlines often raises the question of "overbooking." When more tickets are sold than there are seats on a flight, it is rarely due to a failure of the reservation system. More likely, it is a deliberate policy based on statistical evidence that a few ticket holders will not show up for the flight.

DATA PROCESSING AND MIS

It is now appropriate to reiterate and expand upon a few points made in Chapter 1 regarding the relationship between data processing and MIS. Figure 3–10 illustrates a point made earlier: it is difficult, if not impossible, to separate data processing and MIS. They are more like end-points of a continuum, with no clear dividing line between them, than they are like separate entities.

Both data processing and MIS are concerned with information technology—hardware, software, and processing methods—and

FIGURE 3–10. Data processing and MIS.

MANAGEMENT

TECHNOLOGY

DATA PROCESSING ────────▶ MIS

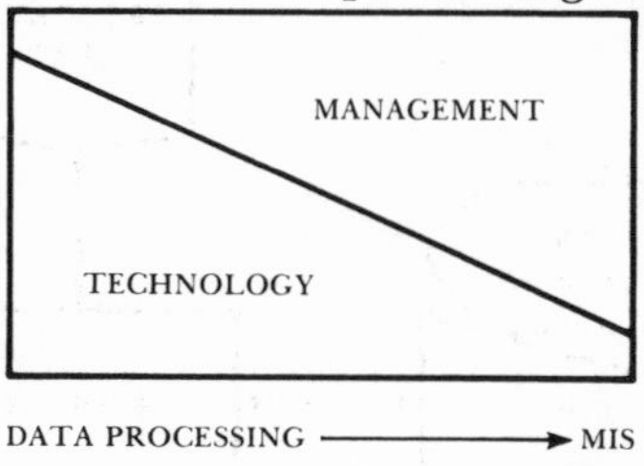

information management—the use of information to achieve organizational goals. But they are not concerned with these matters to the same degree. Data processing is more heavily oriented toward technology while MIS are more involved in management concerns. In the next chapter, we explore one of the most important concerns of management: decision making.

NOTE

1. Cards, tape, and disks are used here, as earlier, as the representative media of off-line, on-line sequential access, and on-line direct access storage. The reader can make substitutions as necessary for MIS that use different media. For example, some MIS use magnetic drums instead of disks, but the processing principles are the same.

CHAPTER 4

Decision Making

In Chapter 1, an MIS was defined, in part, as "an organized set of processes ... to support ... decision making within an organization." The key to providing this support is an understanding of how decisions are made: Do managers pick the best possible solution or merely one that works? To what extent do managers analyze quantitative data and to what extent do they rely on intuition? By what means are data manipulated to answer critical questions in the decision process? And, for the MIS manager, how can decision making be enhanced by a computer-based information system? Although these questions cannot be answered completely in the limited space available here, it is possible to survey the more important aspects of modern decision making by omitting details of actual computational procedures. In most cases, these computations are performed by computer and the user can obtain assistance in applying them from specialists in the MIS office.

THE DECISION ENVIRONMENT

There is a tendency, on the part of MIS specialists and other quantitatively oriented managers, to forget that not all decisions can be "programmed." Indeed, in planning for the support of organizational decision making, it is as important to recognize the limitations of computers as to know their capabilities. Figure 4-1 shows how managers' knowledge of cause-effect relationships and their preference for outcomes can combine to create different decision environments.

When managers have a definite preference for outcomes— high profits over low profits, few production defects over many defects, and so on—*and* they have complete knowledge of the factors that cause these outcomes, they can literally *compute* the best course of action to follow. This is the environment in which computers and quantitative methods flourish. There are numerous standard computer programs available that can compute the order quantity to minimize inventory costs, the shipping routes to minimize transportation costs, the product mix to maximize profits, the allocation of resources to minimize project time, and the solutions to many other similar problems.

In other situations, the preference for an outcome may be equally clear but the knowledge of how to achieve such an outcome is less than complete. Many personnel decisions fall into this caregory. The objective to hire a marketing manager who will increase sales may be abundantly clear, but the choice of the person to fill that position cannot be computed. Instead, the decision makers exercise *judgment;* they consider the information available on each candidate and make their decision subjectively. MIS are not excluded completely from such judgmental decision processes. MIS may be used to locate candidates from among current personnel or used to create files on other candidates who apply or are suggested by placement services. Nor are such decisions always nonquantitative. Some highly structured organizations, notably the military, attempt to quantify personal and professional attributes and base personnel decisions on numerical scores.

FIGURE 4-1. Decision environments. *Adapted from J. D. Thompson, Organizations in Action (New York: McGraw-Hill, 1967), p. 134.*

PREFERENCE FOR OUTCOMES

		CLEAR	UNCLEAR
KNOWLEDGE OF CAUSE-EFFECT RELATIONSHIPS	COMPLETE	COMPUTATIONAL	COMPROMISE
	INCOMPLETE	JUDGMENTAL	INSPIRATIONAL

More recently, there have been attempts to make judgmental decisions directly by computer. The computer programs involved *simulate* rather than *replicate* human judgment; that is, the computer model will make the same decision as a human might, although it obviously cannot duplicate the free-form, associative thought processes of the human mind. Imitation of human decision making by computer is called *heuristic* programming. Graduate school applications, bank loan applications, and other large-scale personnel decisions ordinarily made judgmentally have been made heuristically by computers with success. Heuristic programming is undoubtedly on the frontier of MIS evolution and holds great promise in the support of managerial decision making.

A particularly frustrating decision environment exists when managers know exactly how to achieve certain outcomes, but their preference for any given outcome is unclear. For example, in the 1960s, IBM undoubtedly possessed the knowledge—and the ability to apply it—of how to achieve monopolistic control of the computer industry. But did IBM prefer such an outcome? Clearly, it had a preference for the high profits that accompany such control but, just as clearly, it had a distinct preference to avoid the antitrust suits that would inevitably follow. The situation called for a *compromise:* a trade-off between market share and the tolerance of the federal government.

Compromise decisions are quite common in the public sector, where conflicting or unclear preferences are present in almost every situation. Individual freedom versus public safety, environmental concerns versus economic benefits, defense spending versus human services, and other such philosophical differences constantly face elected and appointed decision makers in government. The dispute over preferences cannot, of course, be resolved by MIS, although MIS may help gather and analyze data on public opinion. But, once preferences are established, the decision environment shifts back to the computational quadrant and MIS become an important, almost dominating, factor in the decision process.

Pity the poor decision maker in the environment depicted in the lower right-hand corner of Figure 4–1. He (or she) is unsure of what he prefers and even if he did have a preference he would not know how to achieve the desired outcome. Faced with such a decision, most of us simply raise our eyes heavenward and mur-

mur, "Help," hoping for an *inspirational* answer to our problem. Once again, such situations are somewhat more common in the public sector. Should a friendly but totalitarian foreign regime be supported or not and, assuming it should, how can it be kept in power? Should unemployment really be eliminated and how can that be done without excessive inflation? At present, MIS are all but helpless in solving these and similar dilemmas. Human decision makers must resolve preferences to the extent that the environment shifts to the judgmental or computational.

The matrix of decision environments is a convenient model for explaining decision situations, but it has several shortcomings that should be mentioned. First, the scales of preferences and outcomes are not dichotomous as shown in the drawing—that is merely a pedagogical convenience. In reality, they are continuous with only the extreme end-points shown. There are many shades of grey between the black and white of "complete-incomplete" and "clear-unclear." Obviously, the extent of MIS help in these in-between situations also varies continuously from much to little or none. Second, the matrix gives no clue to the *frequency* of each decision environment. The organization—a bank, for instance— that habitually finds itself in a computational situation will undoubtedly make a heavier commitment to MIS than, say, the State Department, which through no fault of its own is more likely to find itself in an inspirational environment. An organization's decision environment is a major factor in the design of its MIS.

DECISION STRATEGIES

There is another dimension to the matrix of decision-making environments that is particularly relevant to the computational cell. The additional dimension, shown in Figure 4–2, describes the extent of a manager's knowledge of the external conditions that will prevail at the time the decision is carried out. This knowledge of the future—of the *state of nature* that will exist—ranges from *certainty* (perfect knowledge) to *uncertainty* (no knowledge whatsoever) with a middle ground of *risk* (probabilistic knowledge).

DECISION MAKING UNDER UNCERTAINTY

When managers have no knowledge of future environmental factors, they tend to be guided by their personal philosophy to-

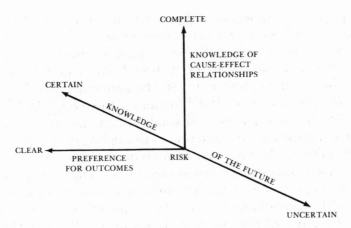

FIGURE 4-2. Dimensions of the decision environment.

ward success and failure. For some, the rewards of success dominate the decision process while others are more motivated by fear of failure. To illustrate, consider the case of an electronics manufacturing firm that wishes to enter the growing market for personal computers. Three alternative courses of action have been proposed: to manufacture its own brand of personal computer, to manufacture accessories to be used with the personal computers of other manufacturers, or to become a supplier of circuit boards and subassemblies used by other manufacturers. The states of nature that might prevail in the future concern the action of the computer industry leader. If the industry leader enters the market, it would seriously damage sales of other personal computers but might create good markets for accessories and subassemblies. If the industry leader stays out, the firm's own personal computer could be a big seller and there would be a greater market for subassemblies to other manufacturers, but lower overall sales of personal computers would hurt the sales of accessories. The electronics firm, of course, does not know what the industry leader will do and its management feels that its decision must be made before the industry leader's plans become known. The estimated profits (or loss) from each combination of an alternative and a state of nature are shown in the form of a *payoff table* in Table 4-1.

The Maximax Strategy

"Maximax" is an abbreviated expression for "maximize the maximums"; that is, evaluate each alternative in terms of its

TABLE 4–1.   Payoff Table for an Electronics Firm

Alternative	State of Nature	
	1. INDUSTRY LEADER ENTERS MARKET	2. INDUSTRY LEADER DOES NOT ENTER MARKET
1. Manufacture own personal computer	($250,000)	$1,200,000
2. Manufacture personal computer accessories	$600,000	$ 450,000
3. Supply subassemblies to other manufacturers	$400,000	$ 500,000

maximum possible payoff and select the one with the highest maximum. A manager of the maximax philosophy would view the courses of action for the electronics firm as shown in Table 4–2. Such a manager would naturally favor the manufacture of personal computers, since it is the alternative with the highest potential profit.

Maximax is often referred to as the strategy of the complete optimist. Only favorable outcomes are considered, even if they happen to require different states of nature. In order to achieve the maximum profits for the first and third alternatives, the maximax manager must assume that the industry leader will *not* enter the market; however, the maximum profit for alternative 2 is based on an assumption that the industry leader *will* enter the market. Such inconsistencies will not deter a true optimist, of course, but they may be bothersome to the information analyst trying to design a system to support this manager's decision making.

TABLE 4–2.   Maximax View of Expected Profits

ALTERNATIVE	MAXIMUM PROFIT
1. Manufacture own personal computer	$1,200,000
2. Manufacture personal computer accessories	$ 600,000
3. Supply subassemblies to other manufacturers	$ 500,000

THE MAXIMIN STRATEGY

"Maximin" is a shortened version of "maximize the minimums." In this case, the decision maker considers only the *worst* possible outcome for each course of action and selects the one with the highest minimum. For the electronics firm, a maximin manager would consider only the outcomes shown in Table 4-3 and would elect to manufacture accessories for the personal computers of other manufacturers.

If a maximax is a complete optimist, a maximin is obviously a complete pessimist. Maximin managers are no more or less logical than maximax managers—both require the state of nature to vary freely in order to support their payoff assumptions—they simply have a different philosophical outlook. There are, perhaps, more managers of the maximin persuasion (how many times have you heard, "If we do this, what is the worst thing that can happen?"), but our society tends to glorify the risk-takers, the maximax managers who go for the big payoff. The football coach who calls for a long pass on fourth-and-one from his own 20-yard line will be hailed for his courage—especially if the pass is successful—but the coach who punts in the same situation is more likely to enjoy a long career.

THE OPPORTUNITY LOSS CRITERION

Some decision makers prefer to view alternatives in terms of their opportunity loss instead of their payoffs. Opportunity loss is the difference between the best payoff for a given alternative under a specified state of nature and the payoff for each other alternative under that same state of nature. For the electronics

TABLE 4-3.   Maximin View of Expected Profits

ALTERNATIVE	MINIMUM PROFIT (LOSS)
1. Manufacture own personal computer	($250,000)
2. Manufacture personal computer accessories	$450,000
3. Supply subassemblies to other manufacturers	$400,000

firm, Table 4–4 shows that, if the industry leader enters the market and the firm manufactures accessories (alternative 2), there is no opportunity for higher profit, and the opportunity loss is zero. However, if the firm decides to manufacture its own personal computer and the industry leader enters the market, it loses $250,000 when it could have made $600,000 by manufacturing accessories—an opportunity loss of $850,000. Finally, the opportunity lost by the decision to become a subassembly supplier is the $600,000 of alternative 2 less the $400,000 of alternative 3 or $200,000. Opportunity losses when the industry leader does not enter the market are computed similarly as differences between the best payoff ($1,200,000 for making the firm's own personal computer) and the payoffs for the other alternatives.

The use of opportunity loss to evaluate alternatives is often called "minimax," which stands for "minimize maximum opportunity loss." For the electronics firm, the maximum opportunity loss for each alternative is shown in Table 4-5. A minimax strategist would select the third alternative based on its low maximum opportunity loss.

The minimax strategy often turns out to be a compromise, as in this example, between the completely optimistic and completely pessimistic outlooks. The philosophical foundation of minimax is still somewhat pessimistic, however, in that it seeks to minimize loss.

TABLE 4–4. Opportunity Loss for an Electronics Firm

	State of Nature	
Alternative	1. INDUSTRY LEADER ENTERS MARKET	2. INDUSTRY LEADER DOES NOT ENTER MARKET
1. Manufacture own personal computer	600,000 −(250,000) 850,000	1,200,000 −1,200,000 0
2. Manufacture personal computer accessories	600,000 − 600,000 0	1,200,000 − 450,000 750,000
3. Supply subassemblies to other manufacturers	600,000 − 400,000 200,000	1,200,000 − 500,000 700,000

TABLE 4-5. Minimax View of Opportunity Loss

ALTERNATIVE	MAXIMUM OPPORTUNITY LOSS
1. Manufacture own personal computer	$850,000
2. Manufacture personal computer accessories	$750,000
3. Supply subassemblies to other manufacturers	$700,000

DECISION MAKING UNDER RISK

The quality of decision making can be improved by additional information about the possible states of nature. Indeed, one of the major objectives of decision makers is to reduce or eliminate uncertainty. Uncertainty is reduced when probabilities can be assigned to the occurrence of each state of nature. For example, in the electronics firm case, it may be determined that the probability that the industry leader will enter the market is .6 (six chances out of ten), which implies a probability of .4 (the remaining four chances out of ten) that it will not enter the market. In this case, the probabilities represent the subjective estimate of the decision maker based on an evaluation of the industry leader's historical market activity and perhaps indications found in its current activities.

EXPECTED VALUE CRITERION

When probabilities can be assigned to the states of nature, the appropriate decision criterion—irrespective of the decision maker's personal philosophy—is the *expected value* of each alternative. An expected value is the weighted average of the payoffs for a given alternative under the various states of nature. For alternative number 1, the expected value is the payoff when the industry leader enters the market weighted (multiplied) by the probability that the leader will enter the market, plus the payoff when the leader does not enter the market weighted by that probability. In numbers, the expected value is

$$(-250,000)(.6) + (1,200,000)(.4) =$$
$$-150,000 + 480,000 \qquad = \$330,000$$

This and other expected values for the alternatives under consideration by the electronics firm are shown in Table 4-6.

The three alternatives now represent expected profits of $330,000, $540,000, and $440,000, respectively. The best decision, of course, is the one with the highest expected value—to manufacture personal computer accessories.

DECISION TREES

In its simplest form, a decision tree is merely a graphical representation of a payoff table. Figure 4-3, for example, shows exactly the same information included in Table 4-6. In keeping with conventional decision tree notation, alternatives are shown as arcs (lines) designated with an A, subscripted to identify specific alternatives (A_1 is the first alternative, A_2 the second, and so on). Similarly, states of nature are shown by arcs with a subscripted S. When probabilities are assigned to states of nature, they are shown on or near the arc; in this example they appear under the arc, just below the identifying S. The shape of the nodes is also governed by convention—squares represent *decision nodes* (where the decision maker has a choice of alternatives to follow) and circles represent *chance nodes* (where probability determines which state of nature occurs). The number in each chance node represents the expected value for the alternative that terminates in that

TABLE 4-6. Payoff Table with Expected Values

	State of Nature		
Alternative	1. INDUSTRY LEADER ENTERS MARKET. PROBABILITY = .6	2. INDUSTRY LEADER DOES NOT ENTER MARKET. PROBABILITY = .4	EXPECTED VALUE
1. Manufacture own personal computer	$-250,000$ $\times \quad .6$ $-150,000$	$+$	$1,200,000$ $\times \quad .4$ $480,000$	$= 330,000$
2. Manufacture personal computer accessories	$600,000$ $\times \quad .6$ $360,000$	$+$	$450,000$ $\times \quad .4$ $180,000$	$= 540,000$
3. Supply subassemblies to other manufacturers	$400,000$ $\times \quad .6$ $240,000$	$+$	$500,000$ $\times \quad .4$ $200,000$	$= 440,000$

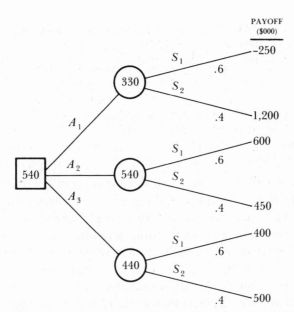

FIGURE 4-3.   Decision tree with simple probabilities.

node. A decision is reached by looking forward from a position at the decision node and selecting the alternative that leads to the highest expected value. The number in the decision node represents the expected value of that alternative. In this decision tree for the electronics firm example, the number 540 in the decision node means that alternative 2, with an expected value of $540,000, should be selected.

When decisions are complex, the decision tree format gives a much clearer picture of the factors that determine the optimum alternative. Suppose, for example, the electronics firm's decision were complicated by the industry leader's involvement with the manufacture of a microprocessor suitable for use in personal computers. Entry into the microprocessor market will alter the probability that the industry leader will enter the personal computer market, and the electronics firm should revise its decision process accordingly. We will call production of a microprocessor "indicator number 1" and note it by I_1. Indicator number 2 (I_2) is *not* producing a microprocessor.

The management of the electronics firm knows that the industry leader makes about 70 percent of its own components. Therefore, if it is going to enter the personal computer market (S_1), there is a .7 probability that it will make its own microprocessor (I_1). In statistical notation, this is written as $P(I_1|S_1) = .7$ and read as "the probability of indicator 1, *given* that state of nature 1 is a certainty, is 70 percent." By deduction, $P(I_2|S_1) = .3$, or, there is a 30 percent chance that the industry leader will not make its own microprocessor even if it does enter the personal computer market.

The electronics firm management also knows that about 20 percent of the industry leader's output consists of components or subassemblies used in products it does not manufacture. This suggests that there is a probability of .2 that the leader will produce microprocessors even if it does not enter the personal computer market, or, $P(I_1|S_2) = .2$ and $P(I_2|S_2) = .8$.

It is now possible to compute the probability of I_1 and I_2 as weighted averages of the conditional probabilities. The probability of I_1 is found by $P(S_1)P(I_1|S_1) + P(S_2)P(I_1|S_2)$ or $(.6)(.7) + (.4)(.2) = .42 + .08 = .50$. The probability of I_2 is $P(S_1)P(I_2|S_1) + P(S_2)P(I_2|S_2)$ which also happens to be .50.

It is clear that the electronics firm can improve its decision situation by waiting to see what the industry leader does with respect to microprocessor production. But a six-month wait is not without penalty. Other firms may get a competitive jump and the cost of implementing the final decision on short notice may be increased by overtime labor and priority shipments of material. For these reasons, the electronics firm assigns a cost of $50,000 to the option of waiting six months to observe the microprocessor indicator.

The decision tree reflecting this new development is shown in Figure 4–4. An important difference between this and the previous decision tree is the substitution of conditional probabilities for the simple probabilities associated with the states of nature. The whole purpose of waiting for the indicator is to reduce uncertainty about the state of nature. We therefore expect revised, improved probabilities for S_1 and S_2. The revisions based on the indicators are written as $P(S_1|I_1)$, $P(S_2|I_1)$, $P(S_1|I_2)$, and $P(S_2|I_2)$. One example will serve to illustrate the computation of revised probabilities:[1]

$$P(S_1|I_1) = \frac{P(S_1)P(I_1|S_1)}{P(I_1)}$$

$$= \frac{(.6)(.7)}{(.5)}$$

$$= .84$$

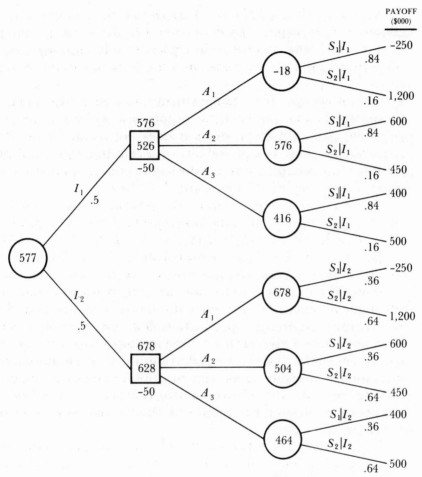

FIGURE 4-4. Decision tree with revised probabilities.

Other revisions of the state-of-nature probabilities can be verified by substituting the appropriate subscripted variables and their respective numerical values.

The decision tree is interpreted as follows: If the industry leader begins to produce microprocessors (I_1), then manufacture personal computer accessories (A_2) with the expectation of a net profit of \$526,000 (i.e., \$576,000 − \$50,000). If the industry leader does not produce microprocessors within six months (I_2), then manufacture the complete personal computer (A_1) and expect a net profit of \$628,000 (i.e., \$678,000 − \$50,000). The expected value of the overall decision is the equally weighted (.5 for I_1 and .5 for I_2) average of \$526,000 and \$628,000: \$577,000.

This analysis also resolves the decision, shown in Figure 4-5, to wait or not wait for the indicator. Since the expected value without the indicator is $540,000 and the expected value with the indicator, including the $50,000 penalty, is $577,000, it is wiser to wait and let the decision be guided by the indicator.

Decision tree analysis has wide application, especially in marketing where indicators predict consumer attitudes toward a product. Decision trees help justify (or reject) decisions to conduct market research by showing the effect such additional information will have on the profits expected by marketing different products.

DECISION MAKING UNDER CERTAINTY

When the state of nature is known with certainty, the emphasis shifts from the selection of an alternative to the computation of outcomes. The decision itself is usually obvious under certainty; the challenge comes in developing a model that will yield the answer. When the decision situation is unique, management scientists or operations researchers may be required to develop an appropriate model. Fortunately, many decisions can be supported with standard models that require only brief familiarizations and a little practice on a computer terminal. A few examples of commonly used modeling techniques will serve to illustrate the process of decision making under certainty.

LINEAR PROGRAMMING

The name "linear programming" refers to the formulation (programming) of a decision situation with first-order (linear) equations expressed in terms of certain decision variables. The

FIGURE 4-5. Decision to wait for indicator.

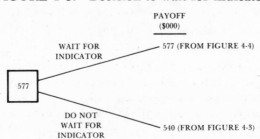

equations are solved simultaneously to give not just the best of two or three proposed alternatives, but the *best of all possible solutions* to the problem. Models that yield a best possible solution directly are called *optimization models*. It has been estimated that 15 to 20 percent of all businesses use linear programming, which makes it one of the most popular of all optimization techniques.

Linear programming can be used to find the optimum mix of products to manufacture under certain production constraints, the most profitable combination of investments that meets a client's investment philosophy, the least expensive shipping plan for a distribution network, and the solutions to many other typical problems. Most such problems involve numerous variables and constraint equations and, for all practical purposes, must be solved by computer. It is possible, however, to make a graphical analog of the way problems are solved by linear programming if the problem is restricted to only two variables and a few constraints. One such problem is presented in Table 4-7.

The production manager of an optical company has some idle time available each week on the grinding and polishing machines. The company wishes to use this time to produce camera lenses. A type *A* lens yields a profit of $15 and requires two minutes of grinding time and ten minutes of polishing time. The type *B* lens brings a profit of $12 and requires three minutes of grinding and six of polishing. The firm can sell all the type *B* lenses it can make, but the demand for type *A* lenses is only 275 per week. Based on the limited grinding and polishing time available and the limited demand for type *A* lenses, how many of each type should be manufactured to maximize profits? The graphical solution to this problem is shown in Figure 4-6.

TABLE 4-7.   A Product Mix Problem

| PROCESS | Requirement (Minutes) | | Available Time (Minutes) |
	LENS *A*	LENS *B*	
Grinding	2	3	940
Polishing	10	6	3080

Profit: $15 for each *A* lens, $12 for each *B* lens

Maximum demand for *A* lenses is 275/week. All *B* lenses made can be sold.

Problem: How many of each type lens should be made in order to maximize profits?

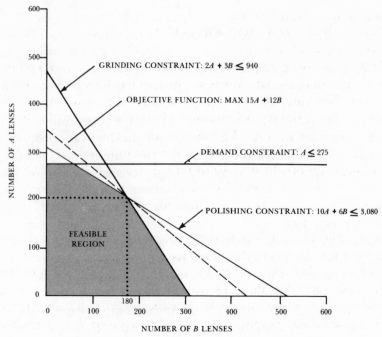

FIGURE 4-6.   Linear programming graph.

The constraint on grinding time is expressed as $2A + 3B \leq$ 940, meaning that two (minutes) times A (the number of A lenses made) plus three (minutes) times B (the number of B lenses made) must be less than or equal to 940 (minutes of grinding time available). The line from 470 on the A axis to 313 on the B axis represents combinations of A and B lens quantities that will require *exactly* 940 minutes of grinding. The area below the line represents combinations that use *less than* 940 minutes. The polishing constraint and the A-lens demand constraint are plotted similarly. The shaded area defined by the overlap of the three constraints is known as the *feasible region*—the combinations of A and B quantities that meet all three constraints. Somewhere in this region is the optimum combination.

Profit for this problem is given by $15A + 12B$, or 15 (dollars) times the number of A lenses plus 12 (dollars) times the number of B lenses. The objective is to maximize this expression, hence it is called the *objective function* and written as MAXIMIZE $15A + 12B$.

The optimum combination is found by plotting the slope of the objective function and moving it as far from the origin (the lower left-hand corner of the graph) as possible, staying within feasible region. For this problem, the optimum combination is where the objective function, shown by a dashed line, just touches the corner of feasible region at $A = 200$, $B = 180$. The solution to the problem, therefore, is to manufacture 200 type A lenses and 180 type B lenses for a profit of $5,160. No other feasible combination of A and B lenses will bring as much profit.

INVENTORY ANALYSIS

Every organization that maintains inventory faces the problem of striking a balance between certain _ordering_ and _carrying_ costs associated with inventory. Ordering costs are administrative expenses generated by the placing of an order and are independent of order size. Ordering costs argue for very large orders which would have to be placed only infrequently. Carrying costs are based on insurance, taxes, storage fees, and other costs directly related to the quantity of inventory. Carrying costs argue for very small orders which obviously would occur more frequently than large orders.

Figure 4-7 shows that carrying cost is a straight line function

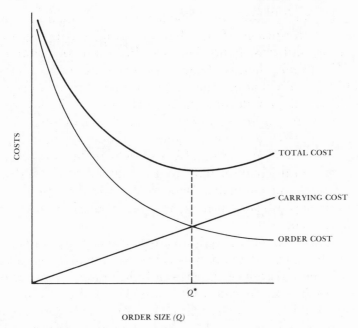

ORDER SIZE (Q)

FIGURE 4-7. Minimizing annual inventory costs.

that increases constantly with order size. It costs twice as much to carry, say, 100 units as 50; three times as much to carry 150; and so on. Ordering costs follow a curve that decreases more and more gradually as order size increases. In the extremes, one could place very small orders every day or one very large order once a year. The *total* cost curve represents the sum of the annual ordering and carrying costs for any given order size. The optimum order size is the quantity that minimizes total cost.

The relationships shown in Figure 4–7 have been expressed mathematically in Figure 4–8. The optimum order size, usually called the *Economic Order Quantity* or *EOQ*, is given by the square root of two times the annual demand for the item times the cost of placing an order divided by the cost to carry one item in inventory for one year. This formula can be used by anyone who is certain of the demand and costs and who has a pocket calculator.

The basic EOQ model is *deterministic;* that is, the variables involved are known with certainty and can assume only one specific value each in the computation of the EOQ. More sophisticated analyses of inventory introduce *probabilistic* values for some variables. Such factors as the shipping time and the demand during shipping time may vary from period to period. If shipping time exceeds the expected time or if demand suddenly increases before an order arrives, inventory may not be sufficient to satisfy demand and a stock-out will occur. Stock-outs result in back orders, loss of good will, possibly the loss of the order, or, at worst, the loss of the customer. In order to avoid these losses, inventory managers carry some additional numbers of items called *safety stock.* The optimum level of safety stock can be determined from an analysis of the probability distributions for demand and shipping time, the penalty perceived for a stock-out, and the cost of carrying safety stock.

FIGURE 4–8.   Optimum order size.

$$Q^* = \sqrt{\frac{2DC_o}{C_k}}$$

where Q^* is the Economic Order Quantity (EOQ)
$\quad D$ is the annual demand for the item
$\quad C_o$ is the cost of placing an order for items
$\quad C_k$ is the cost of carrying one item in inventory for one year

Present Value Techniques

It would seem that, when future costs and revenues are known with certainty, the choice between competing investment opportunities would be simple. Surprisingly, it is not, and many poor financial decisions are made because of a lack of knowledge of the appropriate decision techniques. For example, consider the two projects shown in Figure 4-9. Project number 1 involves fairly high start-up costs, but low maintenance costs over the life of the project. Project number 2 is exactly opposite: low start-up costs

FIGURE 4-9. Financial decision without discounting.

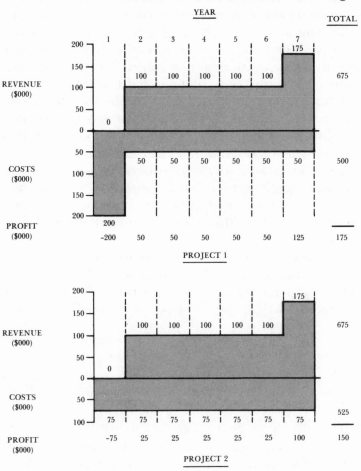

and high maintenance costs. Both projects produce identical yearly revenues, including the salvage value of capital investments received in the final year.

From a superficial review of the data presented in Figure 4-9, it would seem that project number 1 is the more profitable by $25,000. After all, total revenues are the same but total costs are $25,000 higher in project number 2. But this reasoning ignores the *time value* of money. We know that a dollar in hand today is of more value than a dollar payable one year from now. But how much more? Assuming that one could invest today's dollar at 15 percent, it would be worth $1.15 in one year. Conversely, the dollar payable in one year is worth the amount that, if invested today at 15 percent, would yield exactly $1.00 a year from now. That amount is known as the *present value*. The present value of one dollar payable one year from now, using an interest rate of 15 percent, is 86.9565¢.[2] It can also be said that this is the value of $1.00 *discounted to the present* at the rate of 15 percent.

When the revenues and costs of the two projects shown in Figure 4-9 are discounted at 15 percent, the cash flow chart appears as shown in Figure 4-10. Total profit is still the relevant criterion, but profit is now expressed as the difference between the present value of revenues and the present value of costs—a difference referred to as the *net present value*.

Two facts are apparent in Figure 4-10. First, neither project is nearly as profitable as first imagined and, second, our superficial analysis led to the wrong decision—we should have picked project number 2!

Present value methods are now so universally accepted and so simple to use that they have been programmed into many hand-held calculators. They are, of course, also incorporated into the model bank of MIS for the convenience of terminal users.

ADMINISTRATIVE BEHAVIOR

Before leaving the subject of decision strategies, it should be pointed out that the objective of choosing the one best alternative is considerably easier to achieve in the closed environment of a book than in the open environment of the real world. In the real world, the combinations of alternatives and states of nature may be too numerous to consider. Certainty and deterministic conditions also occur much less frequently in the real world than we are

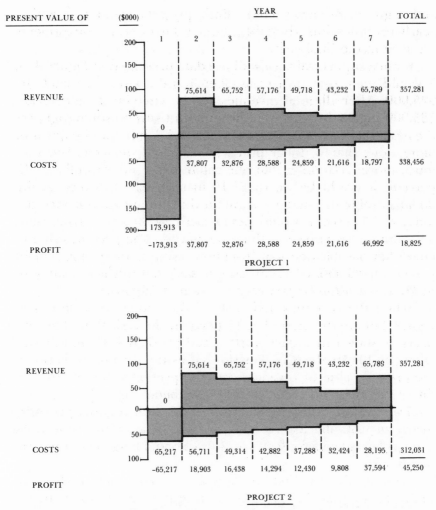

FIGURE 4-10. Financial decision with discounting.

sometimes led to believe. And many variables are difficult or impossible to express in the quantitative terms required by these analyses. How would you, for example, estimate the value of good will created by landscaping the physical plant of a firm?

The result is that many managers prefer intuitive methods over the more analytical methods presented here. It can be argued, of course, that intuition *is* an analytical process—we simply are not yet able to discern the steps involved. This is an area of great interest in the subject of heuristic programming mentioned earlier.

There is also evidence that managers do not really attempt to optimize, to find the best solution. Instead, it is argued, they *satisfice;* that is, they accept the first solution that satisfies certain acceptance criteria. Personnel managers, for example, cannot possibly consider every potential candidate for a job opening. Rather, they establish criteria for experience, education, and other relevant attributes and then hire the first candidate who qualifies.

The tendency to satisfice instead of optimize is called *administrative behavior* by behavioral scientists. Administrative behavior unquestionably occurs, but certainly not to the exclusion of quantitative techniques. The current popularity of quantitative topics in business school curricula and the increasing availability of computational power, both of the hardware and software variety, tend to relegate satisficing to a "second choice" role behind optimizing. Even when satisficing is appropriate, as in the personnel example above, many managers will compromise by selecting a number of satisfactory alternatives and then optimizing from among those selections.

OTHER DECISION TOOLS

In addition to those decision methods selected to illustrate decision making under uncertainty, risk, and certainty, two other decision tools merit discussion because of their widespread use and great value in the support of decision making. They are *statistical methods* and *simulation.*

STATISTICAL METHODS

In conversational English, most of us use the term *statistics* to refer to numerical data—as in labor statistics, population statistics, baseball statistics, and so on. To the management scientist, however, *statistics* refers to the branch of mathematics concerned with probabilistic concepts. The decision tree analysis discussed earlier, for example, is based upon probability and is properly included in the field of statistics.

Other statistical tools enable managers to predict future events and thus reduce uncertainty over the state of nature. For example, a marketing manager may hypothesize several levels of demand for a product as possible states of nature. With no way of knowing just which state will exist, the selection of an alternative must be guided by minimax, maximin, or some other philosophical approach to decision making under uncertainty. However, if a single level of demand can be predicted, then the decision can be made, under certainty, by a method such as linear programming.

It is obvious that the quality of any decision based on a prediction is directly dependent on the accuracy of that prediction. Accuracy in turn is dependent on the quality and quantity of data collected, chance, and the method of prediction. One such method of statistical prediction is the process of *estimation*.

ESTIMATION

In statistics, estimates are made of some population characteristic based upon knowledge gained from a sample of that population. For example, the estimated mean age of household heads within an insurance sales region could be estimated from a survey of a few hundred households. A few *thousand* households would improve the accuracy of the estimate, but, as the number of households surveyed increases, the cost of the survey also increases. There are statistical methods to determine the appropriate sample size based upon the maximum allowable error of the estimate.

An estimate expressed as a single value is called a *point estimate*. Thus, to continue the example above, if a survey of 200 households indicated a mean age of 41 years for the head of the household, then the point estimate for the mean age of the heads of all households in the region would also be 41 years. Point estimates are convenient for use in deterministic models where a single value must be substituted for an unknown, but they are also risky in that they give no indication of possible deviation from the estimated value.

A more informative form of an estimate, but one that is more difficult to incorporate into analytical models, is the *interval estimate*. Thus, one might say that the mean age of all heads of households in the region is 41 years *plus or minus*, say, 1.7 years. The amount added and subtracted to give the interval is based upon three things: the size of the sample, the inherent variability of the population as exhibited in the sample, and the degree of confidence desired by the decision maker. Small samples, much variability, and high levels of confidence all contribute to large intervals. Large samples, little variability, and a willingness to accept a lesser degree of confidence all tend to reduce the interval. Sample size, as noted earlier, can be computed; variability is expressed by a statistical measure called the *standard deviation* which can be computed from the sample data; and confidence is usually expressed as a percentage of 90, 95, or 99 percent. A 95 percent confidence level for an interval estimate means that the decision maker is 95 percent certain that the population mean falls within the stated interval about the sample mean.

Estimation is usually based upon *current* observations of the variable to be estimated. It is also possible to predict based upon *past* observations of the variable under examination. This form of prediction is called *trend analysis*.

TREND ANALYSIS

Trend analysis is appropriate for predictions into the future when there is evidence that the future is at least partially determined by the past. Population growth, for example, reasonably can be predicted on the basis of the past, but one might be less willing to predict next year's snowfall based on historical data. Annual gross sales, the number of people who participate in various recreational activities, the number of computer systems in use, and other similar facts of interest can be predicted fairly well by trend analysis.

In trend analysis, a decision maker seeks to "fit" a line to a plot of data. For simplicity, an example using a straight line will be used, although many trends are explained better by curved lines. "Curve fit" programs in the MIS model bank can determine the type of line that best fits the data. Figure 4–11 shows how a straight line has been fitted to a plot of annual attendance at an amusement park.[3] Based on a straight-line projection of attendance, park management could expect 2.60 million visitors in 1982.

Trend analysis is easy to understand and to use, but it is very susceptible to sudden environmental changes that may make the estimate totally wrong. For example, consider the net earnings of the Polaroid Corporation for the years 1975 to 1978. Figure 4–12 shows that a linear trend analysis of net earnings would have predicted a 1979 figure of $132 million. Yet Polaroid's actual net earnings for 1979 were around $37 million! Clearly, the condi-

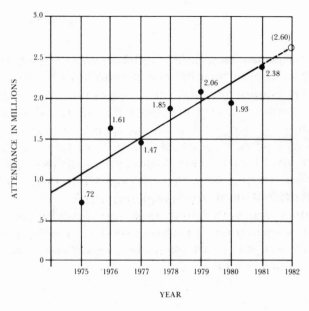

FIGURE 4-11. Trend analysis of amusement park attendance.

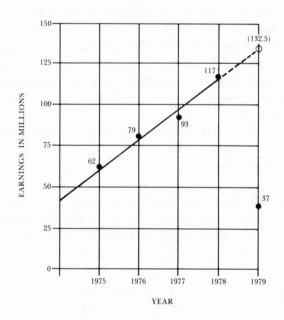

*From *Business Week*, March 2, 1981.

FIGURE 4-12. Trend analysis of Polaroid's annual net earnings.

tions that led to the steady increases between 1975 and 1978 had changed and should have been incorporated into any model to predict 1979 net earnings.

REGRESSION ANALYSIS

Regression analysis is closely related to trend analysis in that it also predicts on the basis of historical data. But where trend analysis relies on the past performance of the *predicted* variable, regression analysis uses other, related variables to make the prediction. In this way, sales of television sets might be predicted on the basis of total population, disposable income, interest rates, and other such variables. Like trend analysis, regression analysis is not restricted to straight line, or linear, relationships. But, unlike trend analysis, there may be more than two variables involved in regression analysis. Again, for the sake of simplicity, a linear example will be used and, to permit a graphical solution, only two variables will be considered. Neither of these conditions poses a serious problem to computer applications of regression analysis, which can accommodate a variety of curvilinear relationships and do not use graphical solution methods.

Table 4-8 shows the number of hot dogs sold at a major league baseball park and the home team's winning percentage as of that date. Regression analysis will permit the concessions manager to predict the number of hot dogs to be prepared for each game (the *dependent* variable) on the basis of the team's current winning percentage (the *independent* variable). The results of such an analysis are shown in Figure 4-13.

TABLE 4-8. Hot Dog Sales and Winning Percentages

DATE	WINNING PERCENTAGE	SALES (IN THOUSANDS)
Apr. 15, 1980	.250	9.9
Jun. 1, 1980	.375	11.4
Aug. 1, 1980	.533	12.8
Sep. 15, 1980	.482	11.5
Apr. 15, 1981	.667	13.9
Jun. 1, 1981	.571	13.5
Aug. 1, 1981	.510	13.4
Sep. 15, 1981	.425	12.4

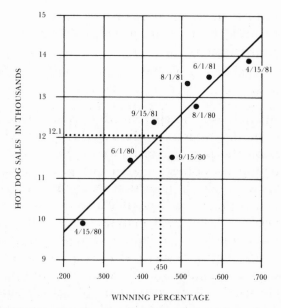

FIGURE 4-13. Regression analysis of hot dog sales.

A *regression line* fitted to the hog dog/winning percentage data shows that if the team's current percentage is .450, past performance suggests the sale of approximately 12.1 thousand hot dogs. This is called *simple* regression because it employs only one independent variable. Of course, there are other variables that affect hot dog sales—such as the weather, the opponent, the team's involvement in the pennant race, and so on—as evidenced by the fact that all plotted points do not lie exactly on the regression line. The inclusion of such additional independent variables requires a form of analysis called *multiple* regression which, as suggested earlier, is difficult to portray graphically, but not particularly demanding of a computer analysis.

The examples of regression and trend analysis presented here are comparable to the point estimates discussed previously. It is also possible to construct intervals about regression and trend analysis predictions. In the hot dog example, the concessions manager might wish to operate at the upper end of a 95 percent confidence interval to reduce the chance of running out of hot dogs. The refinement of the prediction by including additional independent variables and the use of a confidence interval would greatly reduce uncertainty over the demand for hot dogs.

SIMULATION

The models described up to this point are more or less standard mathematical or statistical techniques. They can be included in the model bank and used in a variety of situations with little effort other than entering data according to a specified format. They also are *static;* that is, they show a final solution with little attention to what may have transpired en route to that solution. There are many decision situations in which no standard model applies or in which a *dynamic* model—one that shows and considers intermediate results—is necessary. The technique of *simulation* is particularly appropriate in these cases.

Simulation imitates the actual transactions in an organization. A simulation of inventory, for example, might consider the depletion of inventory each day as orders are filled, the reordering of stock, the delay while awaiting replacement stock, daily costs of carrying inventory, and the daily starting and closing stockage levels. Annual costs and average stockage levels would be determined from the daily figures. On average, the results of this simulation would be the same as the results of the inventory analysis described earlier, but the simulation would point out more clearly the peaks and valleys of inventory over the course of the year.

Simulation is particularly helpful in unstructured decisions such as those encountered in financial planning. A static financial plan might ensure annual receipts that cover annual expenditures, but financial managers must also be assured of adequate funds to meet day-by-day demands. The simulation of daily receipts and expenditures will show the requirement for cash reserves and how much money can be placed in term investments.

The key to simulation is the determination of these daily figures—demand on inventory, receipts, expenditures, and so on. Average values are probably known, but they have the same disadvantage of static models: they do not reflect daily fluctuations. Simulation solves this problem by generating a value for each variable as the variable occurs. If daily demand on inventory has been found to vary from 15 to 60 units, then the simulation model will generate a number between 15 and 60 to subtract from the previous day's balance.

The mechanism for assigning values to a variable in simulation is called a *process generator.* The inputs to a process generator are *random numbers* and the outputs are values of the variable to be simulated. A simulation that uses random numbers in this fashion is referred to as *Monte Carlo* simulation—in recognition of the element of chance that is introduced into the model.

Once again, the computer application for simulation is mathematical, but the process can be explained in simpler terms graphically. Figure 4-14 shows how random numbers between zero and one can be converted to daily demand for inventory when demand varies from 15 to 60. In this example, a random number of .63 results in a demand for 32 items. As many different variables as necessary may be simulated in this way and incorporated into the model.

Of course, it is unlikely that demand for inventory on the day in question really will be 32. The value of simulation lies not in its ability to predict specific outcomes but in the way it shows the results of the interaction of a number of probabilistic variables. Since no single iteration of the simulation model is likely to reflect the actual situation, it is common to run hundreds or even thousands of iterations. The resultant hundreds or thousands of answers form a distribution of possible outcomes. Perhaps a simulation of a certain inventory policy (the level of safety stock, the reorder point, and the order size) shows that the level of inventory never falls below 52 items. The inventory manager may wish to

FIGURE 4-14. Process generator for demand on inventory.

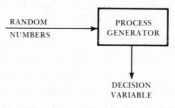

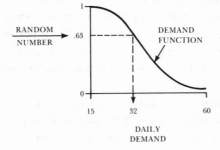

simulate different policies until a lower minimum is reached and stock-outs are still held to an acceptable level. Notice that simulation does not lead directly to a *best* solution. Simulation is not an optimization model like linear programming. It is merely *descriptive;* it describes the situation defined by the decision maker. It is up to the decision maker to alter the situation in order to improve the solution.

MIS AND DECISION MAKING

The decision tools discussed in this chapter all can be used without computers or an MIS. The techniques involved have been known for years and years and are all described in standard textbooks on statistics and management science. But, like the examples used here, textbook examples are invariably simple and admittedly unrealistic in comparison to real world situations. A linear programming solution for a real optical company might involve dozens of product variables and hundreds of constraint equations. While it is theoretically possible to solve such a problem manually, the hundreds of thousands of individual calculations involved would take so long and would be so error-prone as to preclude any manual attempt.

Other decision tools increase in complexity similarly when employed in the real world. One iteration of a simulation model may require values for ten or twenty variables. And it is not uncommon to run through several hundred iterations just to get a *starting point* for the model. Even the daily interval mentioned here is an oversimplification; a production simulation can use intervals of only a few seconds—and then simulate a monthly period! The present value model explained here used an *annual* compounding period. But we know that most financial institutions now compound *daily* or even continuously—for perhaps thousands of accounts! Clearly, these models too are impractical in a manual mode.

It is the computer that has raised management science models from the level of theoretical curiosities to the practical decision-support tools they represent today. And it is the MIS, which collects these models into a readily accessible bank, that makes management science techniques available for organizational decision making. And, as we shall see in the following chapter, it is the manager who is ultimately responsible for applying these techniques.

NOTES

1. The revision is based on *Bayes' Theorem,* an explanation of which may be found in any college-level statistics text.
2. This value is obtained by $P = F/(1 + i)^n$, where P is the present value, F is the future sum, i is the annual interest rate, and n is the number of years. For this example, $P = 1/(1.15)^1 = .869565$. This formula can be modified to take into consideration periodic compounding of interest, which has been omitted here for the sake of simplicity.
3. The exact placement of the line in Figure 4-11 is determined by the "least squares" method, which minimizes the sum of the squared deviations of each plotted point from the line.

PART II
The Management of MIS

Up to this point, the focus has been on the *technological* aspects of MIS—computer hardware and software, data processing, decision models, and so on. There is also a *behavioral* side to MIS, one that deals with human and organizational issues. Humans are involved in MIS as users and managers, while organizational issues stem from the need to integrate MIS personnel and equipment into the organizational structure.

In this book, where computers are viewed primarily in their MIS support role, the major behavioral concerns are for managers. It is important to remember, however, that the larger social issues concerning computers deal with invasion of privacy, unemployment due to automation, and the consumer's view of computers as impersonal and dehumanizing. The omission of these issues from this discussion does not diminish their significance; they simply do not have a direct bearing on MIS.

Because of MIS, management and organizations are different today than they were 15 or 20 years ago. Traditional roles and organizational structures have been altered. In Chapter 5, the role of MIS in management and the impact of MIS on traditional management functions are explored. Organizational and person-

nel implications are discussed in Chapter 6, and a new role of
management—that of managing the MIS itself—is addressed in
Chapter 7.

Not all managers have welcomed the changes brought about
by MIS. Some, to be sure, have adapted well. Others have resisted
and still others have sought to avoid involvement with MIS. Resistance has been crushed by the computer revolution of information management, and avoidance is virtually impossible in a contemporary organization. Managers must either adapt or be replaced by those with the skills—now taught in every graduate and
undergraduate business curriculum—to use MIS to their advantage. Part II details the changes in management and organization;
the decision to adapt or not is left to the reader.

CHAPTER 5

MIS and Management

There are two important management implications of MIS: the *role* of MIS in management and the *impact* of MIS on management. The role of MIS is to serve managers, to help them discharge their managerial responsibilities with greater efficiency and productivity. But in doing so, MIS alter the techniques and methods used by managers and, invariably, alter the nature of management itself. This is the impact of MIS.

THE NATURE OF MANAGEMENT

The management implications of MIS are so broad that it is helpful to have some framework for organizing and analyzing them. There are two common approaches to explaining management that serve this need rather well: the *process* view, which describes management as a cycle of job-independent functions common to all managers, and the *hierarchical* view, which considers differences in responsibility based upon organizational levels.

THE MANAGEMENT PROCESS

Although management scholars do not agree on the exact number or definitions of functions in the management process, Figure 5-1 is representative of the responsibilities usually attributed to management.

PLANNING

The management process is guided by goals and objectives that originate with owners, government, society, or management itself. In the planning function, managers translate these goals and objectives into specific courses of action. For example, the board of directors' goal to increase a firm's market share may result in plans to expand production capacity, intensify promotional activities, or improve product design. Similarly, the federal government's objective to reduce air pollution may require plans to modify the production process in a steel mill. And management's

FIGURE 5-1.   The management cycle.

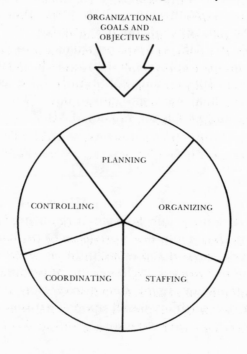

own goal to reduce the amount of returned merchandise may lead to plans for new quality control procedures.

By definition, planning is a future-oriented function. For organizations to survive in a constantly changing environment, managers must anticipate changes and plan accordingly. Some automobile manufacturers in the seventies failed to anticipate decreased fuel supplies, consumer preferences for small cars, and government regulations on safety and fuel economy. The difficulties of these companies in the eighties is a reflection of their poor planning in the seventies.

ORGANIZING

In a narrow sense, organizing refers to a structuring of resources—the establishment of divisions, departments, sections, and so forth, to carry out organizational plans in the most efficient manner. The body of knowledge on how best to accomplish this structuring is known as *organization theory*. The *classical school* of organization theory considers purely structural factors such as span of control, chain of command, and specialization of labor. The *behavioral school* adds human considerations and the very important concept of the *informal organization*. A more contemporary view, the *systems school*, considers the flow of resources—capital and labor—through the organization.

In the broader context of the management process, organizing includes the identification of all the resources needed to carry out the plans developed in the planning function. A plan to introduce a new product line, for example, requires the identification of appropriately skilled labor by personnel managers, material and equipment by production managers, sources of capital by financial managers, and potential markets by marketing managers.

STAFFING

While staffing is generally used to describe the acquisition of just human resources, in the management process it is also used generically to include the acquisition of all of the resources identified during the organizing function. Managers in the various functional areas of an organization discharge their staffing responsibilities by recruiting personnel, purchasing material, raising capital, and acquiring other necessary goods and services.

COORDINATING

Coordinating is sometimes called "leading," "activating," "directing," or even "communicating." By any name, it refers to the actual execution of the plans made earlier in the management process. As coordinators, managers ensure that organizational resources are utilized in an efficient, cooperative manner. The alternative terms for this function reflect the need of managers to communicate instructions to subordinates and to motivate subordinates to accomplish the goals and objectives upon which plans are based.

CONTROLLING

Managers control organizational activities by comparing actual performance to planned performance—and initiating corrective action to remedy any discrepancies. Controlling is usually considered the last step in the management process, but it is also involved in the other management functions. For example, the standards against which actual performance is compared are developed during the planning function and should be written into the plans. Control is also exercised during the organizing function by setting quality and performance standards for personnel, material, and equipment. As these resources are acquired during the staffing function, control is exercised again by screening personnel, inspecting material, and testing equipment. Finally, as plans are executed and resources are converted into goods or services in the coordinating function, actual performance data are collected for comparison, during the controlling function, against projected performance.

THE MANAGEMENT CYCLE

When the comparison of actual performance to planned performance reveals a discrepancy, controlling can be thought of as the *first* function of management as well as the last. For discrepancies must be remedied, and this usually involves new plans or modification of existing plans. To illustrate, suppose actual sales fall short of projected sales. First, the projections should be reexamined. Are they reasonable? Are they based on correct input and valid computations? Have they been accurately communicated to the sales force? And so on. Assuming the standards are valid, why are the actual sales low? Is advertising sufficient? Is the product faulty? Is the sales force competent? In short, what has caused the discrepancy? When the problem has been isolated, new plans must be formulated to correct the situation. Additional resources must be identified and acquired, the new plan must be executed, and the new results must be compared to the expected performance.

In addition to complete cycles through the five functions of the management process, there are often shorter cycles within and between functions. For example, a common planning tool is the milestone chart which shows the expected completion dates for key events, such as the hiring of personnel, the testing of new equipment, and so forth. However, many of these events are first identified during the organizing function. Clearly, managers must "back up" and complete the plans after some initial work on organizing. And staffing, the acquisition of resources, often reveals flaws in organizing, the identification of resources, that require remedial work in that function. And so it is with other functions as well. The management process is never really completed but cycles endlessly through and between its various functions.

THE HIERARCHY OF MANAGEMENT

A second approach to viewing the nature of management is based upon the organizational level from which managers operate. Traditionally, three levels are considered: top, middle, and supervisory or first line. Of course, the actual _number_ of managers in an organization is a function of size and organizational complexity. A very small, single-function organization, such as a gas station, may have only one or two managers; while a very large, complex organization, such as an automobile manufacturer, may have hundreds. The relationship between management levels and the number of managers can be explained in terms of the outlook or _planning horizon_ of managers. Regardless of the exact number of managers in an organization, those at or near the top will be concerned with long-range, _strategic_ plans; those in the middle will be concerned with short-range, _tactical_ plans; and the lowest level will be concerned with day-to-day, _operational_ plans. In the extreme, even a sole proprietor, as perhaps the only manager in the firm, must divide his or her time among these three outlooks.

The levels of management and the corresponding planning horizons are shown in Figure 5-2. The hierarchy of management typically is depicted as a pyramid to reflect the proportion of managers at each level.

THE RELATIONSHIP BETWEEN PROCESS AND HIERARCHY

The hierarchical view of management is important for two reasons: information needs tend to be different at different levels of management and the amount of time devoted to any given function of management varies considerably with the level of management. The differences in information needs are the basis for the MIS support levels described in Chapters 8 and 10; the way managers allocate their time to management functions is shown in Figure 5-3.

The usual presentation of planning, organizing, staffing, coordinating, and controlling as equal slices of the management pie may be aesthetically pleasing, but it is also somewhat misleading in implying that those functions place equal demands on managerial resources. When the management functions are shown in approximate proportion to the time managers spend on each, it can be seen that there are differences both among functions and among management levels. These differences can be interpreted by MIS planners in at least two ways.

First, a strong case can be made for allocating MIS resources in proportion to the importance of the supported function at each management level. According to this line of thinking, which equates importance to the amount of time spent, one-half of the MIS resources allocated to serving top management's information

FIGURE 5-2.   The hierarchy of management.

LEVEL		OUTLOOK
TOP		STRATEGIC
MIDDLE		TACTICAL
FIRST-LINE		OPERATIONAL

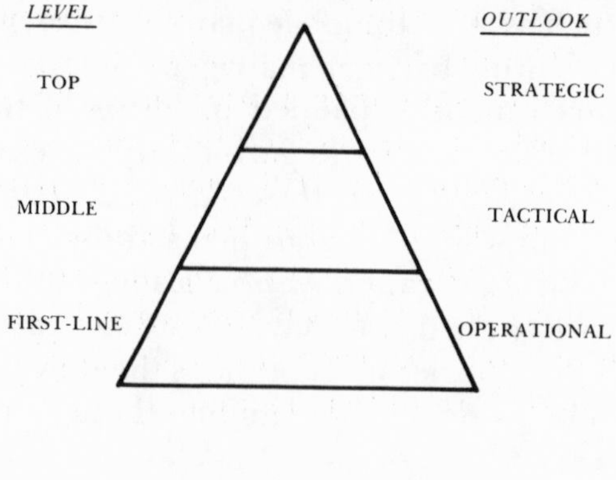

FIGURE 5-3. The allocation of managers' time. *From* Management Information Systems, Instructor's Guide, *by Raymond McLeod, Jr.* © *1979 Science Research Associates, Inc. Adapted by permission of the publisher.*

needs should be in support of strategic planning. Yet planning, and strategic planning in particular, is the most innovative and creative of all the management functions. But computers, and therefore MIS, are literally incapable of innovation or creativity.[1] This poses an interesting dilemma for MIS designers: should MIS be directed into a role in which they do not perform well or should they be restricted to areas of proven success?

Many designers opt for the second choice on the theory that freeing managers from mundane or highly structured responsibilities which can be accomplished within the MIS framework gives them more time to devote to creative activities. Managers and MIS in such organizations coexist in a symbiotic relationship—each performs independent but equally important tasks for their mutual well-being.

The current state of the art in computer and MIS design suggests that a third, compromise, approach is now possible. There will always be a requirement for human creativity—a *person* must first recognize the potential of a corporate merger, a change in fashions, an impending political situation, or any of the hundreds of other strategic planning considerations. But the fact that such creative activities must be initiated by humans does not completely rule out participation by MIS. Once a manager has proposed a merger, he or she can use the MIS to collect facts, analyze alternative financing schemes, select the optimal course of action, and simulate the merged activities before actually implementing the plan. This interaction between managers and MIS is a key element in the role of MIS in management.

THE ROLE OF MIS IN MANAGEMENT

There are three basic MIS activities involved in support of the management process: report generation, inquiry processing, and data analysis. All MIS activities support all the functions of management to some degree, but certain activities are of greater importance in some functions than in others. Figure 5-4 shows the most common interactions between MIS activities and management functions.

REPORT GENERATION

Reports are the primary means of disseminating information in an MIS. Reports are usually classified according to their frequency, level of detail, and the degree to which they anticipate an information need.

SCHEDULED REPORTS

Scheduled reports are produced at regular intervals (daily, weekly, monthly, etc.) to satisfy recurring needs that were fully anticipated at the time the MIS was designed. Periodic sales reports, financial statements, inventory records, and other such re-

FIGURE 5–4. Management functions and MIS activities.

| | MIS ACTIVITY | | |
MANAGEMENT FUNCTION	REPORT GENERATION	INQUIRY PROCESSING	DATA ANALYSIS
PLANNING	◒	●	●
ORGANIZING	◒	●	◒
STAFFING	◒	◒	○
COORDINATING	●	◒	○
CONTROLLING	●	◒	◒

● EXTENSIVE APPLICATION
◒ MODERATE APPLICATION
○ LITTLE OR NO APPLICATION

ports fall into this category. Scheduled reports are distributed routinely and require no initiative on the part of managers who receive them.

Often the value of scheduled reports is diminished simply because they are routine. If familiarity does not necessarily breed contempt, neither does it stimulate interest. Many managers become so used to ignoring frequent, bulky, scheduled reports which contain much information they do not need that they do not bother to use such reports to find information they do need. MIS personnel may not be able to change managers' attitudes toward scheduled reports, but they can at least review report content with interested managers periodically to confirm the need and applicability of the information provided.

UNSCHEDULED REPORTS

Unscheduled reports also satisfy anticipated needs, but are not produced unless called for. For example, a computer program to generate a listing of employees' job skills would have been prepared during MIS development, but the listing itself is not needed unless the personnel department is trying to fill a vacancy. When the need arises, the report can be requested and provided within a very short time—hours, perhaps.

The responsibility for the success of unscheduled reports rests primarily with the managers who need the information the reports provide. Obviously, if a manager is unaware or forgets that a certain unscheduled report is available, he or she will not request it. MIS personnel can help by circulating lists of available reports and by briefing new managers on kinds of reports and other services offered by the MIS.

SPECIAL REPORTS

Special reports are prepared to satisfy unanticipated needs. For example, the discovery of a hazardous substance in a manufacturing process might prompt a request for a report on absenteeism and medical claims by personnel who work with the substance. In all probability, no program exists to prepare such a report and one must be designed, coded, tested, and debugged (corrected) before the report can be produced. Depending on the availability of data, the complexity of the programming, and the urgency of the information need, the preparation of a special report can take days or even weeks.

Of course, once the program to produce a special report has been prepared, it will be kept on file and can be run again on call to produce an unscheduled report or run routinely to produce a scheduled report. In the example above, employees' medical claims would probably be monitored on a regular basis for some time after the hazardous substance had been eliminated.

REPORT DETAIL

Reports can also be classified by their level of detail. Reports that give all available information, such as every sale made by each member of the sales force, are called *detail reports*. It is rare for managers to need this kind of information, although it is quite common for MIS to produce it. More often, management needs are served better by *summary reports* which use statistical summary measures (averages, ranges, deviations, etc.) to reduce report volume. Sales data, for example, might be summarized by listing only the monthly totals for each salesperson or the mean dollar value of sales in each of several sales regions. Still better for most management needs are *exception reports* which list only information that falls outside certain management-defined parameters, for example, only those sales persons whose actual sales vary more than plus or minus 10 percent from their quotas.

MANAGEMENT USE OF REPORTS

As the primary means of disseminating information in an MIS, report generation can be expected to have broad application to the functions of management. Although this is generally true, in practice the greatest need for disseminating information occurs in coordinating and controlling, and it is there that reports are employed most advantageously.

The significance of report generation in coordinating is more apparent when it is recalled that coordinating includes the function of communicating. Reports are often the means of communicating the nature of a task to be performed, the materials to be used, and the destination of the goods to be produced or the recipient of the services to be provided. This kind of report is particularly significant at lower organizational levels where coordinating occupies such a large proportion of managers' time. Examples of reports that support the coordinating function may be found in the discussion of the production subsystem in Chapter 11.

Coordinating reports flow downward in an organization, conveying the implementing instructions of plans from higher to lower levels of management. Reports in support of the controlling function tend to flow upward as supervisory managers report the accomplishment of tasks, the consumption of resources, the result of quality inspections, and the disposition of the output of goods and services. Middle-level managers, who tend to spend more time on controlling than on any other function, compare these reports of actual performance to standards established during planning.

Reports are of more limited use, but still helpful, in the management function of planning. Plans that involve projections into the future often are based on historical data captured in previous reports. For example, an insurance firm may plan for future expenses on the basis of historical trends in the number of policy holders, claims, and settlements. Special reports can be prepared to present these data in a format convenient to the planners or they can be retrieved directly through inquiry processing.

Organizing may also be facilitated by historical data. While it is unlikely that a plan will exactly duplicate some previous mix of resources, most organizational activities can be broken down into tasks identical or similar to some performed in the past. In these cases, the resource requirements of the planned activity can be synthesized from data on actual expenditures for those past tasks. Many manufacturing processes can be organized in this fashion. Calculators, for example, may be unique in appearance and function, but they are made up of more-or-less standard components under established production methods. Resource requirments for a new calculator can be determined quite accurately from old production reports. Once again, the required information may be presented in a special report or obtained directly from an inquiry.

Staffing is difficult to support with any MIS activity because it is so often requires data from sources external to the organization. Although an organization may maintain data (and thus be capable of reports) on vendors, employment agenices, and financial institutions with which it has dealt in the past, there usually are no data in the MIS on the thousands of other suppliers with which it has not dealt. While managers may be guided in the selection of a supplier based on a history of timeliness, quality, service, and price in past dealings with their organization, it would be a mistake not to consider the other, perhaps equally dependable, suppliers simply for lack of MIS-furnished data.

Not all resources are acquired externally. In the case of personnel, managers can be aided by reports on employees such as the job skill listing suggested earlier. Of course, the promotion of in-house personnel simply creates openings elsewhere in the organization, but usually at a lower level where the personnel selection decision is easier and less critical.

INQUIRY PROCESSING

Inquiries have already been mentioned as alternatives to special reports. Indeed, inquiries, as the term is used here, can be thought of as special reports that are programmed by the end user—usually a manager who can access an on-line, direct-access storage device via a terminal. The use of data base management systems (DBMS) greatly enhances inquiry processing. With a DBMS, managers can generate special reports on virtually any subject with a few simple commands. Of course, the basic data needed to produce these reports, usually captured in transaction processing, must be in the database. More is said on DBMS in Chapter 9.

Since inquiries are alternatives to special reports, managers should consider the advantages and disadvantages of each before deciding which to use. Three factors influence the choice: the ability of the user to process an inquiry, the urgency of the information need, and the volume of the expected output.

Special reports require no data processing skills or equipment on the part of the user whereas inquiries require some familiarity with the DBMS and access to a terminal. Managers who already fear or mistrust MIS usually opt for special reports.

Inquiries produce results in seconds or minutes as opposed to the days or weeks required for a special report. Even if time is not critical, inquiries allow much greater freedom of expression by the user. A request for a special report must be thought out in great detail with particular attention given to the content and format of the information desired. In most organizations, a special report request must be made in writing and approved by a responsible person or committee. If the requested information turns out not to satisfy the information need completely, most managers are reluctant to make a second request which calls attention to their original mistake. Inquiry processing permits managers to experiment with different data formats, to follow up interesting results with additional inquiries, and to organize data for analysis.

Inquiries tend to be limited in output volume. CRT terminals display perhaps one page of material at a time and typewriter terminals are very slow. If output is voluminous or very specialized (hard-copy graphs, multiple copies, wide-paper format, etc.), special reports may be more appropriate. Of course, inquiry output can be sent to a more versatile output device, but the interactive nature of inquiry processing is sacrificed in the process.

Management Use of Inquiry Processing

Figure 5-4 shows that inquiry processing is used primarily in support of planning and organizing, although it certainly is the most flexible of all MIS activities and can support any management function. One reason that inquiry processing is not used more in support of coordinating and controlling is that those functions are already supported well by report generation. This may change, however. As managers develop inquiry processing skills for planning and organizing, they become dissatisfied with the restrictions inherent in report generation and seek to apply their new skills to more traditionally supported functions such as coordinating and controlling. But, while the use of inquiry processing is increasing dramatically with the proliferation of terminals, it is doubtful that it will ever replace report generation completely.

The ability to pose follow-up inquiries, that is, to have interactive access, is especially beneficial in the planning function. For planning is the least structured of all management functions and it is a rare planner who completely anticipates all the information needed to develop a plan. More likely, as the plans begin to take shape, additional information needs arise. The planning function would be seriously impaired if information were available only in reports or, worse, if planners failed to consider some information because it took too long to process it.

The ability to search large volumes of data and select elements that meet certain criteria is extremely difficult to do manually and equally easy to do by inquiry processing. This is precisely what is required in the organizing function: managers must review un-counted previous operations in search of activities similar to those planned for the future. It is like trying to find a name in a tele-phone directory when you know only the telephone number. Yet this would be a relatively simple task—to associate a subscriber with a telephone number—for a terminal user accessing a tele-phone directory data base. It is also easy for a manager organizing the production of a new model automobile to query a data base for previous examples of, say, front wheel disc brake assembly operations.

When information requirements for staffing, coordinating, or controlling are brief, inquiry processing may be the best way to satisfy the requirement. Questions such as, "Do we have an em-ployee who speaks Spanish and has a degree in mechanical en-gineering?" or "What is the status of job number P4702-C?" or "What percentage of allocated funds has been expended on ad-vertising to date?" may be answered readily—provided the data have been captured and stored in an accessible device in some structured manner.

DATA ANALYSIS

In Chapter 1, it was noted that some transformation processes are more sophisticated than others. Storing, retrieving, sorting, duplicating and classifying data are important but simple pro-cesses. They make data available in a convenient form, but they do not add new information; they expand quantitative limits to han-dling data, but they do not qualitatively add to the information data convey. By contrast, processes such as calculating and sum-marizing improve data management quantitatively *and* qualita-tively. There is a synergistic effect by which the processed data convey more information than that contained in the individual, unprocessed data elements. Data analysis is the application of these more sophisticated transformation processes to increase the information content.

In scientific usage, analysis means to break down and examine in detail. Similarly, data analysis is the examination of subsets of data with the purpose of discerning hidden meaning. For exam-ple, automobile sales data are a mass of numbers representing sales by model, color, year, options, and so forth. One analytical approach to such data would be to isolate and examine sales of, say, four-door sedans. If sales of four-door sedans for the past six years have been .53, .62, .71, .69, .74, and .80 million, a *trend analysis* could be used to predict next year's sales to be approximately .85 million (trend analysis and other similar techniques are discussed in Chapter 4). Additional analyses may refine this estimate by considering the effects of exogenous factors such as trends in family size, age of automobile buyers, economic activity, and other relevant variables.

Mathematical models form the basis for most data analyses. The more commonly used models—trend analysis, linear regression, linear programming, and inventory analysis—are usually kept in a *model bank* on an on-line storage device. Computer programs that require one of these models simply call the appropriate model out of the bank when it is required for data analysis.

The model bank can also be accessed interactively from a terminal. In a logical extension of inquiry processing, a manager not only can tailor reports to specific information needs, he or she also can call up a mathematical model to perform a detailed analysis of those reports without ever leaving the terminal. For example, many manufacturing firms determine an optimum mix of products from an analysis of the costs of the resources involved and the profit margin of each product. An inquiry can isolate those costs that are changing and the production manager can use a linear programming model to determine a new mix based on the revised data.

Not all models can be preprogrammed and stored in the model bank—any more than all reports can be anticipated. Some situations require unique models, just as some information needs require special reports. When managers themselves possess the skill to develop such models—as they frequently do in research and development or engineering departments, and less frequently in other departments—it is a good idea to provide them microcomputers or "smart" terminals with which to program their own models. Of course, just as special reports can evolve into scheduled or unscheduled reports, a "unique" model might have subsequent applications. The developer of a unique model may keep it on a cassette or floppy disk compatible with the terminal or microcomputer used as an input device, but if it appears that there are organization-wide applications of the model, it should be turned over to the MIS department for documentation and inclusion in the model bank. Models incorporated into an MIS in this manner are still readily available to the developer.

MANAGEMENT USE OF DATA ANALYSIS

As the most creative of management functions, planning is most likely to require information that is not readily apparent in the raw data. Thus, it is not surprising that data analysis is especially supportive of the planning function. The future orientation of planning also demands an MIS capability to predict—one of the primary applications of the mathematical models incorporated into data analysis. Some of the more common uses of data analysis in planning include scheduling production, locating new facilities, routing materials, scheduling investments, and developing marketing campaigns. Many of the decision-making techniques discussed in Chapter 4 can be applied to these and other planning tasks.

Other management functions are supported to a lesser degree by data analysis. Certain financial models are useful in identifying sources of capital in the organizing function, and the controlling function frequently involves data analysis to pinpoint the source of a discrepancy between actual and projected performance. Coordinating sometimes involves data analyses similar to those used in planning, but on a greatly reduced time schedule. In fact, some management theorists view coordinating as one end of a continuum with planning at the other end. As plans become shorter and shorter in range, planning gradually evolves into execution. Many processes, particularly in manufacturing, require extremely short range plans, often measured in seconds or less, to control equipment and material used in the production process. These "plans" are based on a real-time analysis of data gathered from the process itself. For example, in automated photo processing, the time to develop pictures is determined by the rate at which film responds to the developing chemicals rather than by a preset time. Computer control of operational processes such as these is generally considered to be apart from the MIS.

THE IMPACT OF MIS ON MANAGEMENT

The specter of a computer takeover has been a real concern to blue collar and clerical workers for some time. Although it has received less attention, a similar concern exists among many managers who view MIS as a threat to their jobs. Are managers threatened by MIS? Certaintly computers *do* replace some workers; do managers face the same fate? MIS have been with us long enough that we need no longer speculate on these questions—the evidence now exists to determine just what impact MIS have had on management.

EARLY PREDICTIONS

In the late fifties, two management scholars predicted that computers (the term "MIS" was not yet popular) would take over much of the decision making by managers. The result, they said, would be that first-line management could handle these programmable decisions while top management would assume responsibility for the nonprogrammable decisions; middle management would, in effect, be "squeezed out."[2] The effect they predicted on the traditional management pyramid is shown in Figure 5-5.

By the early sixties, however, predictions were beginning to take on a different tone. It became apparent that, for the moment at least, computers were not *replacing* managers but were being *used* by managers. Instead of changing the numbers or organizational level of managers, computers seemed to be changing the way managers performed their jobs. This led to predictions that computers and MIS (a new term for that time) would result in a new elite class of managers skilled in computer operations and the quantitative methods typical of computer-supported decision making.

FIGURE 5-5. The impact of computers on management.

TOP

MIDDLE

FIRST-LINE

TRADITIONAL

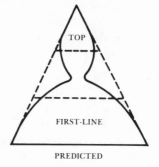

TOP

FIRST-LINE

PREDICTED

CURRENT OBSERVATIONS

Management research during the seventies and into the eighties reveals that early predictions of a reduction in middle management simply have not materialized. By 1973 it was seen that there had been no reduction either in the total number of managers (corrected for growth) or the number of middle managers. But if this is comforting news at first, it soon begins to raise doubts. After all, computers are expensive and, if it still requires the same number of managers to get the job done, why have computers? How many times have we heard, "A computer will save time and money," only to find later that we have the same (or greater) number of employees and it is costing more to get the job done?

The answer lies in the quality and quantity of work accomplished. It is true that the number of managers has not decreased, but they now base decisions on a more thorough and accurate analysis of data than was previously possible. And if these decisions do not result in immediate, dramatic increases in profits or decreases in cost, it is because the environmental conditions have changed. The legal and social environment places ever-increasing demands on managerial resources. The competition, too, is making decisions based on more thorough and accurate, computer-assisted analyses. A modern management needs MIS not so much to get ahead, but merely to hold its own in a changing environment.

While the erosion of middle management did not materialize, the predictions of changes to the scope of management did. There *is* a new elite of innovative, creative, mathematically oriented managers and, ironically, they are *middle* managers—the very group that was supposed to be squeezed out. As predicted, first-line management did assume responsibility for programmable decisions, but this merely relieved middle management of routine tasks and freed it for more creative activities, such as planning.

If one were to generalize on the relationship between computer-assisted decision making and management levels today, the result would be as shown in Figure 5-6: top management tends to deal primarily with nonprogrammable decisions involving environmental data that are not readily available in the MIS; first-line management deals mainly with programmable decisions

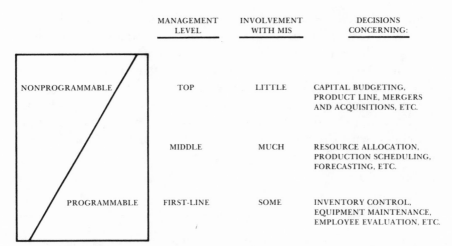

	MANAGEMENT LEVEL	INVOLVEMENT WITH MIS	DECISIONS CONCERNING:
NONPROGRAMMABLE	TOP	LITTLE	CAPITAL BUDGETING, PRODUCT LINE, MERGERS AND ACQUISITIONS, ETC.
	MIDDLE	MUCH	RESOURCE ALLOCATION, PRODUCTION SCHEDULING, FORECASTING, ETC.
PROGRAMMABLE	FIRST-LINE	SOME	INVENTORY CONTROL, EQUIPMENT MAINTENANCE, EMPLOYEE EVALUATION, ETC.

FIGURE 5-6. Management levels and decision making.

supported so well by MIS that they require little management intervention; and middle management may encounter decisions that are either programmable or nonprogrammable, but make good use of MIS-furnished data and models.

The kinds of decisions made by middle management require a greater degree of interaction with MIS than that of other management levels. MIS do not yet have the environmental data required by top management and, once programmed, first-line managerial decisions are made more or less automatically. That leaves middle management to query the data base, to format reports along previously unconsidered lines, to call upon the model bank in data analysis, and to simulate various alternatives. Indeed, recent studies reveal middle management as the single largest user of MIS, and the author's own study of over 150 business and governmental organizations in the late 1970s showed that 58.2 percent considered middle management to be the principal beneficiary of MIS (22.2% named top management and the remaining 19.6% picked first-line management).

Another reason for the lack of any decrease in total or middle manager numbers is that computer and MIS facilities themselves must be managed. Every organization has a few managers, usually *middle* managers, to look after its data processing and MIS activities. So that, while the *net* change in the number of managers is insignificant, it may be the result of an increase in the information management function at the expense of decreases in traditional areas of management. The numbers are small, however, and losses have been absorbed through attrition rather than by some wholesale firing of unnecessary managers.

The introduction of a new management responsibility—that of managing the MIS—raises more than just questions concerning the number of managers. It also poses an organizational problem: where to put the equipment and personnel, managers included, associated with the MIS. These and related organizational issues are discussed in the following chapter.

NOTES

1. It must be conceded that there have been a number of "successful" experiments in computer-generated art and poetry; the author knows of no success in applying this capability to normal management activities.
2. Harold J. Leavitt and Thomas L. Whisler, "Management in the 1980's," *Harvard Business Review* 36 (Nov.–Dec. 1958):41–48.

CHAPTER 6

MIS and Organizations

The management function of organizing was identified in Chapter 5 as, in a narrow sense, the structuring of organizational resources. If one were starting a new organization from scratch, two immediate structural questions concerning the MIS would arise: who is to be responsible for MIS and how is the MIS office itself to be organized?[1] There are other organizational implications of MIS, such as how the number and qualifications of managers in, say, marketing are affected by MIS, but they are relatively minor compared to the two basis questions.

RESPONSIBILITY FOR MIS

In organizing, the question of who is responsible for MIS is essentially the same as, "Where should the MIS office be located?" Historically, this question has been resolved on the basis of who was to use the system and which existing organizational entity possessed the expertise to operate such a system. Since traditional relationships often exert a powerful influence on current organization, it is useful to look at the historical evolution of MIS office location.

FIRST GENERATION COMPUTER LOCATION

Responsibility for computer operations, and later for MIS, is related to the familiar classification of computers by "generations." First generation computers were direct descendants of special-purpose scientific computers, and early business applications stressed the kind of numerical analysis typical of scientific applications. Since the "number people" in business tended to be in the accounting department, it is not surprising that accounting first became responsible for computer operations and that payroll, billing, and other accounting applications dominated the early business use of computers. A typical organization chart of the first generation is shown in Figure 6-1.

SECOND GENERATION COMPUTER LOCATION

By the second generation of computers, other considerations began to influence computer location and responsibility. First, departments of marketing, production, and personnel recognized the potential of computers and generated demand for computer resources. Second, greater reliability and easier programming techniques reduced dependence on a few highly trained specialists in the accounting department. This prompted some large organizations, where the increase in demand exceeded the increased capacity of second generation computers, to decentralize data processing activities by locating additional computers in other functional departments. In many organizations, however,

FIGURE 6-1. First generation computer location.

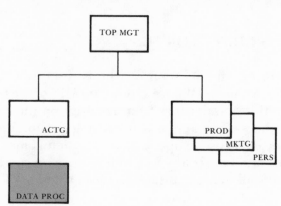

second generation computers were adequate to handle all organizational data processing. These organizations simply upgraded the accounting computer, and the accounting department became a data processing service center for the entire organization. The two versions of second generation organization are depicted in Figure 6-2.

THIRD GENERATION COMPUTERS AND MIS

The nearly simultaneous appearance, in the mid-1960s, of third generation technology and MIS had a profound impact on organizational structure. The then vast capacity of third generation computers and the broad application of information processing to management functions made for a happy marriage. MIS concepts of corporate data bases, model banks, and other shared capabilities made enormous demands on hardware, but, in most cases, a single computer facility could handle all of an organization's needs. But, if centralization was an obvious choice, the assignment of MIS responsibilities was not. Those organizations that had centralized under accounting in the second generation saw no compelling reason to change and, once again, upgraded and expanded their service center concept. The organizations that had decentralized found that functional departments were unwilling to yield their DP activities back to accounting. Account-

FIGURE 6-2.   Second generation computer location.

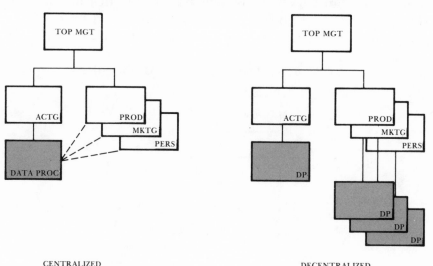

CENTRALIZED   DECENTRALIZED

ing would give priority to its own applications and other users would be slighted, or so the argument went. Whether this was true or not—and the success of many organizations with accounting-based MIS would suggest that it was not—it led to the formation of independent MIS offices. Although it may have been done for the wrong reasons, independent MIS organization has proved to be a more stimulating alternative and has produced more innovative information systems than accounting-based locations. The author's study of MIS in the late 1970s found that approximately one-half of the organizations had independent MIS offices, about one-third still located MIS in finance or accounting, and the remainder, usually specialized governmental organizations, employed other locations. More important, managers of independent MIS reported greater return on investment and greater system performance than did managers of accounting-based systems. The centralized, independent MIS of the third generation is shown in Figure 6-3.

CURRENT ORGANIZATIONAL STRUCTURE

A few years ago, MIS scholars were ready to wrap up the organization location issue and put it on the shelf with other apparently resolved questions. But once again, technological advances have given managers new options. In particular, advances in data communications and the development of minicomputers and microcomputers have rekindled interest in decentralization. The ring and star distributed systems discussed in Chapter 2 are examples of decentralized systems facilitated by new technology.[2]

FIGURE 6-3. Third generation MIS location.

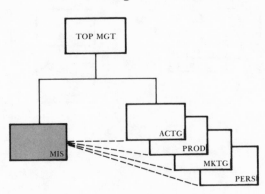

Since the current alternatives also involve differences in the organization of the MIS office itself, it is more convenient to examine the two issues together.

ORGANIZATION OF THE MIS OFFICE

Activities in an MIS office fall into four categories: *administration, systems analysis and design, programming,* and *systems operation.* Administration involves the coordination of the other three activities, data base management, liaison with other departments, and representation of MIS matters to upper levels of management. Systems analysis and design includes the identification of information needs and the planning for a set of integrated computer programs to satisfy those needs. In programming, programs based on the analysis are coded into a programming language, tested, and debugged. Finally, systems operation involves the running of programs on computer hardware and the dissemination of the resultant output.

While these functions are common to all MIS, they do not always lead to similar organization. Figure 6-4 shows three different approaches to MIS office organization—still others are possible.

The MIS office in Figure 6-4a is organized along activity lines. The separation of design, programming, and operations is considered to be a security measure—no one person has access to all of the steps necessary to defraud the system, and collusion is thought to be more difficult between members of different divisions. Organizing for security is particularly important in financial institutions such as banks and insurance companies.

The second organization, shown in Figure 6-4b, employs teams of programmers and analysts organized along project or functional lines. This organization sacrifices some security for the cooperation, understanding, and efficiency that result from a habitual working relationship between the teams and the corresponding functional department heads or project managers. This organization is particularly well suited to heterogeneous or high technology firms where MIS applications tend to be very specialized.

The third variation of MIS office organization, shown in Figure 6-4c, is based upon an increasingly popular belief that new

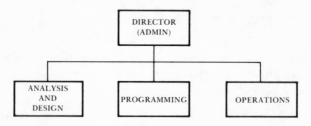

FIGURE 6-4a. Current MIS organization—activity orientation.

FIGURE 6-4b. Current MIS organization—project orientation.

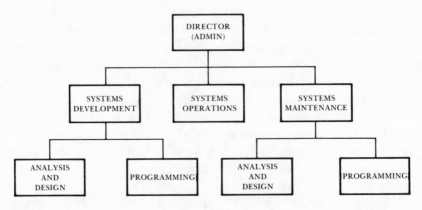

FIGURE 6-4c. Current MIS organization—life-cycle orientation.

systems development is essentially different from the maintenance of existing systems. At one time, it was almost axiomatic that the best programmer to modify or correct a program was the one who wrote it. The problem with this approach is that programming is a very mobile occupation and the original programmer may not be around when modifications are required. Also, the increased capacity and speed of contemporary computers makes it unnecessary for programmers to employ the statement-saving shortcuts that once made maintenance so difficult for a different programmer. In fact, current techniques of *structured programming* trade brevity and efficiency for format and clarity. Structured programs are much easier for a second programmer to follow and changes are less likely to bring about undesired results. Consequently, many MIS offices now treat program change and modification as a separate function. This type of organization is most applicable where new systems development is particularly difficult or demands rare skills not found in all programmers and analysts. New or less-skilled personnel may start in the maintenance division and move on to development if their progress warrants such a move.

MIS PERSONNEL

Another organizational consideration of MIS involves the classification of personnel who work in MIS, either in the MIS office itself or in functional departments. Some reference has been made already to administrators, programmers, analysts, and operators. The degree to which these personnel are specialized is, to a large measure, determined by the size of the organization and the extent of MIS activities. In a very small organization, the administration of MIS may be merely an additional duty of another executive, for example, the controller; programmer and analyst responsibilities may be vested in a single person, a programmer-analyst who maintains vendor-supplied software; and the actual operation of equipment may be handled by a few persons who double as data preparation personnel. In very large organizations, the four basic activities may be further broken down into more specialized positions requiring hundreds of persons. This discussion treats activities and subactivities as separate job positions, but it must be remembered that virtually any combination of responsibilities is possible to meet constraints on the number and capabilities of personnel involved in MIS.

ADMINISTRATIVE PERSONNEL

There is usually one high-level executive responsible for MIS in an organization. This person could be the chief executive officer but more likely is a vice-president for services, an executive vice-president, or, in those organizations that retain an accounting orientation to MIS, the controller or the vice-president for finance. The responsible executive may chair an *MIS Committee* which is made up of the heads of user departments (or their representatives) and the Director of MIS.[3]

The *Director of MIS* is the highest ranking MIS professional in the organization. He or she is responsible for the attainment of goals and objectives established by the MIS Committee. Goals and objectives in MIS set standards for systems development, operating costs, error rates, security, and timeliness. The director also has normal department head responsibilities for personnel administration, office management and the budget.

In organizations with central data bases, and even in some without, there is also a position for a *data base administrator* (DBA). The DBA is second in importance only to the director of MIS and, in fact, may be the deputy director. It is the responsibility of the DBA to standardize data codes, establish the overall schema of the data base, control access to the data base, and maintain security of the data base.

SYSTEMS ANALYSIS PERSONNEL

Systems analysis involves two different but related tasks. First, someone must articulate the need for information and, second, someone must conceive a means of satisfying that need. Both tasks are the responsibility of systems analysts, but in large organizations there may be different descriptions for each job. The responsibility for identifying information requirements rests with an *information analyst,* while the design of a computer-based solution is accomplished by a *system designer.* The information analyst is the more functionally oriented of the two. In fact, the information analyst may even be a member of the functional department (marketing, production, finance, etc.) that initiated the request for information. The information analyst provides liaison between the user and the designer to explain the capabilities and limitations of the MIS to the user and to translate the user's request into specific MIS requirements for the designer. The systems designer then determines the data requirements, the transformation processes that convert data into the desired information, and the form and content of the output. Even when this distinction between information analysts and systems designers is not made, it is a good idea to have in each department a designated point of contact who has some background in MIS and whose job it is to coordinate functional applications with the systems analysts.

Programmers

In general terms, programmers translate the English-language statements of systems designers into computer-language statements. *Application programmers* write programs for the basic data processing and MIS applications in the organization, while *systems programmers* write control or service programs (see the discussion of application and systems software in Chapter 2). Although there is usually a requirement for some systems programming in every MIS, more sophisticated systems software, such as compilers, operating systems, and data base management systems tend to be prepared by computer manufacturers or software vendors. In those organizations that separate systems development from systems maintenance, there are also *maintenance programmers*. In general, application and maintenance programmers have similar qualifications.

Operators

Managers using remote terminals sometimes forget that computer *operators* are still necessary. *Console operators* monitor a CRT display unit that gives information on the status of work in progress and requirements for human assistance. For example, the CRT may display a list of jobs in queue, the identification of remote users, or the need to load a certain file onto an external storage device. Other operator personnel keep high-speed printers in supply of paper and distribute printer output. A special category of operator, the *librarian,* maintains custody of off-line files, programs, and systems documentation.

Data preparation personnel are frequently classified as operator personnel for the simple reason that they often, in fact, operate keypunch machines, key-to-tape or key-to-disk devices, and other types of data preparation equipment. The role of operators as data preparation personnel has been diminished somewhat by advances in optical character recognition equipment which requires no special data preparation. Also, data preparation personnel are often found in functional departments as opposed to the MIS office. Of course, the latter point does not mean they are not MIS personnel, but it does make them different from most other operator personnel.

Users

Users are perhaps the most important of all categories of MIS personnel. And users *are* MIS personnel, even though most would not consider themselves as such. Certainly, MIS are pointless without users, and, in a well-run MIS, users play an important role in systems design and operation. It is a user who first establishes an information need and, in many systems, a managerial user may prepare and enter data (via a terminal), write simple programs (also on a terminal), and even operate some equipment (the terminal again). The MIS director who views users as external to the system is on the road to failure.

CURRENT ORGANIZATIONAL STRUCTURE— A SECOND LOOK

When the variations in MIS office organization and the placement of MIS personnel are considered along with the previously mentioned technological advances, there are numerous possible ways to tailor the organizational structure of MIS to meet the needs of the firm. Instead of attempting an exhaustive listing of combinations, three examples will be used to illustrate the flexibility of MIS organization.

Figure 6-5 shows the organization of a state division of motor vehicles. Numerous branch offices throughout the state use remote job entry equipment to enter vehicle registration data and to receive titles, license tag renewals and other output. Terminals in the branch offices are used for inquiries that require no output documents. The MIS is centralized in the state headquarters because all branch offices have identical information needs and require access to a common data base. Because of the homogeneous

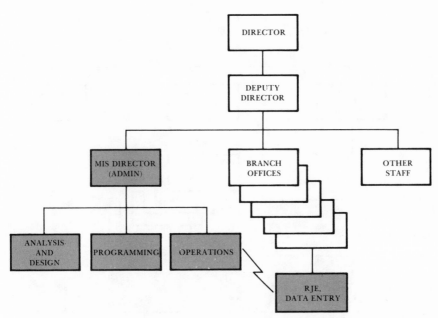

FIGURE 6-5. MIS in a state division of motor vehicles.

nature of the applications, there is no need to form specialized teams of programmers and analysts, and a certain degree of security is obtained by separating programming, analysis, and operations. Other than users and data preparation personnel in branch offices, all MIS personnel and activities are centralized.

The bank organization shown in Figure 6-6 is quite the opposite of the motor vehicle division organization. The bank also has branches but has no central computer. Instead, each branch has a minicomputer that is part of a ring distributed system. Each branch has a data base of its own accounts, data from which are also available to other branches in the ring. Branch MIS are organized by activity for maximum security and because banking applications are relatively homogeneous. Although the central office has no computer, it still has an MIS office. The data base administrator in the main MIS office must provide for data security and ensure compatibility of data between branch operations. The main MIS office also has analysis and design and programming responsibilities for common applications, such as statement preparation, computation of interest on loans and savings, credit-card accounts, and so on. Within the guidelines established by the DBA, branch MIS may design and program applications of

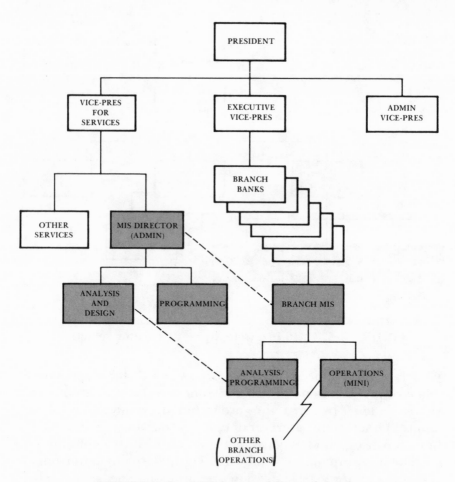

FIGURE 6-6.   MIS in a multibranch bank.

purely local interest. For system-wide applications, such as the payroll or the preparation of accounting statements, the ring system may be made to act as a single large computer through techniques of multiprocessing.

A star distributed system is the best organization for a multiplant manufacturing firm such as the one shown in Figure 6-7. A central MIS office is responsible for the development, maintenance, and operation (on the host computer) of company-wide applications such as capital budgeting, financial statement preparation, and resource allocation. The host computer is also the access point to the corporate data base and model bank. Individual plants also have MIS offices and computer hardware—probably minicomputers. Branch MIS operations may take sev-

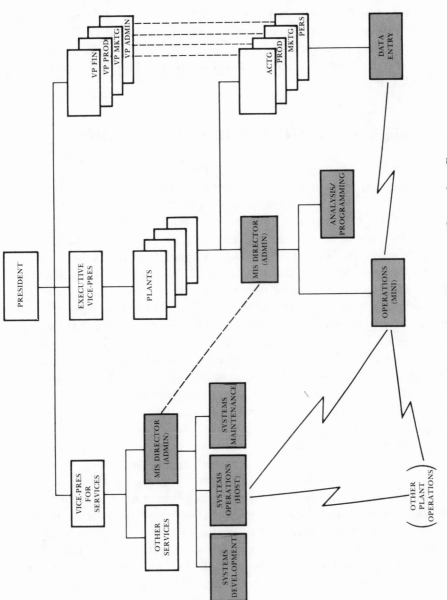

FIGURE 6-7. MIS in a multiplant manufacturing firm.

129

eral different forms. Locally developed programs may draw on the corporate data base for data, locally originated data may be analyzed with programs from the corporate model bank, or both data and programs may be of local origin. In all cases, branch activities are monitored by the central MIS office to encourage the sharing of programs and data and to ensure data base and model bank integrity.

MIS AND ORGANIZATIONAL PHILOSOPHIES

An interesting sidelight to the principal organizational issues concerning MIS involves the effect of MIS on management's attitude toward the centralization of authority and decision making. According to the span-of-control concept in classical organization theory, managers decentralized because of limitations on the number of persons they could supervise. Computers and information systems have the capability of providing information for decision making directly to top managers, without the need for intervening layers of management. Would not these intermediate managers become unnecessary? The predictions that MIS would erode middle management assumed they would. But it has been shown that middle management is more influential than ever. Do computers and MIS promote centralization or not?

It now appears that computers and MIS merely *facilitate* centralization; they do not *cause* centralization. In fact, while this question was being pondered by organization theorists, advances in computer technology that also facilitate *decentralization* were introduced. Large mainframes, high-speed processing, vast on-line storage, data base management systems, and remote data collection all suggest centralization, while minicomputers, microcomputers, and data communications favor decentralization.

Studies have shown that management style plays a much greater role in centralization than does information-processing technology. Autocratic managers of the "Theory X" school tend to have little faith in their subordinates and use MIS to increase their authority. Democratic managers of the "Theory Y" school use MIS to enhance the creative and innovative talents of their subordinates. Either philosophy can be accommodated by MIS; indeed, it is management's attitude toward centralization that influences MIS structure rather than MIS influencing the attitude of management. One thing is certain, however; whether decision making is centralized or decentralized, it is enhanced by MIS.

NOTES

1. The term "office" is used here generically to include division, directorate, department, or any of the other terms used to describe organizational subdivisions. The reader can substitute the appropriate term for his or her organization.
2. "New technology" is used in lieu of "fourth generation" because there is not yet universal agreement on whether or not the fourth generation has arrived. While the first, second, and third generations were characterized by vacuum tubes, transistors, and integrated circuits, respectively, there is no new characteristic technology to describe a fourth generation. Some of the performance improvement criteria (speed, cost, capacity) used to describe progress from one generation to the next have been met by current computers, but others have not. Everyone agrees that current technology has advanced beyond the third generation, but not everyone is willing to call it the fourth. Most likely, there will not be single, dramatic breakthroughs to define future generations. Instead, changes will be gradual and evolutionary. Perhaps only in 1990 will we be able to look back and identify the early eighties as the period of the fourth generation.
3. The MIS Committee is often a continuation of the *MIS Project Management Team* (see Chapter 7) which is formed to guide the development of an MIS project.

CHAPTER 7

The MIS Life Cycle

The introduction of a management information system into an organization is an event of major consequence, equivalent in impact to the introduction of a new product line, the addition of a new plant, or the reorganization of senior staff responsibilities. Yet top managers, who would not dream of undertaking these other projects without the most thorough planning and preparation, often avoid involvement when the "MIS people want a new computer."

A management information system is a vital organizational resource. Like the product line, the plant, and the organizational structure, it will not last forever. It is conceived and developed under certain environmental conditions and, as those conditions change, it will gradually become outmoded. To keep it alive, management must constantly tend it, cycling through successive iterations of a development process to ensure that the MIS continues to meet the organization's ever-changing information needs.

In broad terms, the life cycle of an MIS is no different from the life cycle of any other project. As shown in Figure 7-1, the cycle is initiated by a perceived need and includes phases of planning, development, implementation, operation, and control. Dis-

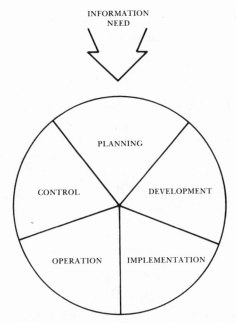

FIGURE 7-1. MIS project life cycle.

crepancies discovered in the control phase trigger further planning and the cycle repeats itself.

The similarity between the project life cycle and the management process described in Chapter 5 is not accidental. Management is responsible for the success or failure of a project and it is
logical to adapt the management process to project management.
In the remainder of this chapter we shall further adapt and refine
that process to describe the management of a specific project—the
introduction of an MIS.

THE PLANNING PHASE

The ultimate success or failure of an MIS may well be determined in the planning phase. While a good plan does not give
absolute assurance of a good MIS, it is extremely unlikely that an
efficient MIS could emerge from a poor plan. The risks associated
with a poor MIS are high indeed; managers can hardly be expected to make correct decisions on the basis of incomplete, un-
timely, or just plain incorrect information. Given these risks, the
decision to introduce a new or modified information system must

not be made lightly. It is appropriate, therefore, that planning begin with a thorough evaluation of the need for a new MIS.

RECOGNIZING THE NEEDS FOR MIS

The general factors that contribute to the need for MIS were discussed in Chapter 1: the nature of modern organizations, the current legal and social environment, advancing technology, and the expanding role of management. These factors may be manifested as more specific needs in different organizations. A few examples of such indications of the need for an MIS will illustrate the point.

THE COMPLEXITY OF OPERATIONS

Many organizations have information-processing requirements that are virtually impossible without computer assistance. Some of the management science models described in Chapter 4 fall into this category. High technology industries, firms with a strong commitment to research and development, and many consulting groups have need of MIS for this reason.

THE VOLUME OF TRANSACTIONS

Other organizations perform relatively simple operations but in such volume as to require computer assistance. Banks, insurance companies, and investment firms are typical of this category.

THE RISK FACTOR

Regardless of the number or complexity of transactions, certain organizations suffer more from errors than others. An error in processing one's electricity bill is inconvenient, but not catastrophic. If the same utility firm errs in dampening its nuclear reactor, the results could be disastrous. The need for the precision afforded by a computer-based information system in such an organization is obvious.

INTERDEPENDENT OPERATIONS

The requirement to exchange or share information among departments in an organization also suggests the need for an MIS.

The manufacturing firm, with finance, accounting, production, and marketing departments all dependent on one another for information, is in this category.

THE REQUIREMENT FOR SPEED

Sometimes MIS are required for the sheer speed of their operations. Military command and control systems, which may have only seconds to distinguish an enemy bomber from a commercial airliner, have such requirements. And so does that airline company, which also has only seconds to confirm a ticket reservation before a competing request for the same seat is received.

OBJECTIVES OF MIS

Just as managers are guided by organizational goals and objectives in the management process, so MIS planners must establish goals and objectives for the MIS. The two sets of objectives are not unrelated. MIS objectives support organizational objectives, but the former are more specific and, of course, deal with the processing of information. For example, an organizational goal might be to "respond to all orders within three days." This may lead to MIS objectives to "enter all orders into the transaction file within 12 hours of receipt," and to "furnish copies of order invoices to finished goods inventory within 24 hours of receipt," and so on.

It is important to state MIS objectives in behavioral terms to facilitate comparison with actual system performance during the control phase. It is also necessary for both the functional and MIS staffs to agree on these objectives. There is a natural conflict between these two groups: MIS personnel need time and other resources to take care of internal operating requirements as well as to satisfy every other department's information needs. The functional staff just as clearly needs the information requested quickly in order to accomplish its primary activity. The dispute must be resolved early, in the planning phase, before irreconcilable differences are permanently built into the system.

FEASIBILITY STUDIES

Having established the need for an MIS and further identified specific objectives of the proposed system, MIS planners must next answer the question, "Can this be done?" Many organizations will have established standards for the form, content, and methodology of a feasibility study. Typically, such a study addresses three kinds of constraints: *technical, economic,* and *behavioral.*

TECHNICAL FEASIBILITY

An MIS is technically feasible when state-of-the-art hardware and software can accomplish the objectives of the system. Technical limitations are imposed by the number of remote terminals a computer can accommodate, storage space, access time, computational speed, data base management capabilities, and so forth. Technical feasibility is rarely a problem in commercial applications, although there are still a few scientific applications that push technological limits.

ECONOMIC FEASIBILITY

Having been assured by your friendly systems engineer that *nothing* is technically infeasible for his company's products, your next question should be, "Yes, but can I afford it?" Again, most firms will have standard procedures for evaluating investment opportunities to include the not inconsiderable investment in an MIS. These procedures usually take the form of a cost/benefit analysis similar to the one described in Chapter 4. A positive net present value or an internal rate of return that exceeds the minimum standard is a signal to proceed. The difficulty in determining the economic feasibility of an MIS in this fashion lies in estimating the future benefits. Some, like reductions in order-processing costs, can be computed. Others, like the goodwill gained from reducing errors, are more subjective. This problem is not unique to MIS, although it may be less pronounced in other kinds of projects. MIS planners must resist the temptation to overestimate MIS benefits in order to justify a new system.

BEHAVIORAL FEASIBILITY

Any change to the traditional way of doing things in an organization is going to meet with some resistance, but new MIS seem to incur more than their share of resentment. It is appropriate, therefore, to ask, "Is all of this worth the trouble it is going to cause?" The timid souls who respond, "No," need not read on. The remainder, hopefully a vast majority, must face the problem of reassuring threatened employees, retraining others, and, regrettably, letting some go. Often, displaced employees can be absorbed by attrition, and retraining frequently gives employees new, more marketable skills. Others, however, may feel a loss of identity in working with the MIS. And many of the personnel whose jobs are eliminated by the MIS—stock clerks, filing clerks, order and billing clerks, and others—simply do not have the qualifications or the motivation to be retrained for the positions created by the MIS: programming, systems analysis, and similar jobs. It is doubtful that an MIS project has ever been rejected solely on behavioral grounds, but the feasibility analysis should be conducted anyway, just to show where such problems will exist and to give personnel managers time to plan how to alleviate them when they do occur.

THE MASTER PLAN

Assuming that the feasibility study is favorable, it is now time to prepare a document to guide the MIS project through its life cycle. There is no universally accepted format for an MIS master plan, but there are several topics that tend to be included in most plans.

OBJECTIVES

The objectives are the purpose of the project. Even though they have already been established and are known to the MIS planners, they should be reiterated in the master plan, prominently, as guidelines for all involved.

ORGANIZATION

If there is no existing MIS, the master plan should outline the organizational changes that will result from introducing one. The organizational considerations that govern the assignment of MIS responsibility were discussed in the previous chapter. Even if there is a current MIS, and the purpose is merely to modify or upgrade it, there are certain ad hoc responsibilities not readily apparent on the organization chart. These responsibilities are frequently given to an MIS *project management team* such as the one shown in Figure 7-2.

Although an MIS project management team will be constituted differently in different organizations, one important principle should be observed. The chairperson should not have a parochial interest in the system either as the head of a user department or as the head of the MIS office. It is appropriate for these individuals to serve on the team and for their respective staffs to advise the team and each other, but the chairperson should be someone not personally involved and with sufficient authority to resolve disputes among users and between the users and the MIS director.

RESOURCES

Many master plans include at this point an inventory of current resources—equipment, personnel, physical facilities, software packages, and the operating budget—and a list of those additional resources anticipated for the MIS project. This is not a bad idea from the point of view of answering, "Where are we now" and "Where are we going," if that is how the inventory is used. Unfortunately, many MIS project teams view the current resources as constraints which determine the course of the project. When this is done in the interest of holding down costs, it is usually a mistake. It is something of an axiom in the computer industry that one can get more computational power for less money by obtaining new hardware instead of "adding on" to older equipment. Again, there is nothing wrong with taking stock of

FIGURE 7-2. MIS project management team.

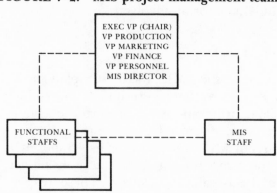

one's resources, particularly in the critical area of personnel, as long as that action does not inhibit the development process.

The point has already been made that control begins during planning, where objectives become the standards against which actual performance will be measured in the future. Such *performance standards* are oriented primarily to the operation and control phases of the MIS life cycle. It is also appropriate to establish standards for the development and implementation phases.

The budget is a control measure that applies to both preoperation and postoperation phases. Expenses are incurred early with the acquisition of specially skilled development personnel (systems analysts and programmers) and perhaps the services of consultants. Major expenses are also incurred during implementation when the site is prepared, hardware and proprietary software are acquired, operators are hired, and the conversion to the new system is effected. Personnel expenses carry over into operation, which has other continuing costs for maintenance and supplies. Finally, the audit of the MIS in the control phase will require still additional funds. These costs can get out of hand quickly if they are not strictly controlled by the MIS project team. As a rough rule of thumb, personnel costs will be between 40 and 50 percent of the MIS budget, equipment costs (rent or depreciation) between 35 and 45 percent, and other costs (maintenance and supplies) will run about 15 percent.

Time often becomes a critical factor in an MIS project, and there are several common methods for exercising control over time during development and implementation. The *milestone schedule,* shown in Table 7-1, provides a calendar of key events and their scheduled dates.[1] Milestone schedules show at a glance whether activities are being completed on time or not, but offer little additional help.

The *Gantt chart,* shown in Figure 7-3, gives essentially the same information found in the milestone schedule, but in a graphical form. The Gantt chart gives a good pictorial representation of the length of each activity, which activities are being conducted simultaneously, and approximately how far along each activity should be on a given date.

The *PERT* (for *P*rogram *E*valuation and *R*eview *T*echnique)

TABLE 7-1. Partial Milestone Schedule for MIS Project

Date	Milestone
Sep. 1, 198__	Start interviews for systems analysts
Oct. 1, 198__	Hire systems analysts
Oct. 15, 198__	Begin information analysis
Jan. 15, 198__	Complete information analysis
Jan. 30, 198__	Begin logical systems design
Mar. 15, 198__	Complete logical systems design
Mar. 20, 198__	Begin preparation of RFP
Mar. 30, 198__	Begin detailed systems design
Jun. 1, 198__	Complete RFP
Jun. 1, 198__	Start interviews for programmers
Jul. 1, 198__	Hire programmers
Jul. 15, 198__	Complete detailed systems design
Jul. 20, 198__	Begin programming
Aug. 15, 198__	Receive hardware bids
Sep. 1, 198__	First progress review
Sep. 15, 198__	Announce hardware contract
⋮	⋮
Jun. 10, 198__	Complete conversion to new system

network, shown in Figure 7-4, is one of the most powerful project management tools. PERT will identify *critical paths* (sequences of activities which, if delayed, will delay project completion), provide a basis for probabilistic estimates of the project completion time, and, when combined with *CPM* (for *Critical Path Method*) techniques, show how resources can be reallocated to speed up a proj-

FIGURE 7-3. Partial Gantt chart for MIS project.

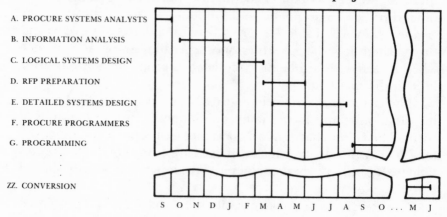

A. PROCURE SYSTEMS ANALYSTS

B. INFORMATION ANALYSIS

C. LOGICAL SYSTEMS DESIGN

D. RFP PREPARATION

E. DETAILED SYSTEMS DESIGN

F. PROCURE PROGRAMMERS

G. PROGRAMMING

ZZ. CONVERSION

S O N D J F M A M J J A S O ... M J

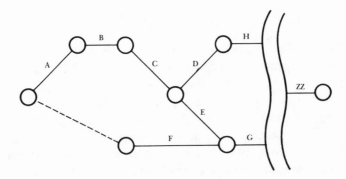

FIGURE 7-4. Partial PERT network for MIS project.

ect or return a delayed project to its original schedule. The details of how PERT and CPM are used in project management are beyond the scope of this book.

THE DEVELOPMENT PHASE

Development of an MIS formally begins when the master plan has been approved by top management, although some preliminary developmental effort is required to ensure proper planning. A tentative system design, for example, must be completed before cost and benefit data can be projected for the economic feasibility analysis. The schedules, too, are dependent upon some rough idea of what is to be done during development.

One very important aspect of development, the selection of a design approach, must also be determined during planning. But, because it is a major development issue, it is treated here, in the discussion of the development phase, along with the other important development activities of analysis and design.

APPROACHES TO MIS DESIGN

MIS planners usually have a good idea of where they want to go, but they do not always agree on how to get there. There are four or five approaches to designing an MIS, each with its own relative advantages and disadvantages, to consider before proceeding further with development. Let us take a brief look at them.

THE TOP-DOWN APPROACH

In the *top-down* approach, the MIS is designed to support the organizational goals and objectives as articulated by top management. Information requirements to support top management are considered first. The processing of this information requires as inputs the information needed by middle management, and so on, until basic transaction data is eventually incorporated into the design. Just as objectives themselves are passed down and given added detail at each level in an organization, the MIS, too, evolves downward, satisfying the information requirements for those refined objectives at each level. For this reason, the top-down approach is also referred to as an *objective-oriented* approach.

Proponents of top-down design argue the logic of supporting organizational goals and point out that the lack of this support is one reason why top management is so apathetic toward present MIS. Opponents generally acknowledge the need to get top management more involved in MIS but point out that the problem lies in the unique, environmental information needs of top management. These needs are not likely to be satisfied by a top-down approach either, and needs of middle and first-line managers, who are heavily involved in MIS, may not be considered fully in the process.

THE BOTTOM-UP APPROACH

Where top-down is an analytic process of breaking down information requirements into more and more detailed components, the *bottom-up* approach synthesizes information needed at higher levels from that already being generated at lower levels. Bottom-up design first satisfies transaction-processing requirements, then summarizes that data for reports to first-line managers, next analyzes information in those reports for middle managers, and so on, until all levels are satisfied. This approach is classified as *problem-oriented* or, because it follows the historical development of MIS, *evolutionary*.

Bottom-up design favors the heavy users of MIS in the middle and lower management levels. If the basic activities of the organization are taken care of, the argument goes, the satisfaction of goals and objectives will follow naturally. Perhaps, but there is still this disenchanted group of top managers not using the MIS because their particular information needs simply cannot be synthesized from transaction data.

THE TOTAL SYSTEM APPROACH

A *systems approach* is one that views the organization as a system in which various resource inputs—labor, material, and capital—are processed into output—goods and services. In a systems approach to MIS design, information is treated as just another resource. All MIS design alternatives use a systems approach to some extent; the *total* systems approach is an extreme that treats the organization as a single, integrated system to be served by a similar, totally integrated MIS.

The total systems approach is aesthetically pleasing to many MIS designers and academicians because it provides a convenient, comprehensive model to explain information flows. It also provides for the integration of MIS applications and the exchange of information between functional departments better than other approaches. The drawbacks to the total systems approach arise when one attempts to use it in the real world. Large, complex, dynamic organizations do not hold still for the five or more years it might take to develop such a system. One attempt by the Department of Defense, a leader in early MIS development, to design a total system for an Army Corps (an organization of hundreds of interrelated units and up to 75,000 personnel) took over ten years and never resulted in the implementation of a *total* system.

THE MODULAR APPROACH

An information system can also be designed on a smaller, more manageable scale by addressing one subsystem or *module* at a time. The modules are usually designed along functional lines of finance, accounting, production, marketing, and so on. Since most organizations are structured along similar lines, this method is sometimes called the *organization chart* approach. Because each module is designed to stand alone, at least until all the other modules are completed, the modular approach is also known as the *integrate-later* approach.

Designing one module at a time places lighter demands on systems development resources, although it usually extends total development time. By following traditional functional lines, the MIS is likely to be less disruptive to the organization and more readily accepted by its users. But organization charts do not fully reflect the interactions between departments, and an MIS designed along functional lines probably will not consider the informal organization and other subtle information flows. Finally, while intentions to integrate later are undoubtedly sincere, the evidence is that this never happens. Independent modules soon develop unique characteristics that make them incompatible with other modules and integration becomes impossible.

An Eclectic Approach

Some MIS scholars attempt to pass judgment on these approaches, branding some "acceptable" and others "unacceptable." There is no reason, however, why MIS planners cannot make themselves aware of the pitfalls of these approaches and, by careful planning, follow any one with success in a given organization. But an even better solution is to select the best features of each and combine them into a new, an *eclectic* approach.

The outstanding feature of the top-down approach is that it recognizes the needs of a heretofore neglected group in MIS: top management. Whether one follows the entire top-down route or not, the information needs of top management must be served. If this means refining information normally used at lower levels, so be it. If it means obtaining and processing environmental data not used at lower levels, that's fine too.

The bottom-up approach provides a strong transactional base and probably lends itself to data base management systems better than the others. An eclectic approach should recognize the fundamental role of transaction processing in organizations and the dependence of supervisory management on that part of an MIS.

At the present stage of MIS development, it is still risky to undertake a total systems approach. Yet there is no reason why MIS planners should not *view* the MIS as a total system even though they may not wish to *design* it as such. For example, informational outputs from production should be recognized as necessary inputs for marketing applications. Provisions for this kind of exchange can be made without creating a monster that is impossible to control.

And lastly, systems theory notwithstanding, there are valid reasons for designing an MIS that reflects organizational structure. In such an MIS, problems or changes in one module will have minimum impact on the overall system. Also, it is easier and more justifiable to run the MIS as a profit center when services are rendered along departmental lines. And modules can be implemented as they are produced, without waiting for the entire system to be completed. An eclectic approach can incorporate modular principles and still integrate later successfully if a total systems view is maintained during the development phase.

ANALYSIS AND DESIGN

In *analysis,* the current system—the manual system in the case of a new MIS or the old automated system in the case of a modification project—is literally taken apart and examined piece by piece, information need by information need. The *design* process is one of assembling a new system that satisfies all these information needs. The actual steps in analysis and design are, of course, considerably more complicated than this simple explanation. They start, in keeping with the problem-orientation borrowed from the bottom-up approach, with an analysis of information needs.

ANALYSIS OF INFORMATION REQUIREMENTS

Managers make decisions on the basis of information available to them. One way to establish information requirements is to examine decision points in organizational activities and determine the information required at each one. For example, the decision on how many copies of this book should be printed is based upon market demand, price, production costs, storage facilities, interest rates, and competition in the field, to mention just a few. If the MIS is to support the manager who makes this decision, it must provide him or her as much of this information as possible.

Each of the thousands of other decisions made in an organization are analyzed similarly. Many of the information requirements will be duplicated in different decision situations, an indication of the need to share information, perhaps through a data base management system. The functional staffs should make these requirements known to the project management team through their representatives. But functional managers are sometimes reticent when it comes to voicing their needs, perhaps because of a lack of understanding of just what an MIS can do for them. It is then incumbent upon the information analysts, who are skilled in both functional and information systems operations, to suggest, prompt, or otherwise draw out of the functional specialists additional information requirements.

LOGICAL SYSTEMS DESIGN

The identification of information requirements establishes *what* the MIS is to do; it is now necessary to define just *how* those information requirements will be satisfied. This step is called *logical* systems design because it reflects the logical relationships between users, operators, equipment, input, output, and processing. It is a deductive process that proceeds from the general to the specific. The general relationships are explained in a *systems flowchart* such as the one in Figure 7-5, which shows a portion of an ordering subsystem. Systems flowcharts are prepared in close cooperation with functional users, who provide input on current manual procedures, desired improvements, personnel capabilities, operational requirements, and other matters not generally known to the MIS staff.

The systems flowchart is user-oriented. Since the application is to be automated, the logical system also must be defined with a data processing orientation. Programmers need to know specific relationships such as those shown in the *programming flowchart* in Figure 7-6. The level of detail in a programming flowchart is geared to the skill and experience of the programmer who will use it. In the extremes, each symbol in the flowchart may result in a single program statement or the programming flowchart may be only slightly more detailed than the systems flowchart.

The normal flow in a system is from input, through processing, to output. The design sequence tends to flow backwards, from output to input and then to processing.

Output Design.   Output design considers the *content, form, frequency* and the *medium* of output. Content is fairly well established

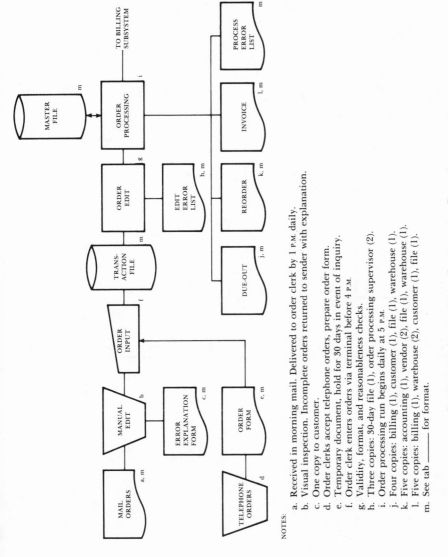

FIGURE 7-5. Sample systems flowchart.

NOTES:

a. Received in morning mail. Delivered to order clerk by 1 P.M. daily.
b. Visual inspection. Incomplete orders returned to sender with explanation.
c. One copy to customer.
d. Order clerks accept telephone orders, prepare order form.
e. Temporary document, hold for 30 days in event of inquiry.
f. Order clerk enters orders via terminal before 4 P.M.
g. Validity, format, and reasonableness checks.
h. Three copies: 30-day file (1), order processing supervisor (2).
i. Order processing run begins daily at 5 P.M.
j. Four copies: billing (1), customer (1), file (1), warehouse (1).
k. Five copies: accounting (1), vendor (2), file (1), warehouse (1).
l. Five copies: billing (1), warehouse (2), customer (1), file (1).
m. See tab _____ for format.

147

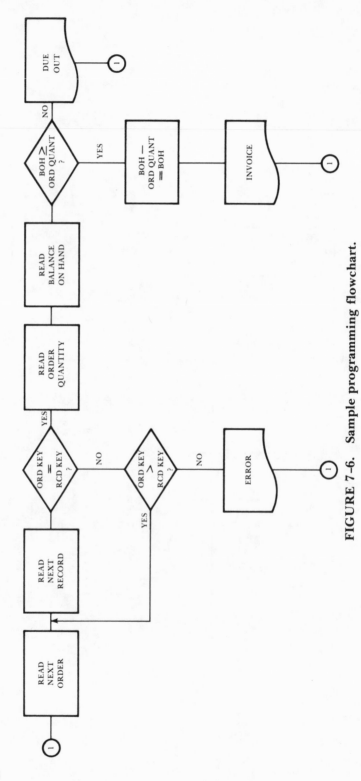

FIGURE 7-6. Sample programming flowchart.

during the information analysis and may be only slightly revised or refined during design. Form treats such matters as column and row headings on reports, spacing, graphic displays, and so forth. Output frequency may be daily, weekly, monthly, "on-call," or, in interactive systems, continuous. Finally, the output medium may be paper, preprinted forms, mailers, video displays, or some combination of these and other media. There are standard forms available to aid in the layout of output, and locally designed forms may be prepared to help organize and collect other output specifications.

Input Design. Output determines input requirements. A weekly production status report, for example, requires input on the type and quantity of items produced during the week, the hours of labor and amount of raw materials expended, the amount and nature of work still in progress, and perhaps the net change to inventory during the week. Some of these data are collected routinely and need only to be made available for entry into the MIS. Other requirements may be new and collection procedures must be established for them. In both cases, input design involves the same considerations of output design, but with slightly different emphasis. Content is restricted to only necessary data items, form is motivated by ease of data collection and preparation for entry, input frequency is determined by the output frequency, and the medium is selected for speed and efficiency. In the production status report example, sensors on machinery could count finished items as they are produced and monitor machine activity as a measure of labor.

Process Design. Process design establishes the way in which input is converted to output. To continue the illustration of a weekly status report, an output requirement for the "average hours of labor per item" is computed by dividing the total hours of labor by the total number of items produced. The process must be designed to determine those totals, perform the division, and save the answer for inclusion in the output report.

The design of processes can be very routine, as in the weekly production status report example, or it can be quite complex, as in a marketing research application. Once again, the skill of the programmer dictates the level of design detail required. The complex processes may draw on management science models in the model bank or require the services of a mathematical programmer.

File Design. It is also necessary during logical systems design to determine the number and type of files required in the system. Considerations of the medium and organization of application files are discussed in Chapter 3; the use of data base management systems in lieu of application files is covered in Chapter 9.

PHYSICAL SYSTEMS DESIGN

The physical system consists of personnel, facilities, hardware, and, in the sense that it is recorded on physical media, software. The design of the physical system includes programming and the selection of hardware. Since programming is primarily a data processing function and, aside from the brief discussion in Chapter 3, outside the realm of this book, we will focus on that part of physical systems design of more concern to management: the selection of hardware.

There are two roads leading to the hardware selection decision. One, *sole source,* is convenient, but may be more expensive. The other, *competitive bidding,* requires a good deal of effort, but is probably less expensive.

Sole Source. When an organization has little in-house systems development experience or capability, it may be best to obtain assistance from a computer manufacturer. Early in the logical systems design phase, the MIS project management team contacts an equipment manufacturer and seeks advice on selection of hardware. The choice of manufacturer may be based on reputation for service and reliability, proximity to service facilities, the recommendation of associates, or other valid reasons.

The equipment manufacturer will usually provide assistance in systems design—around the manufacturer's own equipment, of course. The advantages of this approach are convenience, expert advice, and more efficient utilization of manufacturer-supplied software. The disadvantages are limitations on available hardware, operational changes required by the software package, and the automatic exclusion of all other manufacturers—some of whom might have offered better, less expensive alternatives.

Competitive Bidding. When there is a high level of technical expertise already present or readily available from consultants, an organization is usually better off soliciting competitive bids for its contemplated hardware. Realizing that the contract will probably go to the lowest bidder, computer manufacturers have a strong incentive to propose only the most economical configuration that will get the job done. It is therefore particularly important that the systems specifications, as outlined in the *request for proposal* or *RFP*, be as complete as possible. The manufacturer is not responsible for capabilities omitted in the RFP or to provide for unspecified growth and expansion.

The specifications in the RFP should include input volumes and media, the same information for output and files, representative examples of processing requirements, data communications requirements, programming languages to be used, the required delivery date, and requirements for special capabilities such as graphical displays, data base management systems, performance monitors, and so forth. The manufacturer's proposal will recommend a hardware configuration, show how it meets or exceeds the specifications, list other advantages, give a delivery schedule, state the price, and outline financing arrangements (lease or buy options).

The MIS project management team should conduct a formal evaluation of each proposal and select the best according to previously established criteria. In addition to cost, the committee should consider the capacity for expansion, the availability of software support, compatibility with existing hardware and software, the manufacturer's reputation for reliability, service agreements, back-up support, site preparation requirements, and assistance in training.

THE IMPLEMENTATION PHASE

The implementation phase is marked by four major activities: site preparation and installation of hardware, testing and debugging, training, and conversion to the new system. During this phase the organization is most vulnerable to flaws in MIS design and must make the critical, often irreversible, decision to abandon the old system in favor of the new one.

SITE PREPARATION AND INSTALLATION

Although enormous strides in computer design and construction have been made in recent years, computer hardware is still relatively delicate and sensitive to environmental conditions. The environmental control requirements are much stricter for computers than for other industrial equipment. Temperature, humidity, and air filtering specifications of the manufacturer must be followed closely. The extensive cabling network to power and interconnect hardware components is best located under a raised floor to prevent damage and for easy access. Back-up power facilities will guard against the loss or distortion of data in the event of a power failure. Even nylon garments can create static electricity problems and should be avoided by operator personnel.

The manufacturer will perform the actual installation and conduct any necessary electrical checkout. Diagnostic routines will also be run to check the systems and application software furnished by the manufacturer.

TESTING AND DEBUGGING

The testing of application software prepared in-house may begin before the hardware has been installed if comparable hardware is available elsewhere—it is not cost effective to acquire hardware six months early just to begin testing! The errors sought in testing fall into two categories: *syntax* errors and *logic* errors.

Syntax errors are violations of the programming language or the operating system. Misplaced commas, misspellings, the use of reserved words, and other "grammatical" errors fall into this category. Most syntax errors will be detected by the programming language compiler and printed on an error listing. Some syntax errors can be tolerated by the system and will not preclude the successful compiling of the program.

An error in logic is committed when the programming statements are all valid, but, due to some shortcoming of the programmer or analyst, they do not bring about the intended results. To *add* the quantity of a customer's order to inventory on hand instead of *subtracting* it is perfectly acceptable to the computer, although it is likely to cause the inventory manager considerable consternation. Logic errors are much more difficult to detect and will show up only under exacting testing.

The best way to test a program is to run data through it and check the results. Test or dummy data prepared specifically to exercise all parts of the program give a thorough test but are difficult to develop and must be checked manually. An alternative is to use historical data and compare the results to known out-comes. Shortcomings of this method are that it gives no check on new applications and the old input format may be incompatible with the new system.

Debugging refers to the correction of errors, both in syntax and logic. Syntax errors can usually be corrected by editing from a terminal. Logic errors generally force one back into the develop-ment phase for the redesign of the faulty part. It is very important to retest programs after debugging. Seemingly minor corrections have a way of producing far-reaching and unwanted effects.

TRAINING

Although formal training takes place during the implementa-tion phase, the preparation of personnel for the introduction of a new MIS really begins during planning. The first steps involve assurances of job security and solicitation of user support for an MIS. The best way to quash rumors and fears is to keep em-ployees fully informed of the project and the changes it will bring about. Users and other employees at every level should be kept abreast of development progress and encouraged to participate through suggestion programs and cooperation with information analysts. Effort expended by the MIS project management team in these directions early will be well rewarded in the implementa-tion and operation phases.

PROCEDURE MANUALS

Another very important prelude to formal training is the preparation of *procedure manuals*. There are two categories of pro-cedure manuals, those for *users* and those for *operators*.

User manuals explain how personnel in functional depart-ments can interface with the MIS. In some cases, primary job functions may be altered as they are for clerical personnel who perhaps operate terminals and assume data entry responsibilities. For management personnel, the main concern may be how to interpret a certain report, how to call for unscheduled reports, or even how to tap into the data base and prepare special reports.

The responsibility for preparing user manuals lies with the information analysts—the link between users and MIS in this, the implementation phase, just as in the development phase. The manuals should contain step-by-step instructions for each user activity, samples of appropriate input or output documents, trouble-shooting procedures, and the name of the responsible information analyst to contact in case of problems.

Operator manuals contain instructions for the loading of files, the distribution of reports, the scheduling of programs, and other production matters. These instructions are more hardware-oriented than user manuals and are the MIS equivalent of standing operating procedures or SOPs. MIS operator manuals are prepared by systems analysts and should not be confused with equipment operator manuals which are prepared by the manufacturer. Manuals for the operation of equipment are completely hardware-oriented and deal with matters such as console operation, diagnostic checkouts, trouble indicators, and maintenance procedures.

TRAINING SESSIONS

Data-preparation, data-entry, and other clerical personnel should be trained in a formal environment. Some organizations prefer to use information analysts to conduct training while others use regular supervisory personnel. The information analysts are undoubtedly better equipped to conduct such training and are better able to field questions that stray from the immediate topic. The use of supervisors tends to reinforce the traditional chain of command in the organization and serves to dispel some of the mystique that invariably accompanies a new MIS. The supervisors must themselves be trained first, of course, but their involvement in the training process places them on the side of the developers in the all-important commitment to make the MIS a success.

Left on their own, management personnel rarely take the time to attend formal training sessions when, or if, they are scheduled. In this case, the user manuals may be the information analyst's sole opportunity to educate management to the use and benefits of the MIS. In such organizations, many managers never do become users and the full potential of the MIS is never realized. It often requires a decree from top management to get other managers involved, and then only reluctantly, in MIS training. The information analyst who is aware of this reluctance is forearmed and will make the training sessions short, specific, and at the level of the users. If necessary, different sessions should be scheduled for different departments to ensure that only relevant material is presented. This may strike some as being overly deferential to managerial users, but, after all, the purpose of the MIS is to serve managers and that cannot be accomplished without a supportive, well-informed, participative management.

CONVERSION

When all applications have been analyzed, designed, programmed, tested, and debugged; when hardware has been selected and installed in a prepared site; and when users and operators have been trained in the procedures required by the new MIS; it is time to convert or *cut-over* from the old system. In spite of all the preparations, however, it is still possible, even likely, for problems to occur when users, operators, data, hardware, and software are all brought together for the first time under live operating conditions. There are several conversion options available to MIS planners that will reduce the risk of error in a new system.

Parallel Operations

At one time, it was believed that the safest approach to conversion was to run both the old and new systems simultaneously—in *parallel*—until it was satisfactorily established that the new system was producing results that were "reliable," i.e., the same as the results of the old system. When the new system is little more than an equipment upgrade of the old system with no new applications, this is a workable scheme. But when new applications are introduced, there is no basis for comparison to the old system. Also, some organizations, such as banks, might be reluctant to have duplicate financial information around in spite of all safeguards against confusion between "live" and "dummy" output. These objections, coupled with the increased skill of MIS personnel and hardware reliability, have made the parallel conversion all but obsolete.

PHASE-IN OPERATIONS

An MIS is phased-in when the organization converts to one module or application at a time. This conversion is most compatible with the modular design approach and permits modules to be introduced as they are completed. The combination of a modular design and a phased conversion makes the most efficient use of a limited MIS staff. When errors are discovered in phased-in modules, the effects are generally limited to the application area. This advantage is offset, however, by the difficulty of integrating modules when they are introduced over a long period. To alleviate this problem, the most independent modules—billing, accounting records, inventory management, and so forth—should be introduced first, and the most dependent modules—financial planning, production control, and other integrated applications—should come later.

PILOT MODELS

The concept of a pilot model is a familiar one in production management. Small-scale operations are conducted first to confirm that laboratory methods are indeed transferrable to the production process before full-scale operations are begun. This concept is also applicable to MIS where conditions permit. Pilot conversions are difficult in large, homogeneous organizations but may work well where one part of the organization, say, a single plant in a multiplant firm, accurately reflects the operation of the entire organization. In these cases, the MIS can be introduced as a unit without jeopardizing information flows in the whole organization. Needless to say, if the pilot is successful, the remainder of the organization can convert in comparative safety.

IMMEDIATE METHOD

Sometimes, when the new system is dramatically different from the old, or when applications are extensively interrelated, there is no choice but to convert everything at once—immediately.

This is frequently necessary in systems dependent on a data base management system where, in order to implement any one application, all the old application files must be converted to the schema of the data base and are no longer available for processing under the old system. Obviously the risks are much higher in an immediate conversion, but so are the payoffs if the conversion is successful. Applications dependent upon output from other modules are fully operational upon conversion and there is no awkward "in-between" period for users and operators.

PLANNING FOR CONVERSION

The factors that argue for one method of conversion over another are known very early in the system life cycle; indeed, they may be organizational characteristics completely beyond the control of MIS planners. Since conversion methods are related to design approaches (modular design suggests phase-in and total systems design suggests pilot or immediate conversion), the plans for conversion should be made concurrently with the selection of a design approach. Both decisions take place during planning and should be incorporated into the master plan.

THE OPERATION PHASE

The operation of an MIS is an organization-wide activity involving both user and MIS personnel. In the most liberal interpretation, the reading of a report by a marketing manager or the querying of the data base by a personnel manager is as much a part of MIS operation as the processing of an inventory report or the coding of order data. The way users interact with MIS is covered in subsequent chapters and the operation of the machine room is of interest primarily to data processing personnel. There is one aspect of operations, however, that is of interest to everyone associated with the system: the security of the MIS.

PHYSICAL SECURITY

The physical components of an MIS are as vulnerable to loss, damage or destruction as any other physical asset and must be protected accordingly. Fire, flood, or other natural disasters can result in the loss of both equipment and data. Equipment losses can be recovered by insurance and replacement may result only in an inconvenient loss of time, but data are often irreplaceable and must be protected by other means.

In batch processing, transaction documents are retained to permit reconstruction of a transaction file, and the old master file is usually kept for a few cycles to facilitate the preparation of a new master file in the event of a catastrophic loss. In transaction processing, the master file may be copied periodically (at the time transaction documents are destroyed) to give a back-up capability. Obviously, these back-up files and documents must be stored in a location and manner to preclude a simultaneous loss of primary and back-up data. A fireproof vault some distance from the processing area would satisfy these conditions.

In addition to natural disasters, MIS are sometime threatened by deliberate acts of sabotage. Equipment can be protected from sabotage by passive measures such as locating the machine room away from normal traffic flows and "hardening" the facilities against fire or minor explosions. Active security measures include the use of guards, combination locks at entry points, visitor logs, and other means of restricting or discouraging illegal access.

It is more difficult to protect data from sabotage, particularly in a distributed system where there are many points of access to data banks. Data can be protected by the use of passwords, a "read-only" access mode, access limited to specific applications, and the continual screening of employees who are given access to the system. The last measure is particularly important since most acts of sabotage against data are committed by persons who are authorized access but have become disgruntled for some reason. For example, an employee who is given a one-week termination notice probably should have his or her access restricted at the time of notification. The revocation of access privileges means that passwords must be changed, a step that should be taken periodically, say, monthly, in any event.

OPERATING INTEGRITY

Even if natural disaster and sabotage were not threats to MIS, systems managers would take precautions to preserve the integrity of information. Some information is confidential because it contains data of a personal or proprietary nature. Personnel records and financial statements fall into this category and should be protected against unauthorized access, however innocent it may be.

Another reason for guarding the integrity of the system is the increasing vulnerability of organizations to computer crime. It has been estimated that only 5 to 10 percent of computer fraud is even detected and the annual losses to such crimes by U.S. businesses is well over $1 billion. Computer fraud ranges from the seemingly innocent use of computer facilities for personal business to multi-million-dollar thefts of company funds.

MIS must also be protected against errors that result in losses to the organization. Undetected logic errors and rare, but possible, internal processing errors can result in direct losses through overpayments and billing mistakes or they can lead to losses indirectly by providing faulty information to decision makers.

Obviously, it is best to prevent the loss of operating integrity by denying unauthorized access, thwarting computer crime, and eliminating errors. But when prevention is less than perfect, there is still a chance to head off future losses if detection methods are successful.

ACCESS LOGS

Access logs show the time, date, duration, and user identification of access to the MIS. Increased activity by a user or unusually long access times are cause for suspicion. Exception reports can be prepared from access logs to show deviations from past activity or from group norms. In most cases, of course, there will be a valid reason for such use but there is also an increased opportunity to detect the one abuser of the system.

ERROR DETECTION

Errors can be detected at various stages of processing. *Verification* as a means of detecting data preparation errors was discussed in Chapter 3. Some input errors can be caught by *editing*. For example, a personnel application involving the use of a social security number would be designed to accept only nine numerical characters as input. This does not insure that the nine digits are correct, but it does screen out gross errors.

A *reasonableness check* ensures that data are within certain reasonable limits, such as zero to $20 for the hourly wage rate in a payroll system. Reasonableness checks can be employed at any stage of the system—during input, processing, or output.

A *totals check* compares beginning and ending totals, of inventory, for example, to the net change created by all the transactions. Any difference is an indication of an error, probably the loss of one or more transactions during the update process. Totals checks are quite common in financial applications.

Check digits guard against transmission errors when data are moved from storage to the CPU and back again. A check digit is an extra digit determined by an arithmetic manipulation of numerical data, say, the result of alternately adding and subtracting each digit in a number. Any change in the check digit is an indication that the number was somehow altered during transmission.

THE CONTROL PHASE

Control of MIS begins during planning and is exercised to some extent in every phase of the MIS life cycle, just as control is included in each phase of the management process discussed in Chapter 5. During planning, control standards are established as objectives of the system and periodic evaluations of the MIS are scheduled. One type of evaluation, the *progress review,* occurs during the development phase. Another, the *acceptance test,* takes place during implementation. Shortly after implementation, early in the operating phase, a *postinstallation review* is conducted. Periodic *audits* are administered at regular intervals, usually six months or one year, for the remaining life of the system.

PROGRESS REVIEWS

It would be very unusual for an MIS project to proceed precisely on schedule in exact conformance to the master plan. More likely, some activities will be delayed, others will proceed more rapidly than planned, new or revised information requirements will precipitate design modifications, and environmental changes will force a restatement of objectives. The purpose of a progress review is to bring these changes to light, to revise the master plan if necessary, and to redirect development efforts when that is required.

Progress is measured by comparing the amount of work completed to the amount scheduled for completion using a milestone schedule or Gantt chart. Discrepancies are resolved by modifying the schedules or reallocating development resources. Also, the expenditure of funds is compared to the budget and any necessary adjustments are made. Any changes in either the schedule or the budget must be conveyed to all affected parties.

Deviation from schedules is to be expected and, unless major discrepancies arise, is not a cause for concern. More worrisome are modifications caused by changing information requirements. The MIS project management team should establish change policies very early and enforce them strictly during development and operation. Once the logical design is completed, any changes desired must be fully justified by the originator and approved by the MIS project management team. Changes are usually judged more harshly than original proposals, since changes may render some completed work useless and result in disproportionate expenses. At some point, the MIS project management team must draw the line on changes and approve only those brought about by environmental conditions beyond organizational control.

THE ACCEPTANCE TEST

The acceptance test is the final activity before conversion to the new MIS. In a modular design, there will be an acceptance test for each module, as it is introduced. An MIS introduced as a total system can be tested in its entirety.

The acceptance test is a *systems* test, to include user personnel, which must satisfy the MIS project management team that the MIS (or module) is ready for implementation. In contrast to testing and debugging, which detects errors in programming only, the acceptance test evaluates user procedures, personnel training, operator procedures, the analysis and design effort, data communications, and every other aspect of the system to include a recheck of the program testing done earlier.

The acceptance test may be designed by MIS personnel, but it should be conducted by an agency with less personal involvement. The MIS project management team may form an ad hoc acceptance test team expressly for this purpose. As in all evaluation, there must be clear, quantitative standards for acceptance (or rejection) prior to the test. Error rates, turnaround time, and measures of accuracy provide unambiguous standards for comparison.

THE POSTINSTALLATION REVIEW

When operation of the new system is *technically* satisfactory, that is, when personnel are achieving expected speed and accuracy in entering data, all programming errors are corrected, and users are accustomed to the new output, it is time to evaluate the system in *behavioral* terms. In brief, is the system accomplishing what it was intended to do? There are several criteria applicable to the postinstallation review.

Cost/Benefit Analysis

The standard for this comparison is the cost/benefit analysis conducted in the economic feasibility analysis, as modified by changes encountered during development. Since it is frequently difficult to place a dollar value on benefits of an MIS, some organizations treat the MIS as a *profit center* and "charge" customers (users) for MIS services. Realistic charges can be developed from a comparison to fees charged by computer service centers for similar work. Carried to the extreme, the profit center concept gives the user the choice of "buying" MIS services, doing without some or all of them, or even going to an outside agency to obtain computer service. Under this concept, MIS "income" is equated to benefits, and the cost/benefit analysis is greatly simplified. This method obviously works best in those organizations already using the profit center concept in functional departments.

Attitude Surveys

The cost/benefit analysis validates the economic feasibility study; it is just as important to validate behavioral feasibility. One way to do this is to survey the attitude of users toward the MIS. The design of survey questionnaires is itself a highly specialized skill and may require the assistance of consultants. Without going into the detail of how survey items are constructed, the questions typically address changes in the volume, quality, difficulty, and enjoyment of work as a result of the new system. A well-designed questionnaire will include items that can be validated from second sources so that differences between actual impact and perceived impact can be determined.

MEASUREMENT

Much of the impact of the new MIS can be measured and compared to projected standards or past performance. For example, if inventory stock-outs had averaged 3.7 per week prior to implementation of the MIS and the objective was to reduce this number to 2.5, a new rate of 2.3 represents both an improvement and the meeting of system objectives. Other measures may be more subtle and more difficult to trace to the MIS. Certainly one expects better information to result in better decisions and ultimately in an improvement in some organization-wide measure such as return on investment. But is it difficult to isolate the MIS contribution to such an improvement.

AUDITS

Historically, *financial audits* were conducted to provide an independent validation of an organization's financial affairs. The auditing concept was expanded after World War II to include *operational audits* of other, nonfinancial activities. More recently, *management audits* have been directed specifically to management practices. The audit of an MIS includes some features of each type of audit.

MIS impact on the finances of an organization in two ways: they represent between 5 to 10 percent of the cost of operating the organization and they are used to maintain the organization's financial records. It is not surprising, therefore, that auditors have had to become skilled in the workings of MIS and that those skills are frequently employed to audit the operation and management of MIS as well.

Auditors may come from *internal* or *external* sources. The source is not important, as long as the auditor is able to maintain an objective point of view. In a small organization, where internal auditors come from the accounting department and where the audit must evaluate the performance of the auditors' peers and superiors, objectivity may be lost, and external auditors are called for. Larger organizations may be able to maintain a full-time auditing group which is, for all practical purposes, external to the activities it audits. The financial auditing practice of using external auditors is so well established, however, that many firms that could maintain their own auditing staff still use accounting firms or management consulting groups to audit their MIS.

PERFORMANCE MONITORS

The auditing of MIS operations may be facilitated by the use of *performance monitors*. There are two kinds of performance monitors: *hardware monitors* and *software monitors*. Hardware monitors are "black boxes" connected to the computer that keep track of active and idle time for various components. For example, a hardware monitor might show that a printer is active 90 percent of the time while the CPU is active only 20 percent. In this situation, hardware efficiency could be improved by adding a second printer.

Software monitors are computer programs that record processing times for application software. Software monitors are used to locate inefficiencies in programming. Software monitors give more specific information than hardware monitors but take up memory space, which itself introduces certain inefficiencies. Hardware monitors do not interfere with normal processing, but cannot reflect on individual programs, since contemporary computers process a number of programs at once under multiprocessing or multiprogramming and the hardware monitor cannot tell which program is running at any given instant.

THE LIFE CYCLE PROCESS

A number of parallels between the management process and the MIS life cycle have been noted already; one further similarity remains. Like the management process, MIS exhibit cycles both through and among the five phases.

The initial complete cycle from planning to control has been described in detail; subsequent cycles are initiated when control reveals discrepancies that require modification of the MIS. The modification must be planned, developed, implemented, operated, and, of course, subjected to control measures. Even if the MIS seems perfect—an unlikely event—environmental changes, such as technological advances in hardware and software, will trigger modifications to the system. While modifications usually do not impact on the whole organization the way the initial introductory cycle does, their impact is significant to parts of the organization and they should be managed just as carefully.

There are also incomplete cycles between phases. The need to cycle between planning and development in order to prepare feasibility studies and schedules was discussed earlier. In the same manner, difficulties encountered during implementation may necessitate return to development, or even to planning, for resolution. And minor operating difficulties frequently can be resolved by backing up to the implementation phase and conducting further training or revising procedure manuals.

The application of the management process to the MIS life cycle is but one link between management and MIS. It is an important one, of course, but one that pales in comparison to the more crucial role of MIS in support of management and, through management, the whole organization—a subject that is treated in greater detail in Part III which follows.

NOTE

1. Only a few events are shown in Table 7-1 to illustrate a milestone schedule. A real milestone schedule for an MIS project might contain hundreds of events and cover a period of three to five years. Other scheduling methods are also simplified for illustrative purposes.

PART III

The Structure of MIS

The study of management information systems is not yet, and probably never will be, an exact science. Scholars do not even agree on the *definition* of an MIS (see Chapter 1), although certain terms and phrases keep reappearing in the many definitions. The problem is compounded by the variety of organizations and environments in which MIS may be found. Even if there were general agreement on what an MIS is, it would be difficult to describe one that would fit every situation.

In spite of these difficulties, the manager who would like to know more about MIS is served well by a description of some MIS—*any* MIS—even if it does not accurately describe the information processes in that manager's own organization. For the importance of MIS concepts to a manager lies not in how to perform some very specific task with MIS assistance, but rather how those concepts can be applied in novel situations. General knowledge enhances creativity whereas specific knowledge can often be restrictive.

With this philosophy in mind, the MIS described in Part III is deliberately general. To be sure, specific examples are used from time to time—especially in Chapter 9 to illustrate the use of data base management systems—but the overall approach is to present an MIS model that the reader can, with a little imagination, bend to his or her own situation.

The model used here to describe an MIS is introduced in Chapter 8. It is a three-dimensional model incorporating processing, different levels of management activity, and the usual functional tasks performed in a typical business enterprise. Little detail is given on processing in this part because the basic processing components, computer hardware and software, and accompanying data processing concepts were described in Part I. The activity levels, which build on management principles discussed in Part II, are covered in Chapter 10. Representative functional applications are described in Chapter 11. As noted earlier, Chapter 9 is devoted to the rather specialized topic of data base management.

CHAPTER 8

An Overview of MIS

It is difficult to describe an MIS in clear, unambiguous terms. For one matter, MIS will differ from one organization to another, taking on characteristics peculiar to role of the organization, the information needs of its managers, and the available technology. We would not expect the MIS of, for example, a large financial institution, to be exactly like that of a major military command.

An MIS is also difficult to describe because much of it is conceptual rather than physical. There is a certain security in dealing with physical components: they can be seen, handled, taken apart to see what makes them work, and sent out for repair when they are broken. Perhaps it is this security that causes many managers to think of MIS only in terms of their physical components—the computer hardware. The conceptual components of MIS—the information flows, the relationships between functional applications, and the managerial decision processes—are less understandable.

Both difficulties can be overcome through the use of an appropriate *model*. Models are abstractions of the real world that both generalize and simplify otherwise complex situations. The reader may be familiar with the use of *iconic* models (which are similar in appearance to the real-world objects they represent) in automobile or aircraft design, and some *mathematical* models were introduced in Chapter 4. The model that will be developed here to explain MIS is of the *analog* variety; that is, it accurately represents how an MIS *works*, but it does not *look* like an MIS. These categories of models are part of a popular taxonomy shown in greater detail in Figure 8-1.

AN MIS MODEL

Models are understandable because they simplify, leaving out unessential elements. It would be of little value to devise a model as complex as the real-world situation it represents. Economic models, for example, are understandable (to economists, at least) only because they omit much detail and embody many qualifying assumptions. So it must be with an MIS model. Once an MIS is stripped down to its essential parts and the interrelationships of key elements are understood, additional detail may be added to tailor it to the needs of a particular organization. Only the stripped-down model is presented here; accessories must be added by the reader!

FIGURE 8-1.   A classification of models.

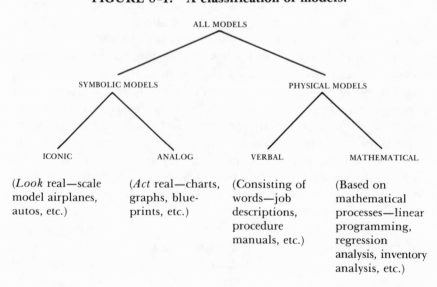

DIMENSIONS OF THE MIS MODEL

Try to imagine a symbolic model of a machined part, such as the crankshaft of an automobile engine. A verbal description would soon become hopelessly bogged down; certainly no machinist could make a crankshaft from such a model. Instead, the designer conveys the shape and dimensions of the crankshaft with an analog model, a drawing in this case. But even a drawing has limitations. It is not possible to show all details of the crankshaft in any one perspective. The standard solution to this problem is to draw the part as it appears in all three dimensions—from the top, the side, and the front. It still takes a certain amount of skill and experience to visualize the end product from these drawings, but the task is greatly simplified.

The crankshaft is comparatively easy to model—it at least is physical. An MIS, with conceptual elements, is more complex but can also be simplified by viewing it one dimension at a time. Of course, the top, side, and front views of the crankshaft are physical dimensions and we do not expect to visualize an MIS in that fashion. Instead, we will view it, conceptually, in a *processing* dimension, an *activity* dimension, and a *functional* dimension.

THE PROCESSING DIMENSION

There are two distinct approaches to processing design in MIS. The older, data processing approach is to use *application-oriented files* while the newer, MIS approach uses a *data base* concept.

The data processing systems described in Chapter 3 are of the application-oriented variety. A typical such system will have a master file for each application—billing, inventory, accounts receivable, payroll, and so on. In processing, an application program oriented to the format of records in the corresponding file updates those records on the basis of transactions that have occurred—charges made to accounts, items added to or deleted from inventory, payments received, hours worked, and so on. Reports generated from these applications may be circulated to interested managers outside the using department, but data usually must be reformatted before they can be used in another application. Although application-oriented files have been identified with data processing methods, they are still appropriate in certain unique MIS applications, such as the processing of a payroll, where there is little or no demand to share data.

The data base approach to processing is shown in Figure 8-2. In addition to the typical input-processing-output elements, this approach incorporates a *model bank*, a *data base management system* (DBMS), and the *data base* itself.

THE DATA BASE

The data base may be thought of as a large, application-*independent* file. The format of records in the data base is not fixed but varies according to the needs of the application programs. Individual records are assembled on a temporary, ad hoc basis for processing. After processing, updated elements are returned to the data base until required again—whether for the same or for a different application.[1]

There are several obvious advantages to such a system. First, much redundancy in the storage of data is reduced. For example, the complete name, address, account number, and other information about a vendor need not be stored in both a purchasing file and an accounts payable file; one record on the vendor can be made available to both applications. Second, maintenance of data is simplified. If the vendor in the preceding example changes his place of business, a single transaction will update the record to the benefit of both applications. Third, processing is speeded up be-

FIGURE 8-2. The processing dimension of an MIS.

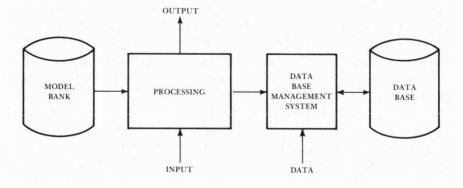

cause only necessary data elements need be drawn from the data base for any given application. For example, in posting payments to vendors, it may be possible to use an abbreviated record consisting only of each vendor's account number and the balance due. Processing in this case is faster than it would be if all data elements pertaining to each vendor were present in the record. Fourth, there is greater internal consistency among data within a data base. If top management were to ask for the number of vendors with which the firm deals, every user of vendor-related data should come up with the same answer. In an application orientation, different users might report different answers, depending on the currency of their files. Last, and by far most important, updated information in a data base is available immediately for other applications. To continue the vendor example, if an update of the accounts-payable application involves a deletion from a vendor's product line, that information is available at once to the purchasing application, and orders for the deleted product can be diverted to a different vendor. In an application-oriented system, the purchasing department might learn of the change from a report and several days could pass before the purchasing file is updated. In the mean time, the purchasing application might be generating orders to a vendor who no longer supplies the product.

There are also some disadvantages to a data base approach. Data security is more difficult because many users have access to the data base. Data of a personal or confidential nature can be protected from unauthorized access, even in a data base, but other data can be compromised or distorted accidently by a legitimate user. Users of accounting applications in particular are uneasy at the notion that users in, for instance, sales, might inadvertently alter the basic financial records of the firm. Also, a data base approach demands much greater standardization of data codes and control over application programs. Production cannot code a date day-month-year while accounting uses month-day-year and both expect to use the same data base. Of course, many MIS managers see increased control as an *advantage* of the data base, although users might disagree. The adoption of a data base must be accompanied by a strong sales pitch to show users the benefits they will receive and to convince them of the need to conform to rigidly defined standards.

THE DATA BASE MANAGEMENT SYSTEM

On the surface, the data base concept is appealingly simple: one merely dumps all relevant data into an accessible container and retrieves that which is needed at the appropriate time. It is roughly analogous to a filing cabinet which, instead of containing neatly alphabetized subject folders (comparable to application-oriented files), is filled with confetti carefully cut from the original documents. All the data are present in both cases, but it is difficult to imagine how an organization could function in the latter instance. Clearly, there must be some structure to the data in the data base and an organized set of procedures to facilitate their recovery. The data base management system satisfies both needs.

The data base management system is a fundamental element of an MIS. It is the integrative link that ties together managers, hardware, and software into a synergistic system. Much more is said on this subject in the following chapter; here it is necessary only to explain the role of the DBMS in the processing dimension.

The DBMS is primarily a software component—a set of computer programs that manages data.[2] Some organizations have developed their own DBMS, but it is more common now to purchase one of the 20 or 30 commercially prepared DBMS. Each DBMS will have its own set of procedures to govern data entry. The procedures give the user certain options to establish relationships between data elements, such as the relationship between a subassembly and the end product in a manufacturing process. In general, these relationships form the basis for data recovery. For example, all subassemblies used in a certain end product can be retrieved or, conversely, all end products that use a certain subassembly can be called out for processing. The instructions that cause data to be retrieved from the data base are incorporated directly into application programs, but they are implemented by the DBMS which amplifies and executes them.

The DBMS also facilitates the return to the data base of updated information. This procedure is different from the initial entry of data and, once again, involves commands incorporated into the application programs and carried out by the DBMS. Examples of data entry, retrieval, and updating are found in Chapter 9.

THE MODEL BANK

The model bank is the repository of application programs in an MIS. Some of these may be very specific and correspond to the programs associated with master files in an application-oriented system. Programs to generate sales reports, billing statements, inventory reports, and the like fall into this category. All that is unique about these programs in a data base system is the inclusion of program statements to create ad hoc records from the data base prior to processing.

Some of the programs in the model bank are much more general and literally may be "models" in the sense of the statistical or management science models discussed in Chapter 4. These programs are available to managers using terminals or microcomputers who may call up a program to analyze data they have collected independently or have obtained from the data base through the DBMS. The same programs may be used as subroutines in application programs. For example, a marketing research program need not have an integral linear regression routine if one is readily available in the model bank.

PROCESSING

The processing dimensions of an MIS now becomes clearer and distinctly different from data processing. Data are entered into the data base and structured according to procedures applicable to the DBMS. These data are stored in the data base where they are available to application programs. The application programs are stored in the model bank and contain program statements which will cause the DBMS to create temporary records for the application. The processing may involve only data from the data base, as in the case of an analysis of existing data, or it may involve additional input, such as transaction data or management-originated data. As in data processing, there will be output in the form of reports, graphs, tables, or video displays as well as changes to the "master file." In this MIS model, however, the "master file" is disbanded after updating and the changes are posted to the data base by the DBMS.

THE ACTIVITY DIMENSION

For the purpose of describing the processing dimension, it is adequate to say that data are transformed into information. But that does not explain the full range of transformation activities. There is another dimension, a hierarchy, in which subtle differences in the transformation processes become evident. While there is no generally accepted scale by which to measure or classify differences in activity levels, they are sufficiently related to the levels of management—*operational, tactical,* and *strategic* to justify using that scale with one important addition: a submanagement level for *transaction processing.* The hierarchy of transformation activities has been added to the previously described processing dimension in Figure 8-3.

TRANSACTION PROCESSING

The transaction-processing activity, sometimes called the transaction-processing *system,* is the foundation upon which

FIGURE 8-3.   The processing and activity dimensions of an MIS.

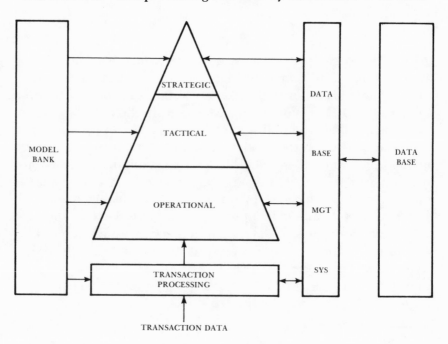

higher level activities are built.[3] The transaction processing activity captures the transaction data from which the data base is created and subsequently updated. The transformation processes at this level are relatively simple; data are prepared, edited, sorted, classified, stored, and retrieved. Computations, if any, are limited to basic arithmetic operations.

Transaction processing is concerned mainly with data collection and recordkeeping; there are few direct benefits to management that accrue from processing transactions. Indirectly, however, much management information can be traced back to transaction processing, which is an input system to the upper, managerial activity levels.

Transaction processing is also responsible for the majority of data base updating. Typical demands on the model bank for this purpose involve data entry programs, edit routines, and various update application programs such as accounts payable, inventory, sales reporting, and personnel recordkeeping. Most of the output from these programs is directed back to the data base and requires no human intervention. In some MIS, there may be additional output in the form of transaction history files and data base back-up files to facilitate re-creation of the data base in the event of a catastrophic loss.

Transaction processing is not solely dedicated to updating the data base and providing input for managerial activities. Much of the basic business of a firm may be carried out by the transaction-processing activity. A bank, for example, would need a transaction-processing activity for clearing checks and maintaining account balances even if it did not ultimately derive management information from those processes. Mail-order firms, credit card companies, insurance companies, and other organizations also depend on transaction processing as their primary means of conducting business. This is not to say that these organizations have no management information needs; they do, of course, but their transaction-processing activities are involved in a great deal more than just the support of those needs.

THE OPERATIONAL LEVEL

Managerial activities are distinguished from transaction processing by the introduction of a decision-making process. At the operational level, decisions tend to be of the programmable variety and, in many cases, are made without human intervention. The assignment of workers and/or machines to a specific job, the reordering of parts and raw materials, and the acceptance or rejection of materials and finished products on the basis of quality all fall into the category of operational decisions.

Input at the operational level comes primarily from transaction processing with only little management-originated data added. Routine decisions of the operational variety can be made almost entirely on the basis of transaction information. For example, information on the consumption of materials out of inventory provides the basis for a decision to reorder. In this example, as well as in other operational decisions, it is important to distinguish between the decision process itself and the establishment of decision criteria. The former is operational in nature while the latter is higher level—tactical in this case. The reorder decision is made when stock reaches or falls below a specified reorder point. The determination of the reorder point is more complicated and involves estimates of annual demand, costs, stock-out penalties, acceptable risk levels, and other management-originated data. These estimates ordinarily are not made at the operational level.

Output at the operational level is consistent with the responsibilities of the first-level managers it serves. Detailed reports may show work begun, in progress, and completed during the reporting period. Or they may show monies received and disbursed. Or personnel gains and losses. Other output, the result of programmable decisions, may be in the form of orders to vendors, work tickets, shipping instructions, or job assignments. And some of this output is processed further for use at the tactical level.

THE TACTICAL LEVEL

The tactical activity serves middle management. Middle managers tend to interact with MIS to a greater extent than do first-line managers. This interaction is especially evident in tactical decision making where the processes themselves may be programmable, but input parameters must be defined by managers. For example, the decision to accept or reject a lot of shear pins may be based on the results of a shear test of a sample of pins taken from the lot—if the mean shear point is within tolerances, the lot is accepted; otherwise, it is rejected. The computation of the mean shear point and the comparison to tolerances is easily programmed, but some middle manager must prescribe the sampling plan, establish a level of statistical significance for the test, and initiate corrective action when the test is failed.

The quality control example also illustrates the increased use of external data at the tactical level. Judgment, experience, and technical expertise are the basis for the manager's inputs in this case—not the MIS data base. This is also true in other applications. Personnel managers may define job qualifications and then let the MIS search the data base for candidates. Financial managers may predict short-term interest rates and then prepare cash budgets with the MIS. And marketing managers may subjectively assess the potential of salespersons as a basis for the MIS to assign them to sales regions.

The interaction of managers with the MIS requires somewhat different processing activities than those found at the operational level. Inquiry processing, in which the data base is searched for items that fall within user-defined parameters, and data analysis, in which the user draws on the model bank for mathematical programs with which to analyze data, are more common at the tactical level. The processing activity of report generation is still important at the tactical level, but reports to middle managers are more likely to be of the exception or summary variety. (The application of report generation, inquiry processing, and data analysis to the functions of management is discussed in Chapter 5.) In most cases, these reports are summarizations or excerpts of detailed infromation reported at the operational level. For example, an operational-level report of sales may be summarized into totals by sales region at the tactical level or abbreviated to show only regions that varied more than 10 percent from their quotas.

The Strategic Level

The differences between strategic and tactical MIS activities lie chiefly in the extent to which external data are used in the decision process and the planning horizon of the using managers. Strategic decision making requires proportionately more external data and tends to be much longer range than tactical decision making. But the processing activities—report generation, inquiry processing, and data analysis—tend to be quite similar.

One unfortunate reason for the similarity between strategic and tactical activities is the gap that has persisted between top-level managers and MIS. Many top-level managers, who reached their present position without the benefit of MIS, are reluctant to change their decision-making habits, and MIS designers, many of whom reached their present position by rising through the data processing ranks, have difficulty in understanding and satisfying top management's need for external data. There is hope for both sides, however. As the MIS-oriented middle managers of the seventies and eighties reach top management positions, and as management-oriented information specialists become MIS directors, the gap is narrowing. The pioneering work on *decision support systems* to serve the long-range, strategic-planning information needs of top management has already been done; general acceptance of such supplements to MIS is not far behind.[4]

THE FUNCTIONAL DIMENSION

The arguments for designing an MIS around functional subsystems have already been made, but even if that design approach is not adopted, there is a certain inescapable functional role in every MIS. The primary purpose of an MIS is to support management, and all but a very few top managers in any organization have a functional outlook. A production manager is unlikely to be swayed by an argument to "collect data this way because it makes it easier for accounting." Nor will a marketing manager willingly forego a certain report because its preparation places some burden on production; and so on. Middle and first-line managers are understandably parochial in viewing their responsibilities. The MIS must satisfy the functional information needs of these managers without degrading the integrative information needs of top managers.

The designation of functional subsystems is somewhat arbitrary and will vary from organization to organization. Smaller organizations, for example, are less likely to have a personnel subsystem, and organizations in the public sector tend not to have a marketing subsystem. The four functions illustrated here are considered to be the most common and will serve as examples even if they may not accurately reflect the functional dimension of a particular MIS.

Figure 8-4 shows the functional dimension of an MIS as it

appears at the transaction-processing level with the four functions of finance, production, marketing, and personnel. At this level, there is no integration of data in processing as each functional subsystem merely captures data for use by nonmanagerial personnel or for entry into the data base. What little integration occurs in transaction processing takes place in the data base as data are stored in such a manner as to make them accessible to various application programs or management inquiries. The transaction-processing level is unique among the activity levels in this "one-way" link to the DBMS.

The managerial activity levels—operational, tactical, and strategic—have a "two-way" link with the DBMS as shown by the example of the tactical activity in the functional dimension in Figure 8-5. Although the functional subsystems are still separate and any one, marketing for example, will produce output oriented strictly to the needs of marketing managers, there is integration in processing because any subsystem can draw on any data stored in the data base. To continue the marketing example, marketing managers must know the future availability of products if they are to take orders for those products from retailers and wholesalers. But production scheduling is a function of the production department. In this model, those schedules are available to the marketing applications just as sales trends are available to production applications to facilitate production planning. The operational and strategic activities would have a similar appearance in the functional dimension but have been omitted from Figure 8-5 for clarity.

FIGURE 8-4. The functional dimension of an MIS at the transaction-processing activity level.

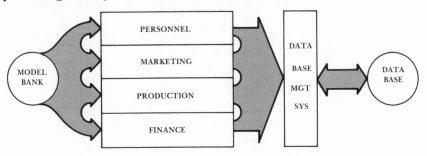

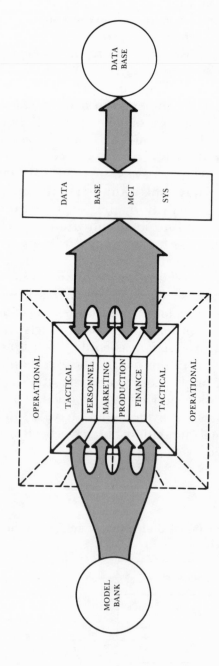

FIGURE 8-5. The functional dimension of an MIS at the tactical activity level.

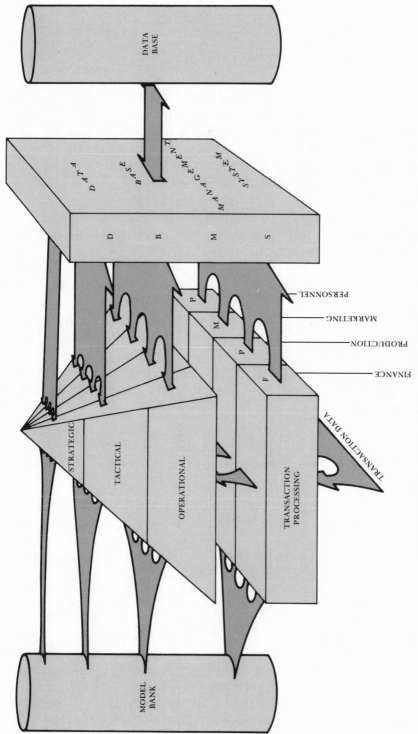

FIGURE 8-6. A three-dimensional view of an MIS model.

A THREE-DIMENSIONAL VIEW

This discussion of the MIS model began with an analogy to machine drawings of a crankshaft in each of three dimensions. Such drawings are often supplemented by a three-dimensional view to aid visualization of the finished product. While the dimensions of the conceptual MIS model do not conform exactly to physical dimensions, it is still possible to view an MIS in all three dimensions. Figure 8-6 is an attempt to do just that.

The model bank and the data base are similar both physically and conceptually: both must be on-line, direct-access storage devices and both must be structured in such a way as to make their contents available to all functions and activities. There are unique functional applications at each activity level, although different applications may involve common models and data.

One very important element of an MIS has been omitted from this model: managers. Managers are the recipients of most of the output of the MIS and provide much of the input as well. How managers interface with the remaining elements of the MIS, through the DBMS and in various activities and functions, is explored in detail in the next three chapters.

NOTES

1. This explanation is figurative. In a literal sense, a data element never leaves the data base. Its value is copied for use in processing and the updated value is written over the former value upon completion of processing.
2. Some DBMS also make use of hardware or "firmware" components. The IBM System 38 is an example of DBMS-oriented hardware.
3. The term "transaction processing," which literally refers to the processing of transactions, should not be confused with the term "*transactional* processing" used to describe a processing mode in Chapter 3. Transactional processing also refers to the processing of transactions, but in the special case of processing them *as they occur,* as opposed to *batch* processing. Transaction processing, as it is used here, may be either batch or transactional.
4. See, for example, Charles L. Meador and David N. Ness, "Decision Support Systems: An Application to Corporate Planning," in the *Sloan Management Review,* Winter 1974.

CHAPTER 9

Data Base Management Systems

As a general rule, the easier and more convenient an MIS component is for the user, the more complex and difficult it is for the systems designers. This is particularly true of data base management systems (DBMS) which give application programmers and managerial users easy access to otherwise hard-to-get data, but which also represent the highest state of the art of systems programming. The details of how systems programmers develop DBMS and integrate them into MIS is beyond the technical and topical scope of this book—the emphasis here is on the use of MIS by managers. But, as in many applications of high technology, the user's benefits are enhanced by a general appreciation of the principles involved. The pilot of a commercial airliner will never have to build or even repair a jet engine, but he is a more professional pilot because he understands how his equipment works. And the manager who uses a DBMS will likewise be more professional in his work if he understands the working principles of DBMS.

DBMS—AN EXPANDED MODEL

The various perspectives of MIS illustrated in the previous chapter show the DBMS only as a box that somehow provides an interface between the data base and the rest of the MIS. The use of the word "system" in DBMS hints at more complexity than that. And, indeed, a DBMS is a system with its own set of interrelated parts, input, output, and other systems characteristics. The additional details and the systems nature of DBMS are shown in Figure 9-1, which views a DBMS as a set of special programming languages and a software management package to complete the interface with the software and hardware of the host computer system. A brief description of these components is helpful in understanding the more detailed explanation of how a DBMS works.

DATA MANAGEMENT ROUTINES

Every DBMS has an integral software or combination software/hardware package to interpret statements in the special programming languages (with one exception) for the operating system of the host computer. That package here is called *data management routines* (DMR).[1] The exception is the device media control language (DMCL) which normally interfaces with the data base directly through the operating system.

It will be recalled that, among other tasks, the operating system of a computer links the various hardware components. Since the data base is in external storage, the operating system must provide the route to and from the storage device. The DMR converts storage and retrieval instructions in DBMS languages so they are understandable to the operating system.

DEVICE MEDIA CONTROL LANGUAGE

Whether in a data base or in more conventional files, data must be structured both physically and logically. Physical structure refers to actual storage locations allocated to data through the use of indexes or key transformation processes. In a DBMS, the assignment of physical storage space to data is accomplished through a *device media control language* (DMCL). While allocation of storage

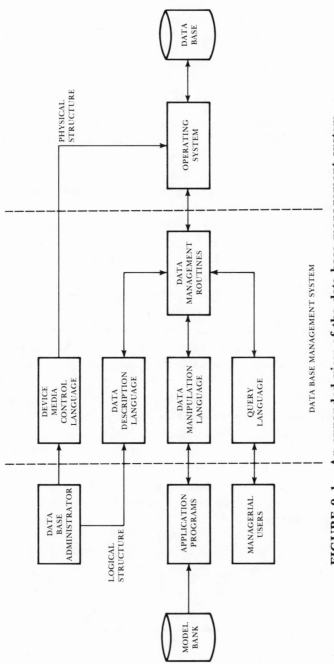

FIGURE 9-1. An expanded view of the data base management system.

187

space is the responsibility of the *data base administrator* (DBA), the actual programming in DMCL may be delegated to a systems programmer.

DATA DESCRIPTION LANGUAGE

The logical relationships between data elements are called the *schemas* in a DBMS and are defined by a *data description language* (DDL). A schema shows element and record formats similar to those in a conventional file. For example, Figure 9-2 shows the schema for a data base on customers of a computer manufacturer. The schema is organized around manufacturer's representatives who have various customers with diverse hardware components. The relationships between records are shown by arrows between *key elements*—those elements by which a record can be addressed. Arrowheads further define the relationships: the single arrowhead from "ACCT NO" to "REP NO" means that each customer can have only one representative, while the double arrowhead in the opposite direction means that a representative may service more than one account. This schema is greatly simplified, of course, to serve our illustrative purposes. An actual schema for such a data base would contain many more record types (application software, servicing office, user association affiliations, etc.) and many more data elements in each record (e.g., representative's office, length of employment, education level, and salary).

In an analogy made popular by James Martin, the schema is often compared to a city map, which shows how various geographic locations are related by streets and other physical features. A city map, also greatly simplified, is shown in Figure 9-3 to illustrate this comparison.

FIGURE 9-2.   Schema for a data base on computer customers.

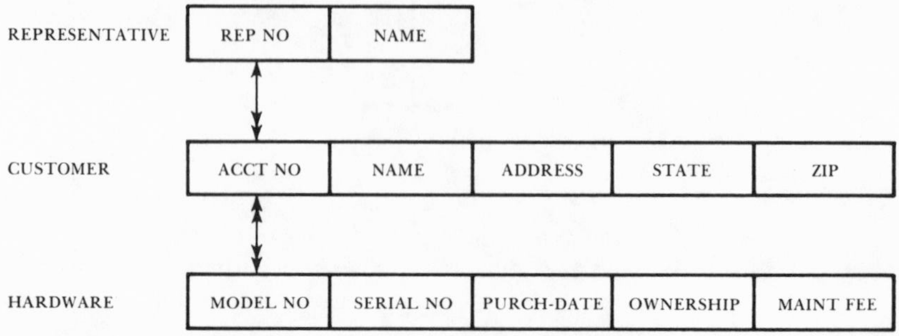

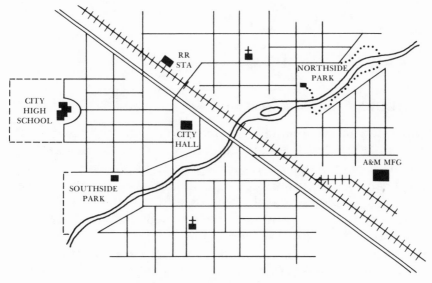

FIGURE 9-3.   A city map.

The schema differs from the format of conventional files in that it merely establishes an overall logical structure; it does not restrict processing to any particular format. Processing formats are defined, also by the DDL, in *subschemas*. A subschema is often described as the *user's* view of data (as opposed to the schema, the DBA's view). Subschemas contain only those records and elements needed for a given application. For example, if the computer manufacturer has an application program to analyze maintenance fees by the state in which leased hardware components are located, only the data elements in the subschema shown in Figure 9-4 would be necessary.[2] To complete the Martin analogy, the subschema is comparable to a route map, such as the one shown in Figure 9-5, which identifies only the streets traveled and key landmarks between two points in the city, for instance, the high school and the northside park.

DATA MANIPULATION LANGUAGE

Application programs communicate with the data base through a *data manipulation language* (DML). Although, like other DBMS languages, there are no universally accepted standards for DML, most DML are now compatible with standard

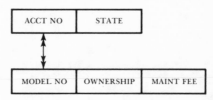

FIGURE 9-4.   Subschema for leased equipment fees by state.

application programming languages such as COBOL and FOR-TRAN. DBMS that use such DML are referred to as *host-language* systems, as opposed to *self-contained* systems in which the DML is a unique application programming language as well as an interface between applications and the data base.

In a host-language system, DML statements are inserted in appropriate places in the application program to identify the schema and subschema required for the applications. Records as defined by the subschema are created as needed and moved to working storage for processing. When processing is completed, updated elements are returned to the data base by other DML statements. Only slight modifications to programming rules, such as starting the DML statements in a different column than, say, COBOL statements, are necessary when using a host-language system.

Self-contained DBMS are usually highly specialized systems developed by large user-organizations to meet unique needs. The original DBMS fell into this category, but now commercially de-signed host-language systems can satisfy all but the most unusual requirements. Self-contained DBMS are not discussed further in this book.

QUERY LANGUAGE

One of the great advantages of DBMS is the opportunity af-forded managerial users to interface directly with the data base without depending upon programmers and analysts for access to data. To facilitate managerial access to the data base, most DBMS

FIGURE 9-5.   Route map from the high school to northside park.

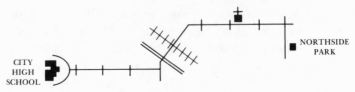

have a *query language* (QL) designed to be used interactively via terminals. QL are characterized by a few simple, yet powerful commands employed in an uncomplicated format. Nonprogrammers usually can be given a working familiarity with a QL in a few hours and the basic sign-on, access, and data analysis procedures can be summarized on several 3″ × 5″ cards for the user's convenience. Of course, more extensive training and experience is helpful if the user wishes to become truly proficient in QL. The use of QL by managers is explained in greater detail later in this chapter.

DESCRIBING THE DATA BASE

The importance of the schema to an effective data base cannot be overemphasized. In preparing the schema, the DBA must anticipate every possible relationship between data elements necessary to satisfy present and future information requirements. Yet the DBA is also motivated to reduce complexity in the data base to conserve storage space, minimize processing times, and improve data management in general.

The relationships required by application programs become evident during the analysis and design phase of the MIS life cycle, but relationships required for management inquiries are more difficult to anticipate. In the latter case, it is particularly important for the DBA to have a strong background in the functional activities of the organization as a basis for decisions on how to define the schema. Since schema definition is so important to management inquiry capability, we will explore the topic in greater detail.

DATA STRUCTURES

Data structures are usually classified as *tree, plex,* or *relational.* In each case, pointers or indexes are used to establish relationships between data elements stored in a direct access storage device, but the effect of the different structures is easier to visualize in diagrams.

TREE STRUCTURES

A data tree, like the decision tree in Chapter 4, is constructed of nodes and arcs. Data trees are usually drawn "upside down" with respect to trees in nature; that is, the *root* node from which *branches* emanate is at the top and the *leaf* nodes are below. A leaf may have only one *parent*, but may have many *children*. A tree illustrating the computer manufacturer's data base from the previous examples is shown in Figure 9-6.

The single parent requirement for customers in this example is easy to maintain, because the schema (Figure 9-2) stipulated that a customer can have only one representative. But hardware presents a problem. No customer can expect to be the exclusive user of a particular model of computer equipment, yet the tree structure requires single parenthood. The solution is to repeat the hardware model in the diagram each time it occurs. In this example, there are three types of hardware (H_1, H_2, and H_3) and type 2 is used by both customers (C_1 and C_2). Therefore, H_2 must appear twice.

Another, more elegant way to show that more than one customer uses H_2 is to *invert* the tree and make H_2 the root, as shown in Figure 9-7. DBMS using a tree structure usually can invert on any key element. Figure 9-7 also shows an inversion placing C_2 at the root. Of course, the DBMS does not literally invert the data tree; the pointers or indexes are merely used in such a way to create the effect of a schema based on a root of hardware models or customers rather than manufacturer's representatives.

DBMS using tree structures may also employ an inversion technique to define subschemas. This is one way in which DBMS avoid the duplication of data used in several applications. Data elements appear in the schema only once, but they may be in any number of subschemas subject only to restrictions imposed when the relationships between elements are defined with the DDL.

FIGURE 9-6.   A tree data structure.

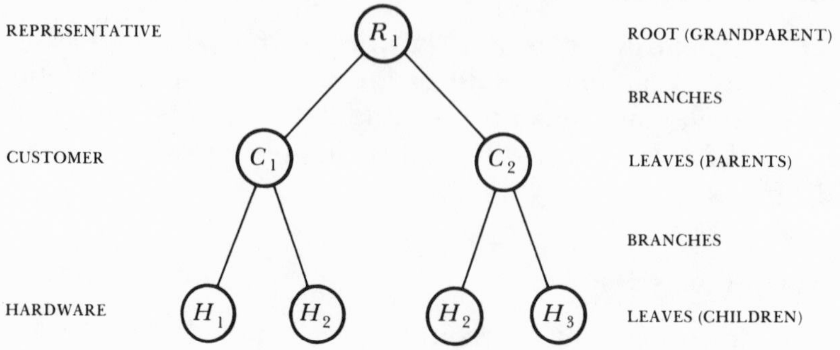

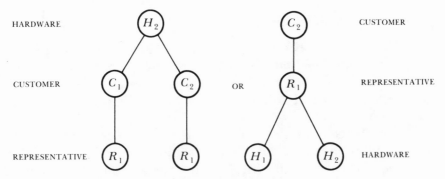

HARDWARE

CUSTOMER

REPRESENTATIVE

CUSTOMER

REPRESENTATIVE

HARDWARE

OR

FIGURE 9-7.   Inverted trees.

PLEX STRUCTURES

It is also possible to show complex relationships in a single diagram if leaves are permitted to have more than one parent. Data structures of this type are called _plex_. Once again, no DBMS literally stores data in either a tree or a plex format, but uses pointers or indexes to create that effect. In general, a plex structure requires more pointers than do tree structures, but some efficiencies are gained in processing. The decision to trade storage space (for the extra pointers) for processing time is made by the DBMS developer during the design phase and is not a matter of choice for the user or even the DBA.

A plex structure for the computer customer data base is shown in Figure 9-8. This diagram is based on the same relationships between the one representative (R_1), the two customers (C_1 and C_2), and the three hardware models (H_1, H_2, and H_3) originally shown in Figure 9-6.

FIGURE 9-8.   A plex data structure.

REPRESENTATIVE

CUSTOMER

HARDWARE

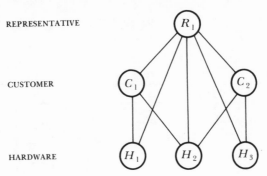

RELATIONAL STRUCTURES

A few DBMS use a data structure that can be represented in flat, two-dimensional tables. The use of tables, or *relations,* gives rise to the term *relational data bases* used to describe such DBMS. A set of relations that describes the data in the computer customer example is shown in Figure 9-9.

In all the examples of data structures, only key elements are shown. Thus, in Figure 9-6, the branch between R_1 and C_1 establishes access not only to the information that C_1 is served by R_1, but also to all the other, nonkey, data elements associated with C_1 and R_1. The same information is accessible in the first relation shown in Figure 9-9. The two keys for representative and customer in each line combine to form a single key by which all data associated with that combination may be accessed (the remaining data elements are not shown). Therefore, the first line in the first relation in Figure 9-9 corresponds to the left branch in Figure 9-6 and the second line to the right branch.

While it appears that data elements in relations are repeated, it must be remembered that these diagrams are aids to understanding; they are not representations of how data are actually stored. Relational data bases are no less efficient in storage than those using a tree or plex structure.

DESCRIBING THE SCHEMA

It was noted earlier that there is no universal agreement on DBMS languages. Not that there has been no effort to stan-

FIGURE 9-9. Relational view of a data base.

REPRESENTATIVE *R*	CUSTOMER *C*
1	1
1	2

REPRESENTATIVE *R*	HARDWARE *H*
1	2
1	1
1	3

CUSTOMER *C*	HARDWARE *H*
1	1
1	2
2	2
2	3

dardize. In the late 1960s, the Conference on Data Systems Languages (CODASYL) formed a Data Base Task Group (DBTG) which developed DBMS language specifications, but the industry has been slow to accept them. Even seemingly unimportant matters, such as calling the smallest unit of data an *element*, a *field* (the IBM term), or an *item* (the CODASYL term) have not been resolved. The description of the schema remains an important task in data base management, however, and, in the absence of a common DDL, we will simply pick one of the more popular DBMS to use for demonstration purposes.

The DBMS demonstrated here is called *System 2000* and the demonstration data base is based on the schema first shown in Figure 9-2. As noted earlier, this schema has been simplified for illustrative purposes and it does not begin to challenge the capability of a modern DBMS. For example, this schema has only three levels (representative, customer, and hardware); System 2000 can accommodate *33* levels! And, while we will introduce only a few entries at each level, the DBMS is constrained only by the limits of physical storage in this respect.

With the understanding that it only scratches the DBMS surface, the computer customer data base schema is described in System 2000 DDL statements in Figure 9-10. Although this schema does not exercise all available DDL expressions, it uses enough to give a general idea of how the DDL is used.

Each line in the schema description represents a *component* and

FIGURE 9-10. Schema description in data definition language.

1* REPRESENTATIVE (KEY INTEGER 9(5)):

2* REPRESENTATIVE NAME (NON-KEY NAME X (25)):

3* CUSTOMER (RG):

    4* ACCOUNT NUMBER (KEY INTEGER 9(7) IN 3):

    5* CUSTOMER NAME (NON-KEY NAME X(20) IN 3):

    6* ADDRESS (NON-KEY NAME X(25) IN 3):

    7* STATE (NON-KEY NAME XX IN 3):

    8* ZIP CODE (NON-KEY NAME X(5) IN 3):

    9* HARDWARE COMPONENT (RG IN 3):

    10* MODEL NUMBER (KEY NAME X(5) IN 9):

    11* SERIAL NUMBER (NON-KEY NAME X(10) IN 9):

    12* PURCHASE DATE (NON-KEY DATE IN 9):

    13* OWNERSHIP (NON-KEY NAME X IN 9):

    14* MAINTENANCE FEE (NON-KEY DECIMAL 9(4).9(2) IN 9):

is identified by a component (C) number. The asterisk that follows the component number is called a *system separator*. Each component also has a name and, in parentheses, a description. Components called *elements* contain data and their description gives the data *picture;* that is, the number and type of characters in the element. A second type of component is called a *repeating group* and contains no data; it merely identifies *data sets* (groups of related data elements) that may be repeated in the schema. The description for a repeating group is simply "RG."

The component descriptions follow strict rules of the DDL. For example, the description of the first element, "REPRESENTATIVE," identifies it as a *key* element of a type called *integer*, meaning that the data tree can be inverted on it and that its value is always a whole number. The picture of this element describes it as having up to five (indicated by the "5" in parentheses) numeric characters (indicated by the "9").

The second element, "REPRESENTATIVE NAME," is not a key element nor is it an integer. It is a *name* and can have as many as 25 alphabetic or numeric characters (including spaces).

Component 3 is a repeating group consisting of components 4 through 14 to include the repeating group described in component 9. By identifying "CUSTOMER" as a repeating group, the DBA is saying that a representative may serve more than one customer, a relationship established earlier by the double arrowhead in Figure 9-2. Similarly, as a repeating group, component 9 permits each customer to have more than one hardware item.

Components associated with repeating groups must be identified with the parent component. This is accomplished by indenting the C-numbers following the first level of repeating groups and with the qualifer "IN 3" to show association with "CUSTOMER" (C3), or "IN 9" to show association with "HARDWARE COMPONENT" (C9). The qualifiers permit the use of common names, such as "ADDRESS" or "ZIP CODE," in more than one repeating group without creating confusion over which repeating group they belong to. Second levels of repeating group elements, such as C10 through C14, are not further indented, but another repeating group associated directly with a representative would be started in the same column as C3.

Because component 7 has only two characters, it uses an alternative picture identification. The use of "XX" to show two alphabetic or numeric characters saves a few spaces over the equivalent

"X(2)" Also, component 8, "ZIP CODE," is described as a name and uses the alphabetic-numeric symbol "X," although it is always numeric. The reason for this is that an integer suppresses leading zeros. As an integer, the zip code 09612 would appear as 9612 which might cause some confusion.

Two descriptions in the hardware repeating group require some further explanation. First, *date* has a fixed format of MM/DD/YY (two digits each for the month, day, and year) and requires no picture. Second, *decimal* is a noninteger number and must show the number of decimal places desired. The picture used for the decimal in component 14 could have been expressed in the alternative format as "9999.99" at a savings of two spaces.

LOADING THE DATA

The 14 DDL statements in Figure 9-10 only describe the *schema;* they do not actually describe the *data* in the computer customer data base. An additional step is required to fill the pictures of the various elements with data. Since this is a rather tedious, repetitive task, we will show only a partial *logical entry* (the System 2000 term for a hierarchical collection of data sets).

Figure 9-11 shows data concerning one customer of a representative named David A. Krause. The customer has three hardware components: an owned CPU Model Z200, a leased printer Model P505, and a leased terminal Model T310.

FIGURE 9-11. **Partial logical entry in a computer customer data base.**

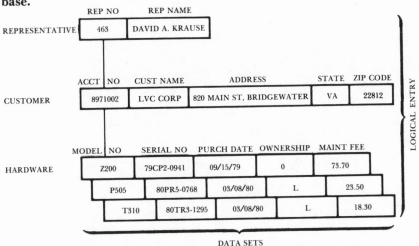

REP NO	REP NAME
463	DAVID A. KRAUSE

ACCT NO	CUST NAME	ADDRESS	STATE	ZIP CODE
8971002	LVC CORP	820 MAIN ST, BRIDGEWATER	VA	22812

MODEL NO	SERIAL NO	PURCH DATE	OWNERSHIP	MAINT FEE
Z200	79CP2-0941	09/15/79	0	73.70
P505	80PR5-0768	03/08/80	L	23.50
T310	80TR3-1295	03/08/80	L	18.30

REPRESENTATIVE

CUSTOMER

HARDWARE

LOGICAL ENTRY

DATA SETS

1* 463*
2* DAVID A. KRAUSE*
3*

4* 8971002*
5* LVC CORP*
6* 820 MAIN ST, BRIDGEWATER*
7* VA*
8* 22812*
9*
10* Z200*
11* 79CP2-0941*
12* 09/15/79*
13* 0*
14* 73.70*

9*
10* P505*
11* 80PR5-0768*
12* 03/08/80*
13* L*
14* 23.50*

9*
10* T310*
11* 80TR3-1295*
12* 03/08/80*
13* L*
14* 18.30*

3*
(Additional customers of David A. Krause)

9*
(Hardware of additional customers)

END*
(Last hardware component of last customer of David A. Krause)

1*
(Additional representatives)

END**
(Last hardware component of last customer of last representative)

FIGURE 9-12.   Data values for computer customer schema.

1*463*2*DAVID A. KRAUSE*

   3*4*8971002*5*LVC CORP*6*820 MAIN ST, BRIDGEWATER*7*VA*8*22812*

   9*10*Z200*11*79CP2-0941*12*09/15/79*13*0*14*73.70*

   9*10*P505*11*80PR5-0768*12*03/08/80*13*L*14*23.50*

   9*10*T310*11*80TR3-1295*12*03/08/80*13*L*14*18.30*

   3* (Additional customers of David A. Krause)

   9* (Hardware of additional customers)

   9* (Last hardware component of last customer of David A. Krause) *END*

1*(Additional representatives)

      •
      •
      •

   9* (Last hardware component of last customer of last representative) *END**

FIGURE 9-13.   Data entry format for loading the data base.

The sample data are shown in a tabular format corresponding to the schema format in Figure 9-12. Notice that a second system separator (asterisk) is used to note the end of each data value as well as to mark its beginning. The word "END" followed by a single asterisk identifies the end of a single instance of the schema, while "END" and a double asterisk indicate the end of the last instance. Repeating groups are easily identified by the absence of data values.

Of course, the tabular format is merely a convenience to illustrate conformity with the schema. The DMR does not need such a format to interpret correctly the DDL statements—the element numbers, asterisks, and the word "END" are sufficient. To actually load this data, then, the programmer can run entries together as shown in Figure 9-13, subject only to a few rules of indentation and the requirement to start repeating groups on a new line.

USING THE DATA BASE

There are two broad categories of data base users: application programmers, who use the data base in lieu of application-oriented files, and managers, who use it to obtain responses to inquiries. As noted earlier, application programmers interface with the data base through a DML while managerial users employ a QL. We will continue the example of a System 2000 data base of computer customers, but because of the similarity between the System 2000 DML and QL, we will illustrate only the use of the query language.

DATA RETRIEVAL

One of the most fundamental, as well as one of the simplest requests that a manager might make of a DBMS is to print or display some of the data stored in the data base. Assume a manager in the computer manufacturing firm in this example is authorized access to the customer data base and has "signed on" a terminal using the proper procedures and passwords for this system. To obtain, for example, a list of all the representatives, the manager need only type:

```
PRINT C2:
```

and the response will be

```
2* DAVID A. KRAUSE
2*     .     .     .
2*     .     .     .
2*     .     .     .
2* (Name of last representative)
```

Of course, this entry assumes the manager has knowledge of the schema and knows that C2 identifies the representatives' names. An alternative entry, which also requires some familiarity with the schema, to produce the same list is:

```
PRINT REPRESENTATIVE NAME:
```

If more than one component is desired, the additional C-numbers, separated by commas, are added to the print command. Thus,

```
PRINT C4, C5:
```

will produce

```
4* 8971002
5* LVC CORP
4*     .     .     .
5*     .     .     .
4* (Last account number)
5* (Last customer name)
```

More often than not, a manager will want only those entries that meet certain conditions. For example, a list of customers served by representative Krause could be obtained with the command

```
PRINT C5 WHERE C1 EQ 463:
```

which means, "Print the customer's name (component number 5) where component number 1 (the representative's number) *is equal to* 463 (Krause's number).

In addition to "equal to," there are five other *binary operators* that limit or define the qualifying conditions. For example,

```
PRINT C5, C10 WHERE C14 LT 25.00:
```

means, "Print the name of the customer and the hardware model number where the maintenance fee is *less than* $25." The remaining operators are NE (for *not equal to*), LE (for *less than or equal to*), GT (for *greater than*), and GE (for *greater than or equal to*).

When there are two or more qualifying conditions, *Boolean operators* may be used to describe the desired relationship. For example, the command to print all leased hardware for the LVC Corporation is written:

```
PRINT C10 WHERE C4 EQ 8971002 AND C13 EQ L:
```

The Boolean operator "AND" means that *both* conditions (belonging to LVC and leased) must be met, and the response will be:

```
10* P505
10* T310
```

The other Boolean operators are OR (*either* condition must be met) and NOT (*neither* condition may exist).

DATA ANALYSIS

Although we normally expect to analyze data with a preprogrammed application from the model bank or a short data analysis routine prepared at the terminal, there is some analytical capability within the QL itself. System 2000 has six *systems functions* which provide summary statistics on data stored in the data base. For example, to obtain the *average* maintenance fee for equipment used by the LVC Corporation, one need only type:

```
PRINT AVG MAINTENANCE FEE WHERE CUSTOMER NAME EQ LVC
CORP:
```

to obtain the response "38.50," which is the arithmetic mean of 73.70, 23.50, and 18.30. This example also illustrates the use of component names instead of numbers in the print command.

The other systems functions are MIN (the *smallest numerical* or *first alphabetical* value that meets the qualifying condition), MAX (the opposite of MIN), SUM (the *total* of numeric values that meet the qualifying condition), SIGMA (the *standard deviation* of qualifying numeric values), and COUNT (the *number* of elements that meet the qualifying condition).

UPDATING THE DATA BASE

Not all managerial users are granted the authority to update the data base. After all, most managers are laypersons in data processing and the data base may contain data vital to the operation of the organization. In the case of the computer manufacturer's data base, for example, it is just as easy to change *every* customer's address to, for instance, 1650 Broad Street, as it is to change just the LVC Corporation's address to that number and street—easier, in fact! Not many DBAs will risk giving this kind of power to every manager who has access to a terminal.

Authority to update the data base can be controlled by passwords and other security measures. For those who have the authority, or for application programmers who routinely update the data base, it is a powerful and valuable tool. We will show just three ways of updating a System 2000 data base: by adding data, changing data, and deleting data.

ADDING DATA

Suppose the LVC Corporation leases a second T310 terminal, serial number 81TR3-0691, on February 14, 1982, with a monthly maintenance fee of $21.00. The representative, David A. Krause, has a password that gives him authority to update his own accounts. He could add data on the new terminal with the command:

```
ADD C9 EQ 10*T310*11*81TR3-0691*12*02/14/82*13*L*14*
    21.00*END*WHERE C4 EQ 8971002:
```

which means, "Add a new repeating group for hardware component (C9) equal to . . . (data set C10 through C14) . . . for the customer (LVC Corp) with account number (C4) equal to 8971002." Notice the similarity between the adding of data to this existing account and the creation of the account during the loading of the data base.

Data are added only as new logical entries or new data sets under existing logical entries. New elements cannot be added to existing data sets. It would be inappropriate, for example, to add C8 (Zip Code) to the data set for the LVC Corporation because it already has a value in C8. The updating of individual elements in existing data sets is accomplished with a *change*.

CHANGING DATA

A data change involves the *replacement* of a current value with a new, or changed, value. Once again, the computer customer data base in System 2000 will serve to illustrate the updating process. In this example, we will assume that the LVC Corporation has moved to 1650 Broad Street, Athens, Georgia, 30601. Representative Krause can make this change with the entry:

```
CHANGE C3 EQ 6*1650 BROAD ST, ATHENS*7*GA*8*30601* END*
    WHERE C4 EQ 8971002:
```

which is virtually identical to the "ADD" format with the exception of the initial operative command, "CHANGE." A less obvious difference is that data values in C6 through C8 already existed for this account and are now destroyed.

A slightly different "CHANGE" format can be used if the change involves only one element. For example, if the monthly maintenance fee on owned CPU Models Z200 is raised to $80.00, the following entry might be made:

```
CHANGE C14 EQ 80.00 WHERE C10 EQ Z200 AND C13 EQ 0:
```

Notice that this changes *all* owned Z200 maintenance fees, not just for the LVC Corporation. If only LVC were involved in the change, the qualifier ". . . AND C4 EQ LVC CORP:" would be added to the command or used to replace the C13 qualifier.[3]

DELETING DATA

Like additions, deletions ordinarily apply only to entire logical entires or data sets, although it is also possible to delete a single data element. To illustrate the deletion of a data set, assume that the LVC Corporation is assigned to another representative after moving from Virginia to Georgia. (In this case, before deleting LVC data from representative Krause's records, we should be careful to assign them first to the new representative before they are erased from the data base.) To delete LVC from Krause's logical entry, we need only enter:

REMOVE TREE C3 WHERE C4 EQ 8971002:

The word "TREE" includes the lower-level data sets for hardware within the customer data set, which is the effect desired in this case. The word "TREE" may be omitted if there are no subordinate data sets. For example, to delete only the P505 printer from the LVC inventory, the following command will suffice:

REMOVE C9 WHERE C10 EQ P505 AND C4 EQ 8971002:

MANAGING THE DATA BASE

The management of data base is the responsibility of the data base administrator. Specifically, the DBA is charged with maintaining the *security, privacy,* and *integrity* of data within data bases. Security refers to protection from deliberate or accidental loss or destruction of data, privacy involves protection from unauthorized access to data, and integrity entails protection from improper changes. These are the same protective measures described in Part II and they apply to systems that do not have data bases as well as to those that do. But they are much more difficult to achieve under a data base concept and by themselves would justify the added position of the DBA.

The DBA is also responsible to ensure the *availability* of data in the data base, and therein lies the problem: increasing availability increases the risks against which data must be protected, and reducing those risks may result in restricted availability. The DBA must establish policies that strike an acceptable compromise between these opposing goals.[4]

Some compromise measures have already been suggested. For example, terminals in user work areas increase availability, but the use of passwords restricts access to data. And even those authorized access can be limited to a "read-only" mode to protect integrity. There are also technical measures to safeguard data integrity when users are authorized to make changes. Nonetheless, there is a basic premise that if one human designs a protective measure another can probably defeat it, and the recent growth of data bases in government and industry has caused much alarm among those responsible for managing data.

NOTES

1. The DMR package is also called the *data base manager* (DBM), a term avoided here because "manager" is used throughout this book to refer to a person rather than software or a software/hardware combination.

2. Notice that ACCT NO and MODEL NO have no direct bearing on this analysis, but they provide access points for STATE, OWNERSHIP, and MAINT FEE which cannot be accessed directly because they are not key elements.

3. Since LVC has only one Z200 CPU, it would be redundant, although not incorrect, to qualify by both ownership and customer name.

4. Some organizations also have a *data administrator* who is responsible for policy in addition to the *data base administrator* who, in such cases, is responsible only for technical matters dealing with the data base and the DBMS.

CHAPTER 10

MIS Activity Levels

The MIS activity levels have been compared to the three levels of management and the submanagement level usually found in organizations. While it is unlikely that MIS designers would actually build four separate modules to support transaction-processing, operational, tactical, and strategic activities, they must keep in mind the special requirements of each activity and ensure that they are met in the final MIS. Table 10-1 shows the differences among activities with respect to certain characteristics of an MIS.

MIS activities can be compared to management in another respect: just as management functions are job-independent and describe the responsibilities of managers across a wide variety of organizations, so MIS activities are independent of functional subsystems and describe similar information-gathering techniques in the various functional departments of an organization. This does not mean that there are not differences among functional subsystems; there are and they are discussed in the following chapter. In this chapter we shall focus only on differences among activity levels.

TABLE 10-1. Representative Characteristics of Activity Levels

Activity Level

CHARACTERISTIC	TRANSACTION	OPERATIONAL	TACTICAL	STRATEGIC
Primary users:	Submanagement personnel	First-line management	Middle management	Top management
Inputs:	Transaction data	Primarily internal data	Mixed internal/external data	Primarily external data
Processing:	Editing, storage, retrieval, file updating	Report generation, programmable decisions	Data analysis, programmable/nonprogrammable decisions	Inquiries, nonprogrammable decisions
Outputs:	Error listings, detailed reports	Detailed reports, information primarily for internal use	Exception reports, information of both internal and external interest	Summary reports, information of both internal and external interest
Planning horizon:	Present	Very short range	Short range	Long range
Major function:	Data collection, recordkeeping	Coordinating	Controlling	Planning

DECISION PROCESSES

Perhaps the single most distinguishing characteristic of MIS activity levels is the manner in which decisions are made at different levels. Most strategic decisions are of the nonprogrammable or *unstructured* variety while most operational decisions are programmable or *structured*. Tactical decisions may be of either kind but transaction processing tends to be more involved with error correction than decision making. The relationship between decision processes and MIS activity levels is the same as the relationship, suggested in Chapter 5, between decision processes and management levels. That relationship is illustrated again in Figure 10-1.

STRUCTURED DECISIONS

Structured decisions are characterized by routine or repetitive applications, well-defined or easily quantifiable input, and relatively simple manipulative processes. The decision to replenish

FIGURE 10-1.   Decision processes at different activity levels.

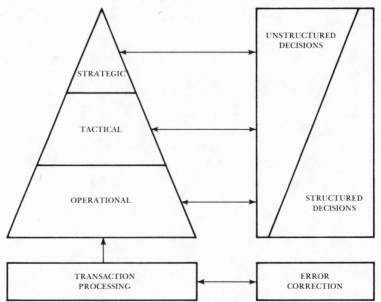

inventory (see Chapter 4) falls into this category: the decision situation may arise every few weeks for each type of item in inventory, inputs are all numerical and easy to obtain, and the computations to determine the amount to order and the time to place the order are not complex. The inventory decision is also one we would expect to be made at the operational level.

The extent to which a decision may be structured is not the sole determinant of the activity level at which it is made, although many decisions in recent years have been delegated to the operational level simply because they are so programmable—the inventory decision illustrates this point as well. Other decisions, however structured or programmable they might be, remain at higher levels either because they are so important to the organization or because they logically fall under strategic or tactical management responsibility. For example, the strategic decision to manufacture a certain mix of products—which can be determined by the structured approach of linear programming—is too critical to the organization to be delegated.

UNSTRUCTURED DECISIONS

Some problems are so unique, so difficult to quantify, or so complex to solve that they cannot be programmed. Consider for example the decision to do business in a foreign country noted for terrorism, corruption, and the repression of civil rights. First, it is a decision that, thankfully, does not occur often and there are probably no precedents on which to rely. Second, there is no way to assess the financial impact of public indignation (or indifference) to the decision. And third, there are moral issues—the personal safety of one's employees in the country, the implied endorsement of the regime, and the possibility of improving (or worsening) the plight of locals who may be hired—which could not be quantified even if they were fully understood.

The fact that this problem is unstructured does not preclude use of the MIS, but it does make such use more difficult. It is possible to construct probability distributions of sales based on public reaction to the decision, calculate increased insurance premiums, weight management's preference for this and other investment opportunities, and construct a simulation model that will show the range and likelihood of these and other variables. The results will not be the answer to the problem, of course; they will be but one input to strategic management's subjective appraisal of the situation. The final decision will be made by a noncomputational process.

Unstructured decisions are more common at strategic levels, but they are by no means excluded from lower levels. The decision to accept or reject an employee's excuse for being tardy is also unstructured but is more common at the operational level. Again, the MIS may be of some help in providing background information on the employee to the supervisor who must make the decision, but the decision itself is not programmable.

PHASES IN DECISION PROCESSES

Over the years, there have been many attempts by philosophers, military leaders, and management theorists to identify steps or phases in decision making. The military staff study format is typical of these efforts:

1. Define the problem.
2. Collect facts.
3. Pose alternative solutions.
4. Evaluate alternatives and select the best.
5. Implement the chosen alternative.

More recently, Herbert Simon classified the phases of decision making as *intelligence, design,* and *choice.* Intelligence is defined as data collection and problem detection, design involves proposing and evaluating alternatives, and choice is the selection of an alternative. The manner in which these phases of decision making are executed is also related to MIS activity levels.

INTELLIGENCE

The data collection aspect of intelligence is actually part of the management function of *control*—that part in which *actual data* are compared to *standard data.* Discrepancies between actual and standard data lead to the other aspect of intelligence— problem detection.

The nature of the data requirements at different levels of MIS activities is shown in Figure 10-2. Transaction processing requires transaction data, which are somewhat outside the external/

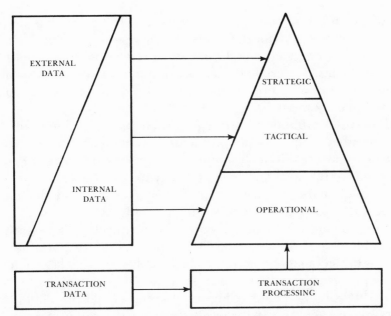

FIGURE 10-2.   Data requirements at different activity levels.

internal classification. Some transaction data are internal—such as hours of labor, production volumes, and so forth—while others originate from external sources—orders from customers, payments received, and so forth. The operational activity level relies mainly on internal data, while the strategic level tends to use more external data. As in decision processes, the tactical level occupies a middle-of-the-road position.

Both actual and standard data can be classified as internal or external. For example, standards for operational control—production quotas, quality standards, and the like—are imposed chiefly from within the organization, although some, such as safety standards or toxic substance levels, may come from external agencies. On the other hand, the strategic level uses mainly external standards imposed by government, industry, or society and has only a few internal, self-imposed standards. Most actual data—production volumes, quality levels, accident rates, pollutant levels, and so forth—are generated internally. In a few instances, such as the interest rate at which debt capital is acquired or public response to an advertising campaign, actual data come from external sources.

Problem identification also varies with the level of MIS activity.

Problems in transaction processing tend to be errors that simply require corrections, not decisions. At the operational level, there tends to be a relatively small number of recurring, easily identifiable problems. Material shortages, equipment malfunctions, and substandard quality are routine, anticipated problems for operational management.

The total number of strategic problems is smaller than the total number of operational problems, but, because strategic problems are more likely to be unique, there may be more *different* problems at the strategic level and they may be harder to detect. Erosion of market share, product obsolescence, and declining stock values are examples of strategic problems.

Once again, the tactical level acts as a transition between the operational and strategic levels. Some tactical responsibilities, such as budget management, produce easily identifiable problems while problems in other areas, such as sales management, are more difficult to recognize. Figure 10-3 shows that problem identification relates to activity levels in much the same manner as decision processes and sources of data.

FIGURE 10-3.   Problem identification at different activity levels.

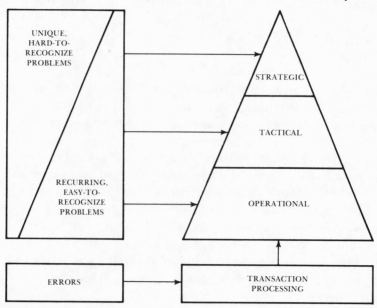

DESIGN

In traditional decision making, the design phase involves the development of several alternative solutions to the problem. In many situations, this is still an appropriate approach. In other problems, however, it is possible to proceed directly to the single best alternative. To avoid the issue of whether one or many alternatives are considered, we will redefine the design phase as one of *model building* or *model selection*. The application of models to decision processes in the various activity levels is shown in Figure 10-4.

There is no special design phase for error correction in transaction processing. Rather, the processing is repeated with corrected data to eliminate the errors.

At the operational level, where certain problems are encountered repeatedly, standard models to solve them probably already exist. Even if they do not, the recurring nature of the problem justifies the effort to develop an appropriate model. For example, every organization that carries inventory needs to know the quantity to order or produce to replenish inventory. Even if EOQ and

FIGURE 10-4. Model usage at different activity levels.

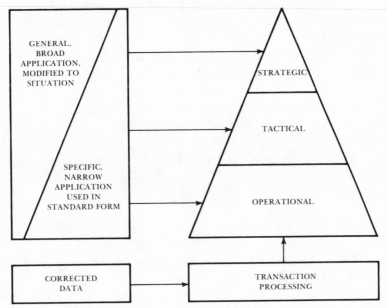

EPQ formulae were not found in every management science text, it still would be worth the effort to develop an inventory model to answer these questions.

The inventory model is very specific and can be applied only to certain inventory problems that meet the assumptions of the model. This is typical of models used at the operational level. Because they are used repeatedly, operational models are more likely to be *selected* from the model bank for use than to be *built* when a problem occurs.

Strategic models are more general in nature, but not necessarily as unique as the problems to which they are applied. There may never have been a merger of an airline and a steel company before, but an organization considering such a move may well base its long-range financial plans on a simulation of the cash flows in an airline-steel conglomerate. The tools to build the financial model—the random number generators, the simulation language, and the cash flow equations—already exist. It is just a matter of using them in a way that describes the merger.

Strategic models may also be more like the traditional evaluation of alternatives. In simulation, for example, the decision maker is not led directly to the best solution but must experiment with variables to determine their influence. In the merger problem, different combinations of debt and equity funding could be inserted into the model for evaluation until an acceptable combination is found.

The tactical activity level represents middle ground in model selection not only because some tactical decisions are based on specific models while others use general models, but also because many tactical decisions require a model that is partially general and partially specific. Linear programming, for example, is a generalized model with broad application in decision making but it also has fairly narrow, specialized applications. The assignment and transportation algorithms are examples of specific application of linear programming techniques.

CHOICE

To the layperson, the selection of an alternative or the approval of model results is the essence of the decision process. To the modern decision maker, however, it may be the most perfunctory of the decision phases. In transaction processing, for example, reprocessed data are simply re-edited and if they meet edit criteria are passed as correct; no choice is presented to a human decision maker.

At the operational level, the structure of the decision process frequently permits the use of optimization models which give the decision maker the best possible solution to the problem. The solution need only be checked for consistency with related operations and adopted. For example, if the EOQ formula, which has been used to illustrate structured, operational decision processes, yields an optimum order quantity of 123, the decision maker may modify that to 120 if the item comes in cases of 12 each. The convenience of working with full cases may offset the slight increase in total inventory costs.

At the strategic level, it is more likely that decision makers will *satisfice;* that is, they will pick the first workable alternative or the best of a limited number of alternatives. The complexity of strategic problems often makes it impossible to conduct an exhaustive evaluation of alternatives. In locating a new plant, for example, an organization cannot possibly consider every available site but selects the first one that meets all criteria or the best of perhaps eight or ten alternative sites.

FIGURE 10-5. Choice criteria at different activity levels.

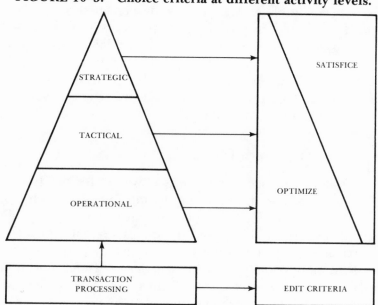

As suggested earlier, the MIS contribution to strategic decision processes may not cover choice at all. Data collected in the intellgence phase and analyzed by a model selected in the design phase may only provide part of the information required for the decision. Then, in keeping with the layperson's image, decision makers weigh that information along with other, nonquantitative data to make their choice.

Figure 10-5 shows how choice processes vary at different activity levels.

ACTIVITY LEVELS ILLUSTRATED

Activities in the four levels of MIS bring together a number of concepts that, up to this point, have been difficult to view as a holistic system. Decision processes, the data base, the model bank, reports, inquiries, data analyses, transactions, internal data, and external data have been discussed either individually or in relation to only one or two other systems components. We will now attempt to illustrate how these components work together as a system.

It is not necessary to analyze every facet of an MIS to demonstrate its systems character; in fact, it is better not to do so. An example of a complete MIS would soon become hopelessly bogged down in detail. Instead, the example used here shows how a single transaction in a hypothetical automobile insurance firm eventually plays a role in decisions and other processes throughout the activity dimension. A flow chart of those processes is shown in Figure 10-6 and is explained, by activity level, in the remaining sections of this chapter.

TRANSACTION PROCESSING

The MIS of the insurance firm is activated, for our purposes, when a policy holder files a claim arising out of an automobile accident ("START," at the left center of Figure 10-6). The claim is mailed to the firm and received by one of several claims clerks. The first action in processing this transaction is to inspect the claim document visually for errors in *form*—usually incomplete data. If errors are detected, the claim is returned to the policy holder with a form letter explaining what corrective action is required.

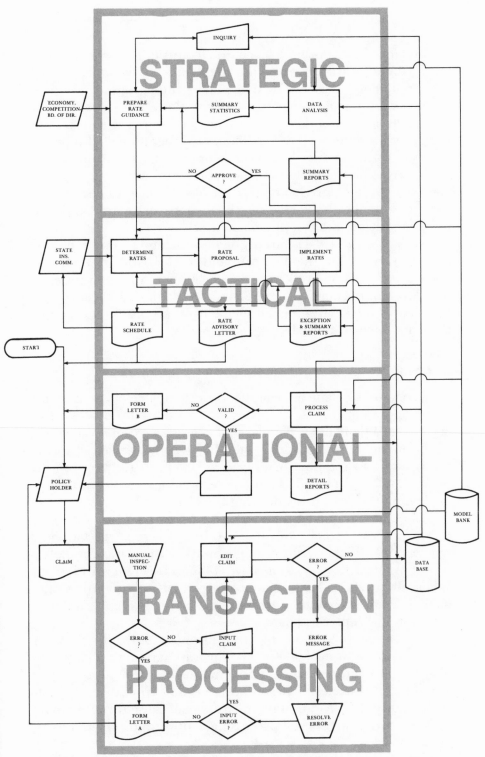

FIGURE 10-6. Activity levels in an automobile insurance company MIS.

If claim data appear to be complete and in proper form, the claim is temporarily entered into the data base via a terminal or other data entry device. The data entry routine calls an edit program out of the model bank to check the claim for errors of *fact*—whether or not data in the claim correspond to similar data in the policy holder's records. The edit program wlll also detect errors in form that may have been overlooked in the manual edit. Input errors on the part of the data entry clerk are easily resolved and the data re-entered, but more serious errors must be referred back to the policy holder. When the data are error-free, they are permanently admitted to the data base.

No *management* decisions are made during the processing of this transaction, but the data base and model bank are used and there is some manual processing in addition to computer processing. Most important, an interface—the claim—has been established with an environmental element—the policy holder—and the system has been fueled.

OPERATIONAL ACTIVITIES

Payment of a claim is a routine, programmable decision found at the operational level. In this example, claims are processed in batches on a daily basis. A claim processing program is called out of the model bank and an ad hoc file of unprocessed claims is prepared from the data base. Checks are prepared and sent to policy holders for valid claims; invalid claims result in a letter explaining the reason for denying the claim.

The decision criteria are fairly simple in this case, consisting only of a series of questions that can be answered "yes" or "no." For example, if the claim is based on a collision, was the policy holder at fault? If so, does she have collision coverage? And so on. When all questions have been answered satisfactorily, the settlement amount is computed by subtracting the deductible amount from the low repair estimate.

Apparently programmable decisions may sometimes turn out to be nonprogrammable. In this illustration, certain conditions may require human intervention in the decision process. For example, excessive estimates, repeated claims from the same policy holder, or other indications of fraud will cause the claim to be removed from the normal processing routine and referred to an investigator.

In addition to the check and form letter, the claim process produces other output. The data base is updated with records of payment, accident statistics are recorded, penalty points are assigned to the policy holder, and so forth. A number of reports will also reflect data from this claim. At the operational level, we would expect a detailed report showing the policy number, the type of claim, the disposition of the claim, the amount paid, and other information relating to each claim processed in this cycle.

TACTICAL ACTIVITIES

Except in cases of fraud or extraordinary losses, middle management does not become involved in the processing of individual claims. Consequently, tactical-level reports are of the exception or summary variety. Typical exceptions include referrals for cancellation action when a policy holder meets management-defined "bad risk" criteria, claims exceeding a specified dollar amount, or claims involving litigation. Summary reports might show total numbers of claims processed by category (collision, comprehensive, and personal liability) and the sum of payments disbursed. These data may be expressed "per thousand policy holders" to make them more comparable with historical data and industry averages.

The original claim, assuming it was an ordinary one that required no individual attention above the operational level, is now absorbed into summary statistics but it is not lost for management decision-making purposes. It contributes a proportional share of the information on which tactical and higher-level decisions are based. One such decision involves the determination of rates charged for various types of coverage.

Rate determination is one of those hybrid, programmable-nonprogrammable decisions peculiar to the tactical activity level. Rates to achieve certain profit objectives literally can be computed from actuarial data and the historical accident activity of the firm's own set of policy holders. But these rates are also influenced by regulations of the various state insurance commissions, which may or may not be incorporated into the basic rate model, and the professional judgment of the managers who prepare the rate proposals, which certainly cannot be programmed.

When the proposed rates are approved, a rate implementation program is called out of the model bank to update data base records with the new rates and to advise policy holders and the respective state commissions of the new rate schedule. Thus the claim that initiated this process plays an eventual role in other functional activities, such as the billing of policy holders according to the new rate schedule.

STRATEGIC ACTIVITIES

It would be extremely unusual for top management to become involved with the processing of a single claim. Strategic decisions in an insurance firm more likely deal with investment policies, affiliations with firms of adjustors, or the extension of coverage to other losses, say, personal property. Yet claim data are available to the strategic level for any or all of these decisions. The claim on which this example is based has already been incorporated into summary reports to strategic management and can be included in data analyses or inquiries as well. Data analysis goes beyond the capability of query language computations and uses either a pre-programmed model or one that is written at the terminal by the using manager. Inquiries are satisfied directly by the data base management system.

One strategic activity in which claim data play an input role is the preparation of rate guidance. The formulation of such guidance is not programmable and we do not expect any first-hand involvement with the model bank. However, a manager at this level may well be concerned about trends in the number of claims, the amounts paid out to claimants, and the extent of injuries in accidents. If there is no scheduled or unscheduled report on these subjects, the interested manager can either ask for a special report or, if possessed of the requisite skills, perform his or her own trend analysis interactively. (See Chapter 5 for a discussion of reports, inquiries, and data analysis.)

Although the preparation of rate guidance involves some highly distilled internal data, it is based more on external data. Top management depends on the environment for most of its data inputs. In this decision, strategic managers will be influenced by economic factors, the rates of competitors, and guidance from their superiors—the board of directors of the firm. Much of this external data cannot be quantified for analytical purposes—the board of directors' instructions to "project an image of personal concern," for example. Other external data, such as rates of inflation and economic growth, may fit perfectly into multiple regression models that predict claims losses. This blending of internal and external data and the mixture of programmable and non-programmable processes makes use of the MIS particularly difficult at the strategic level.

THE EXAMPLE IN PERSPECTIVE

The activity dimension of an MIS is characterized by vertical flows—progressively more refined data and information flow upward through the activity levels and directives and guidance flow downward. These flows have been illustrated in one narrow application in an insurance company, a thin slice, as it were, of the functional dimension. This example illustrates a *production* function in a service industry. Production in manufacturing would, of course, be different, but we would expect the same general processes at each activity level and the same relationships between activity levels. There are other functions as well and they are similarly related to each other and to other industries. We shall explore those relationships in the following chapter.

CHAPTER 11

Functional Subsystems
of MIS

A systems view of an organization permits several options for defining subsystems. One could, for example, construct a perfectly logical model using subsystems based on the flow of resources—labor, money, and material. Levels of management or different approaches to decision making, which were discussed in the previous chapter, are also legitimate bases for describing subsystems. Typical organizational structure and the evolution of MIS, however, argue for another approach: subsystems organized along *functional* lines.

In most organizations, departments are formed by grouping similar functions. An accounting department is made up of those individuals responsible for accounting functions, a marketing department consists of persons who carry out marketing activities, and so on. Not all organizations will have the same functions, of course, but the principle of functional organization will apply nonetheless. As pointed out in Chapter 7, an MIS designed along traditional functional lines may be less threatening to managers who are understandably parochial in their attitude toward information systems. It is much easier to win a manager's support for, say, a production subsystem than for a "middle management subsystem" or a "material resource subsystem."

The division of an MIS into functional subsystems also reflects the evolutionary pattern of information systems. In manual systems, information was exchanged informally—by observation or word-of-mouth—and formally—by written reports or in staff meetings. In the extreme, a sole proprietor with a manual information system had only to *think* about the various functions he or she performed in order to make information from one available to the others. The flow of information between functional areas of a business is illustrated in Figure 11–1.

Ironically, the advent of data processing actually degraded the quality of information exchange in some organizations by interrupting the informal communications channels and inundating management with detail reports. Single-function data processing applications tended to be too narrow and too specific for managers in other functional areas and there was no direct way to exchange information among applications.

The modern MIS comes close to duplicating the sole proprietor's ability to make information from one function immediately available to other functions. The computer at the heart of an MIS does not nearly match the reasoning and associative powers of the human brain (although it is frequently characterized as an "electronic brain" in the popular press), but it does—with the assistance of the data base management system—provide for better information exchange than any manual or data processing system.

Larger organizations also have more complex departmental structure. In a large organization, the production function may be further broken down into engineering, quality control, purchasing, operations, and so on. There is a need to exchange informa-

FIGURE 11–1.　Information exchange among functional subsystems.

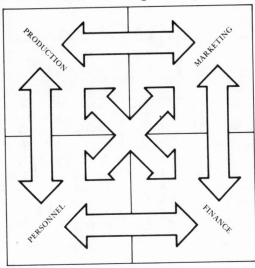

tion among these subunits as well as among departments. The MIS reflects this structure by incorporating specialized *modules* into the functional subsystems.[1] The inter- and intradepartmental information flows in such an MIS are illustrated in Figure 11-2. The departmental modules shown in this figure are merely examples and do not represent a universal MIS design any more than the four functional departments used in this model universally depict organizational structure.

Figure 11-2 shows only the sources and destinations of information in a functional organization; it does not show intermediate storage in the data base or the processes that refine information for specific applications. The succeeding sections of this chapter provide these and other details on functional subsystems of an MIS.

FIGURE 11-2.   Application modules in functional subsystems.

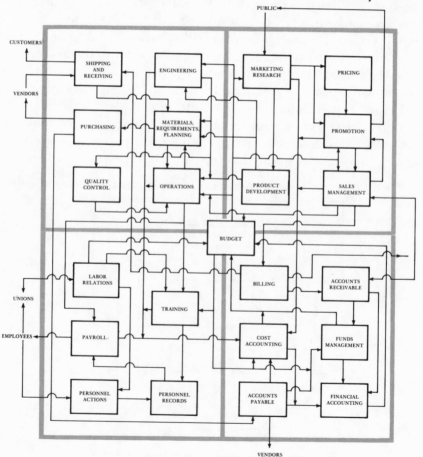

THE PRODUCTION SUBSYSTEM

Production involves the conversion of resource inputs to goods and service outputs. Automobile manufacturers convert labor, capital, and raw material into finished automobiles. Law firms "produce" legal services with the time and professional expertise of their partners. And military units provide national security using labor and capital. While these examples show that a production function can be identified in practically every organization, it is more common to think of production in terms of the

FIGURE 11-3. The production subsystem.

[1]From finance subsystem
[2]From marketing subsystem

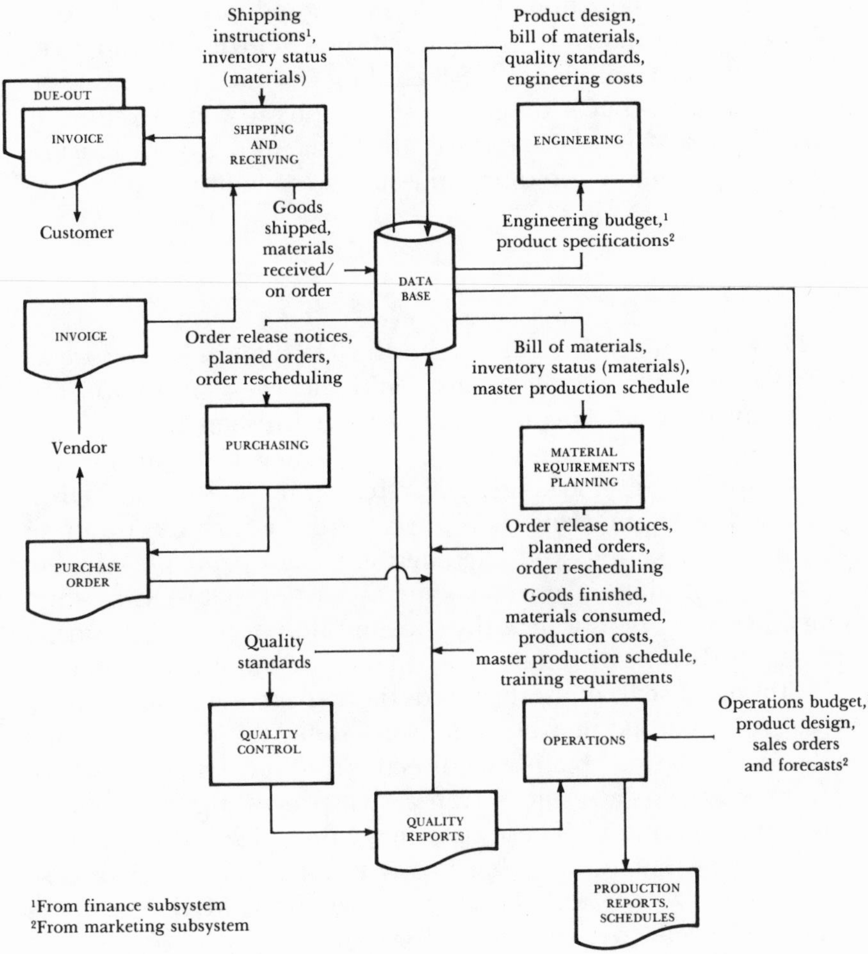

manufacture of goods. Since a service (automobile insurance) was illustrated in the previous chapter and since manufacturing involves a number of functions not found in the production of services (inventory management, for one example), we will assume that the production process reflected in this subsystem yields goods rather than services. A model of a goods-production subsystem is shown in Figure 11–3.

MATERIAL REQUIREMENTS PLANNING

Material requirements planning (MRP) combines two of the most important activities in a manufacturing operation: inventory management and scheduling. The purpose of inventory management is to ensure that raw materials are on hand when they are required for production, that finished goods are on hand to satisfy customer demand, and that the costs of ordering and carrying inventory are minimized. Scheduling complements inventory management in that it determines additions to the inventory of finished goods, but it also ensures the efficient use of production facilities, minimizes idle time, and allows for equipment maintenance.

MRP INPUTS

There are three basic inputs to the MRP module: the *master production schedule, inventory status,* and the *bill of materials.* The master production schedule defines what finished products are needed and when they are needed; it is based upon orders and forecasts from the marketing subsystem. The bill of materials is developed in engineering based upon the product specifications (also from marketing) and engineering design principles. Inventory status (of materials) reflects the receipt of materials by shipping and receiving as well as the consumption of materials during operations. Inventory data are also maintained on finished goods.

Although each input has a definite source in some other production module or functional subsystem, the programs used in the MRP module obtain data directly from the data base, where they are stored as a result of transaction processing or as output from other modules.[2] These data may be used in other applications or appear in various hard-copy reports, but the data base management system makes them available to the MRP module as if they were collected exclusively for that purpose.

MRP Outputs

For this simplified model, there are three primary outputs of the MRP module: *order release notices, planned orders,* and changes as a result of *order rescheduling.* Order release notices are instructions to the purchasing department to order raw materials. Planned orders serve as early warnings to alert purchasing of impending material requirements; any changes to open orders by expediting or de-expediting are made by rescheduling orders.

MRP Processing

For the sake of clarity, the model bank is not shown in Figure 11–3 (or in other figures describing functional subsystems), but it is assumed that each module draws on the model bank for the necessary application programs. In the case of the MRP module, inventory data, such as quantities on hand, quantities on order, and lead time, are combined with scheduled requirements to calculate amounts of materials to be ordered and the timing of those orders. Standard inventory models (see Chapter 4) may be used for lot sizing after all time-phased calculations are made.

OPERATIONS

Operations involves the actual conversion of resources into goods or services. Although operations is "where the action is" in production, it is actually one of the simpler modules in the production subsystem of an MIS. Of course, many manufacturing processes are fully or partially automated and use numeric control or sophisticated devices such as computer-controlled robots. The computer operations in these systems are certainly not simple, but they also are not greatly involved in the production of management information. For this reason, we will not consider further the role of computers in automation.

Operations Inputs

The operations module in this model receives orders and demand forecasts from the marketing subsystem, budgetary data from finance, and product design information from engineering. The operations module also receives a very important feedback input (from the quality control module) in the form of quality reports. Although these reports are shown as documents in Figure 11–3, quality feedback is also furnished in a more immediate form via terminals or verbal reports. Obviously, a manufacturing process cannot be permitted to operate out of control during the time it takes to prepare and deliver a printed report, but must be corrected as soon as possible after deviations from quality standards are detected. The exact method of alerting operations personnel to quality discrepancies varies with different manufacturing processes and products.

OPERATIONS OUTPUTS

Perhaps the most important informational output of the operations module is the master production schedule, described above as an MRP input. Other output from the operations module includes reports on the number of finished goods and the consumption of resources during the production of those goods. This output is *actual* data, to be compared with *standard* or *projected* data for management control. While all of these outputs are stored in the data base for use by other modules and subsystems, many are also incorporated into printed reports for appropriate managers.

OPERATIONS PROCESSING

Programs to generate production reports and to maintain production records are relatively simple. The only unusual feature of operations processing is the variety of input media that may be encountered. Machine time may be input directly from sensors attached to operating equipment, material usage may be obtained by scanning tags affixed to the material, and labor time may be keyed in by workers using special-purpose terminals at the work site. The conversion of the various units by which resource consumption is measured to dollars is accomplished by applying certain standard cost factors.

ENGINEERING

The engineering section, whether included in the production department as it is in this model or organized into a separate department as it is in many large manufacturing organizations, is chiefly responsible for the design of the product and the production facilities. Engineering works closely with marketing in product design and with other modules of production (notably MRP and operations) in facilities design.

ENGINEERING INPUTS

Engineering, to include the research and development function, can be a very expensive activity if not closely controlled. The budget is a particularly important input to engineering for this reason. Although the only other input shown is the product specifications (from the marketing subsystem), engineering will receive many environmental inputs in the form of new developments in materials, manufacturing processes, health and safety standards, and other research findings.

ENGINEERING OUTPUTS

While much of the information processing in engineering is strictly for internal, engineering uses, there are several outputs of great importance to the rest of the organization. Again, cost data is reported to facilitate the management control function. Product-related output includes the design to be followed by operations in production, the bill of materials needed by MRP, and the quality standards to be used in quality control.

ENGINEERING PROCESSING

It is very likely that engineering, particularly if it is organized into a separate department, will have independent computer facilities as well as being a module in the MIS. At the minimum, we would expect engineering personnel to have access to desk-top or microcomputers for immediate and specialized engineering computations. When product design involves complicated graphic displays and other unique processes, a separate hardware configuration may be necessary. Through data communications, engineering can still use the MIS data base and model bank for routine applications, such as costing, but may have its own data base and model bank for pure engineering applications.

SHIPPING AND RECEIVING

The shipping and receiving module is concerned primarily with transaction processing, but it is interesting nonetheless for its interface with two enormously important environmental elements: customers and vendors.

SHIPPING AND RECEIVING INPUTS

In this simplified model, we will consider only two *informational* inputs to shipping and receiving: shipping instructions (from the finance subsystem) and invoices (from vendors). Of course, there is an important *physical* input as well—raw material received from the vendors.

SHIPPING AND RECEIVING OUTPUTS

Information on the receipt of raw materials and the shipping of finished goods is sent, through the data base, to MRP for inventory management. Customers are furnished invoices to reflect the shipment of goods or due-out notices to inform them of shipping delays.

SHIPPING AND RECEIVING PROCESSING

Processing in shipping and receiving, as might be expected of a transaction-processing activity, consists largely of maintaining records. In particular, records of unfilled orders, for which due-out notices were sent, must be maintained to ensure shipment when inventory is replenished. These are routine data processing applications which, as described in Chapter 3, could be run with various combinations of a storage medium and a processing mode but, because of other MIS implications, are probably transactional in this system.

PURCHASING

The purchasing function is an extension of MRP and could easily be included in that module if there were not traditional organizational pressures to retain a separate purchasing section. Indeed, all the inputs to purchasing shown here are MRP outputs: order release notices, planned orders, and rescheduled orders, which are processed into purchase orders issued to suppliers of raw materials.

The environmental interface with suppliers (vendors) is

another reason to maintain a separate purchasing module. MRP is a strictly internal module, but purchasing requires a great deal of external data on type, quality, price, delivery schedules, and availability of raw materials obtained from vendor organizations. As noted previously, purchasing is a particularly good data base application and there may be a separate data base for purchasing in the MIS.

QUALITY CONTROL

Just as purchasing is closely related to MRP, quality control is closely linked with engineering and, in some organizations, is part of the engineering department. It is separate here again to reflect typical organizational structure which seeks to avoid any conflict between the establishment of quality standards (by engineering), the responsibility for quality (operations), and the measurement of quality (by quality control).

The quality control module uses a number of statistical models to determine sampling plans and to establish control limits for the tested attributes of the various products. Depending upon the product and the attribute to be tested, measurements may be made automatically, by computer-controlled equipment, or taken manually. Since testing may be destructive (as in determining the strength of a wire by stretching it until it breaks), statistical inference is especially important to quality control.

THE MARKETING SUBSYSTEM

Since the early 1950s, the marketing function has grown in importance to the point that many companies now speak of the "marketing orientation," the "total marketing concept," or "integrated marketing" as the principal organizational philosophy. In some prominent firms (General Electric, for example), the marketing function even includes inventory management, production scheduling, and the physical distribution of finished goods. Not surprisingly, there are also many MIS in which the "M" stands for *marketing,* rather than *management.*

In an integrated MIS, such as the one described here, who has responsibility for inventory management or production scheduling is less important than how the information needs of those functions are satisfied. So, although the importance of marketing in an increasingly competitive business environment is duly acknowledged, we will follow the more traditional separation of functions with the understanding that the lines separating the functional subsystems in Figure 11-2 are somewhat arbitrary and the reader can move them to describe better his or her own MIS. The more detailed model of this "traditional" marketing subsystem is shown in Figure 11-4.

FIGURE 11-4.   The marketing subsystem.

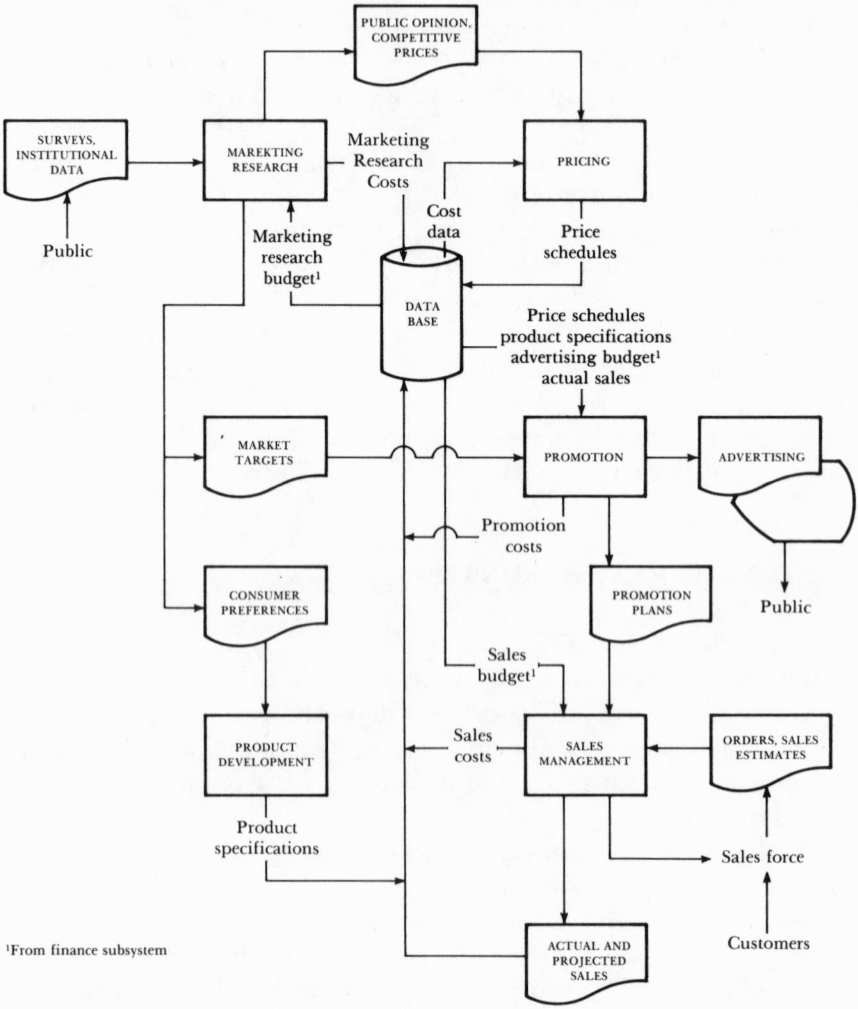

¹From finance subsystem

MARKETING RESEARCH

An important part of the total marketing concept is that marketing activities take place at the *beginning* as well as at the end of the production cycle. In other words, marketing does not merely sell what production produces, it also helps determine what those products are. Marketing research is the first of two marketing modules involved in that determination.

It is not possible to describe here the full range of marketing research activities, but the basic goal is to ascertain what the public wants and how much they are willing to pay for it. If the marketing subsystem provided no other information (and it certainly does provide a great deal more), it would still be a vital component of an MIS.

MARKETING RESEARCH INPUTS

Marketing research depends almost exclusively on external data. Some secondary data, in the form of published institutional or government research on consumer preferences, are available, but most marketing research data are primary; that is, they are collected by the using organization to meet specific information needs. Telephone or mail surveys, interviews, experiments, and direct observation are all means of obtaining data on consumer preferences and buying habits. Like engineering, marketing research is open-ended and not limited by other organizational activities in the way that, for example, shipping and receiving is. This makes the marketing research budget a particularly important input.

MARKETING REARCH OUTPUTS

Since the budgeting of marketing research is so important, we expect a strict accounting of costs to facilitate management control. Most other marketing research output is in the form of written reports on consumer preferences in applicable products, market targets for promotional campaigns, and the value the public places on various products and services. In an automobile manufacturing firm, for example, marketing research may determine that small, fuel-efficient cars are desired; that "two-car" families represent the largest potential market; and that, for an extra $500, the average buyer would rather have velour upholstery and a stereo radio than airbags and crash-resistant bumpers.

MARKETING RESEARCH PROCESSING

The processing of marketing research data relies heavily on statistical models. Much of the analysis is descriptive—tabulating findings, classifying data, constructing frequency distributions, preparing graphical displays, computing measures of central tendency and deviation, and so forth. But much of the analysis will also be inferential—estimating population means from sample data, testing hypotheses about product success, projecting sales from past performance (trend analysis), or projecting sales from other, related variables (regression analysis). Marketing research is one of the heaviest users of the statistical and other quantitative decision-making tools discussed in Chapter 4.

PRODUCT DEVELOPMENT

Product development is the second marketing module involved in the "front-end" of production. The product development section is a link between marketing research and engineering. Its primary function is to translate consumer preferences (from the marketing research module) into *general* product specifications which are refined into *detailed* product design and material specifications by engineering.

The product specifications output of the product development module also contains information on warranties, operating characteristics, and other consumer-oriented information of interest to managers involved in promotion and sales.

PRICING

The role of the pricing module is to fix an appropriate price for each product made by the firm. In microeconomic theory, prices are determined in the marketplace and cannot be controlled by the seller alone. In practice, however, the underlying microeconomic assumptions are not met and the seller has considerable say in setting prices. Advertising, in particular, permits variances from the market price by modifying consumer preference for a particular brand.

Prices are based upon marketing research output on public opinion, the prices of competitors, and the costs of production (from the production subsystem). The determination of prices can be as simple as a percentage mark-up on costs or it may be based on a mathematical model that shows the optimum price under given demand schedules. Whatever the process, the output becomes an important input to the promotion module and the finance subsystem.

PROMOTION

The promotion of a firm's product, one of the most important functions of marketing and of the entire firm, is a creative activity carried on largely outside the MIS. Nevertheless, there are certain inputs and outputs of the promotion module integral to the MIS. Promotion is another open-ended activity in which there are no inherent spending limits and which must be closely monitored to ensure that the firm does not become "promotion poor" any more than it can risk becoming "engineering poor" or "marketing research poor." The control, of course, is a promotion or advertising budget that establishes the standard data against which actual cost data, a promotion module output, are compared.

Other inputs to the promotion module include price schedules (from the pricing module), product specifications (from the product development module), and feedback on actual sales performance (from the sales management module).

While advertisements are not literally developed by programs from the MIS model bank, the management of advertising activities is supported by the MIS. Linear programming models can be used to develop a "media mix" (analogous to the product mix problem used to illustrate LP in Chapter 4) that shows how to allocate limited advertising dollars among the various media in order to maximize returns.

SALES MANAGEMENT

The entire marketing effort ultimately culminates in sales, and the success or failure of marketing is often (unjustly, perhaps) attributed to sales personnel. In a typical manufacturing firm, where products are not sold directly to consumers, sales personnel deal with the purchasing agents of other organizations and must rely more on technical and professional knowledge of their products than on the stereotyped "sales pitch" usually associated with the sale of used cars and patent medicine. This kind of sales effort is much more compatible with an MIS sales management module.

SALES MANAGEMENT INPUTS

Sales management is less open-ended than some other modules, but is still subject to budget control and receives, from the finance subsystem, a sales budget input. In this case, the budget is more than a cost control measure—it also contains confirmed (by top management) sales objectives. Other inputs include plans for the promotion of each product (from the promotion module) and sales estimates and orders (from the sales force).

SALES MANAGEMENT OUTPUT

As usual, budget constraints on the input side must be complemented by appropriate outputs. In this case, the actual cost and volume of sales complete the information needed for management control and projected sales form one basis for sales objectives in the next budget cycle.

Another important output of sales management are quotas, derived from overall sales objectives and other factors, assigned to sales regions or districts. This process is repeated at successively lower levels until even individual salespersons may be assigned quotas.

SALES MANAGEMENT PROCESSING

The techniques of assigning quotas and projecting sales range from the purely intuitive to the highly mathematical. While there is much to be said for intuition, experience, and other intangibles, they are not to be found in the MIS data base or model bank. Instead, the MIS can assist in projections of this type through multiple regression analysis, simulation, or other management science tools of forecasting. Economic conditions, historical sales data, performance evaluations of sales persons, and subjective estimates of sales can all be incorporated into predictive models.

There is still room to modify the resultant predictions by intuition if that is desired.

THE FINANCE SUBSYSTEM

The finance subsystem, as it is defined here, includes the function of accounting—the historical home of data processing. It is not surprising, therefore, to find extensive MIS application in the finance subsystem. As might be expected in view of the data processing history, many of these applications are at the transaction-processing level and are of interest to few outside the lower levels of finance and accounting management. We will touch on some of the functions found at the transaction-processing level in finance, but will be more concerned with higher, managerial activities. The management information flows in the finance subsystem are shown in Figure 11-5.

BUDGET

Responsibility for the preparation and maintenance of the budget typically rests with finance, but, as shown by the positioning of the budget module in Figure 11-2, *all* functional departments have budget responsibilities. The budget is the major control over financial resources and, since other resources can be expressed in monetary terms, the budget is a control measure over those resources as well.

The budget is also a planning tool—a means of implementing plans by allocating resources to various activities in the organization for specific purposes. A plan to introduce a new product, for example, is implemented by a budget (and other directives) authorizing funds for research and development, the acquisition of new equipment and material, the hiring of production personnel, promotional campaigns, and so forth.

BUDGET INPUTS

Budgeting is a cyclical process that starts with budget guidance from top management and projected costs and income from various profit centers. Budget makers also have access, through the data base, to historical cost and income data with which they can check or refine the projections of other functional departments. These inputs are repeated during budget preparation and, as actual data, which may cause budget modification, are collected.

BUDGET OUTPUTS

The budget itself—the document that authorizes organizational elements to expend funds—is the principal output of the budget module. In addition to the hard-copy budget, authorization data are maintained in the data base to facilitate control in other functional departments and to alert the funds management module to requirements for funds.

BUDGET PROCESSING

The development of a budget involves some unstructured decision making—particularly on the part of top management in preparing budget guidance. But, with the exception of the refinement of sales and income projections, which requires the same kind of analytical tools originally used to prepare those projections, the processing of budget data is largely a recordkeeping and report generation activity. In large organizations, however, the sheer volume of data associated with the budget can make even these routine functions a challenging MIS application.

COST ACCOUNTING

In financial control, the budget provides *projected* data while *actual* data are furnished by the cost accounting module. As noted earlier, not all resource expenditures are measured in monetary terms, and some control—over labor, machine time, and raw materials, for example—is exercised outside of the finance subsystem. These expenditures are also converted to dollar amounts and serve as input data to the cost accounting module.

Cost data are maintained in the data base for use in the preparation of future budgets, and discrepancies between actual costs (from other subsystems and modules) and projected costs (from the budget module) are noted in exception reports to appropriate managers.

FUNDS MANAGEMENT

Another finance module with close ties to budgeting is funds management. The purpose of funds management is to ensure that funds are available to meet the financial obligations of the organization while at the same time maximizing the return on idle funds available for investment.

FUNDS MANAGEMENT INPUTS

Funds management, also referred to as capital budgeting, is a high-level activity in an organization and not unexpectedly relies heavily on data from external, as well as internal, sources. External data comes primarily from the financial community— investment opportunities, interest rates, loan opportunities, and so on. Internal data concerns both actual and projected cost and income data. In addition to the cost data already discussed, funds management considers additional costs of interest and dividends paid on bonds and stocks.

FUNDS MANAGEMENT OUTPUTS

The basic output document of the funds management module is the cash-flow budget which shows the amount of cash available for investment or necessary to borrow for each period. An example of an abbreviated cash-flow budget is shown in Table 11–1. Although the cash-flow budget is shown as a document, certain cash-flow data, such as projected income from investments, are made available to the budget module through the data base.

FUNDS MANAGEMENT PROCESSING

There are a number of management science tools useful in the management of funds. Linear programming can be used to develop an optimum mix of long- and short-term investments to meet constraints on acceptable risk and cash availability. Recently, success has been achieved in the simulation of long-range financial planning. And, of course, the computation of present values, internal rates of return, amortization schedules, and compound interest are now commonly available on hand-held calculators as well as in the MIS model bank.

TABLE 11–1.   A Cash-Flow Budget (000's)

	Jan	Feb	Mar	Apr	...	Dec
Balance	—	2	—	4	...	6
Income:						
Accounts Receivable	52	49	65	56	...	50
Interest	8	8	7	7	...	10
Misc	6	5	7	10	...	9
Total	66	64	79	77	...	75
Expenses:						
Wages & Salaries	28	28	29	29	...	30
Accounts Payable	19	16	18	20	...	17
Interest	10	10	8	8	...	6
Dividends	—	—	15	—	...	15
Loan Payment	—	14	—	—	...	—
Misc	7	3	5	6	...	8
Total	64	71	75	63	...	76
Balance	2	(7)	4	14		(1)
Available to invest	2		4	14		
Need to borrow		7				1

FINANCIAL ACCOUNTING

The classification, recording, and summarization of monetary transactions is referred to as *financial*—as opposed to *managerial*—accounting. While there is some management information generated in financial accounting, the primary purpose is to paint a financial picture of the organization for investors, creditors, and to satisfy legal requirements. This is in marked contrast to a purely managerial accounting activity such as cost accounting, although both financial and cost accounting may share certain input data.

Monetary transactions—receipts and expenditures of funds—are made available to the financial accounting module through the data base and maintained in *journals*. Periodically, journal data are used to update basic financial statements such as the *balance sheet* and the *income statement*.

Although the accounting department is a traditional computer user, accounting applications have been somewhat handicapped by longstanding "generally accepted accounting principles" (GAAP), some of which can be traced back to the fifteenth century! One particular problem facing automated accounting is the need for an *audit trail* to back up accounting entries. Random access files are particularly difficult to audit and in many cases processing and storage efficiencies must be sacrificed for compliance with GAAP.

BILLING

The billing module receives sales data (orders) from the marketing subsystem and sets in motion the process of filling those orders and obtaining payment for them. The processing of an order by billing results in a statement to the customer, shipping instructions to the production subsystem, and receivable data to the accounts receivable module.

The billing module also performs a credit check based on limits imposed when an account is established and modified by account status feedback from the accounts receivable module. Although billing is a very routine data processing application, there have been some innovative techniques applied to the credit decision in which human judgment is heuristically mimicked by computer.

ACCOUNTS RECEIVABLE

Accounts receivable is a logical extension of billing (indeed, the two are frequently combined in small firms) in which actual payments are processed. The accounts receivable module is furnished receivable data by the billing module and receives payment from customers. Outputs from accounts receivable include sales income data for budgeting and financial accounting as well as account status for billing.

ACCOUNTS PAYABLE

The accounts payable module is the "cost counterpart" of the accounts receivable module. The purpose of accounts payable is to pay vendors for materials ordered by the production subsystem and to settle other payable accounts—except payroll—in the organization. (For simplicity, only payments for materials are shown in Figure 11–5.)

Payments are made on the basis of invoice data entered into the data base by the shipping and receiving module of the production subsystem or on receipt of the material (also entered by ship-

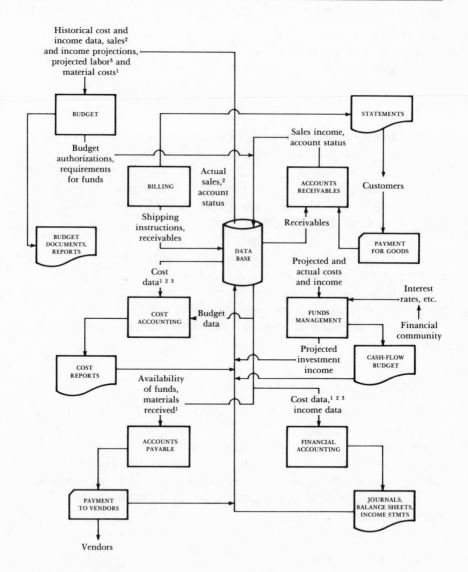

[1]From production subsystem
[2]From marketing subsystem
[3]From personnel subsystem

FIGURE 11-5.   The finance subsystem.

ping and receiving), depending on payment terms. The timing of payments is also influenced by discounts and the availability of funds. Discounts, such as "2-10, net 30" (which means, "2 percent discount if paid within ten days or the full amount if paid between 11 and 30 days"), are usually taken if funds for the budget period have not been expended or can be made available from other sources.[3]

Accounts payable is also a good example of how legal requirements and generally accepted accounting practices complicate an MIS. Although payment data can be stored almost indefinitely in electronic media in relatively little physical space, state statutes of limitations require the maintenance of cancelled checks for an average of six years. This is but one example of legal requirements for retaining records that influence many modules within an MIS.

THE PERSONNEL SUBSYSTEM

The management of personnel information is a subject that has received little attention in systems literature. One reason is that personnel applications tend to be routine recordkeeping activities and make little use of the more interesting management science models applied to the production, marketing, and finance functions. Another reason is that, unless the number of employees is very large, personnel records may be just as easy to maintain manually—easier, perhaps, now with freedom of information and privacy laws. Not only do large organizations achieve certain economies of scale in maintaining computerized personnel records, they are also more likely to find appropriately skilled employees from within their own ranks when job openings occur. The capability to search a personnel data base for, say, an electrical engineer with a graduate degree, top secret military clearance, and fluency in Spanish is not particularly helpful if you have only 25 employees.

LABOR RELATIONS

The labor relations module provides the interface with unions and other worker organizations (see Fig. 11-6). From the union contract, the labor relations module makes available to the rest of the organization specific contractual requirements, such as wage rates, fringe benefits, work conditions, provisions for training, and so on.

Wages, particularly as they may escalate during the contract term, are of great importance to the finance modules of budget and funds management. Work conditions—safety requirements, rest periods, and so forth—are inputs to the operations module of production. And training commitments are also an important

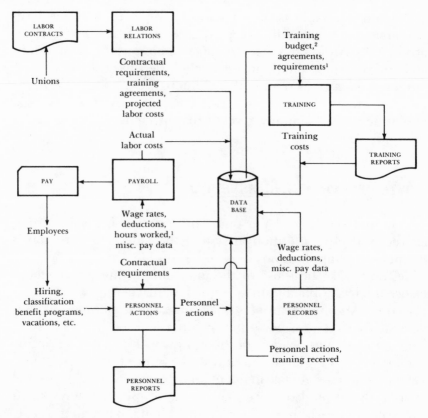

¹From production subsystem
²From financial subsystem

FIGURE 11-6.   The personnel subsystem.

budget input as well as a determinant, along with operations training requirements, of activities in the training module.

PERSONNEL ACTIONS

Labor contracts also provide the basis for many personnel actions such as hiring, classifying, promoting, accruing vacation and
sick-leave time, participating in group medical and life insurance
programs, and so on. Where contractual obligations do not dictate
the administration of these actions, organizational policies must
be established to provide for them.

Personnel actions are summarized for personnel reports but
are made available in detail to the personnel records module.
Reports contain information such as the total number of partici-
pants in a medical insurance program, while personnel records is
concerned whether or not John Doe participates.

PERSONNEL RECORDS

The maintenance of personnel records, still a manilla-folder operation in many organizations, is an excellent data base application. A single data base on personnel data can replace as many as eight or ten application files, all of which duplicate at least some data found in the others. Pay, job skill, training, retirement, medical, and other data can all be collected into single data sets keyed to the employee's name or social security number and assembled into temporary records as required for any application.

TRAINING

In-house training in modern organizations can range from none at all to the operation of college-like facilities. And much sponsored training is conducted by outside agencies on a contract basis or simply by reimbursing the employee for educational expenses.

Training is another "open-ended" activity that must be restricted by budget authorizations. The budget, contractual obligations to train employees, and requirements submitted by other functional departments (mainly production) provide the basis for a training program.

For MIS purposes, we are not greatly concerned about the conduct of training but, rather, about the generation of training information. Like other budgeted activities, the training module maintains and reports costs. And like the personnel actions module, information on individuals—the nature of the training and the level of proficiency achieved—are reported to the personnel records module while collective information is summarized into reports.

PAYROLL

Finally, after exploring the foundations, management, and structure of the modern MIS, we come back to one of, if not *the*, first business data processing application: the payroll. The nature of payroll operations, which may be included in the finance subsystem in many MIS, is well known. Inputs of wage rates, hours of labor, deductions, withholdings, and other data—which are assembled from the data base specifically for payroll processing in this model—are converted into paychecks, earning statements, and summary data for financial accounting records. Actual labor costs are also an input for managerial accounting purposes and for comparison to projected labor costs.

CONCLUSION

This functional model of an MIS is necessarily sketchy. There is no intent to describe every input, output, and process in each special module, many of which—cost accounting, for example—are the subject of entire books but are covered here in a page or two. Instead, the functional model gives the reader an opportunity to place the many diverse topics of this interdisciplinary subject of MIS into context. Which functions use management science models and which are still steeped in data processing methods? How does the MIS fit into contemporary organizational structure? How does the data base concept facilitate the exchange of information among functional subsystems? And, above all, how can the ideas suggested here improve *your* MIS?

NOTES

1. As noted in Chapter 1, systems hierarchy proceeds from the suprasystem to the system to subsystems to subsubsystems, ad infinitum. To avoid this sometimes confusing terminology, the level below the subsystem is called a *module* in this chapter.
2. It is common to refer to "the data base" and to show a single random-access storage device (here and in Chapters 8 and 9) as if all data were stored in a single disk pack. In reality, there may be several data bases in an MIS. In a large organization, one data base may be dedicated to production or even to just MRP. As long as all storage devices are on-line, application programs have the capability of drawing on any one or any combination of data bases. To application programs, the several data bases do in fact appear as one.
3. To not pay until the end of 30 days is, in effect, borrowing the amount of payment at a rate of 2 percent per 20 days or 36 percent, uncompounded (about 43 percent, compounded), per annum!

APPENDIX A

Flowchart Symbols

USAGE

To show *information* or *data flows*. By convention, arrowheads are not needed to show left-to-right or top-to-bottom flows.

To show a *process*. Brief comments inside the box, such as "COMPUTE PAY," further identify the process.

A general symbol for *input/output*. Specific input/output media may be identified with other symbols.

Punched cards. (Also an example of a more specific input or output medium.)

Paper tape.

247

A *cathode ray tube* (CRT); usually as an output medium.

A *document* or the output of a printer.

To show an *on-line* storage device.

To show an *off-line* storage facility, such as a tape library.

To show *manual input*, usually by a keyboard device such as a terminal.

Other *manual operations*, such as the mailing of a bill or the filing of a document.

To show *data preparation*, such as key punching or coding a mark-sense form.

To show a *decision* or *branching operation*. Most commonly, the comment in the symbol will pose a question answerable by "YES" or "NO" to show the branch to be taken.

A *direct access storage device* (DASD) such as a disk pack; a disk or drum file; the data base.

Magnetic tape.

A *data communications link.*

A *terminal*, in the sense of the beginning or end of a program sequence. The comment "START" or "STOP" may be used in the symbol for further clarification.

APPENDIX B

Glossary of Terms

Analog model A physical model that *acts*, but does not necessarily *look*, like the real-world object it represents.

Application-oriented file A file, either transaction or master, that is organized for processing with a specific application program.

Application programmer One who writes application programs, usually in one of the high-level languages such as COBOL or FORTRAN.

Arc A line connecting two nodes in decision trees, network diagrams, or data structures. In network diagrams: an activity.

Assembler language An application programming language in which storage locations and operating instructions are coded with brief combinations of letters and/or numbers and then converted to machine language by systems software called an "assembler."

Batch processing The periodic updating of a master file or data base with data from all transactions that have occurred since the previous update.

Binary operator A mathematical expression that separates data into two categories, such as "that which is equal to some value and that which is not," or "that which is greater than some value and that which is not," and so on.

Binary search A bracketing method of locating a given record in a sequential file packed into a direct access storage device.

Bit   A *bi*nary digi*t;* the presence or absence of an electronic pulse in a designated location within a computer.

Boolean operator   A mathematical expression that classifies data by two or more properties, such as "(both) this property AND that property," "(either) this property OR that property," and so on.

Byte   A group of eight bits, plus a parity bit, usually used to define a single character in a programming language.

Central processing unit (CPU)   The hardware component of a computer, consisting of the controller, the arithmetic and logic unit, and internal storage, that executes programs and manipulates data.

Certainty   A decision-making environment in which the outcomes of future events are known.

Check digit   An extra digit, derived from the existing digits in a numerical data element, that serves as a check on loss or change or numerical data during transmission.

Choice   In the decision-making process: the selection of the best alternative solution to a problem.

COBOL   The *Co*mmon *B*usiness *O*riented *L*anguage, developed by CODASYL between 1959 and 1960. COBOL is particularly well suited to file creation and maintenance.

Compiler language   An application programming language in which instructions are written in near-conversational syntax and then converted to machine language by systems software called a "compiler."

Component   The term, in the System 2000 data base management system, that collectively describes the two basic entries: elements and repeating groups.

Computer   An electronic device that can manipulate data according to programmed instructions and make the results available to a user.

Conference on Data Systems Languages (CODASYL)   A conference, now permanent, convened by the Department of Defense in 1959 to develop a standard programming language the result of which, in 1960, was COBOL.

Critical path   The sequence of activities, as shown on a PERT or Critical Path Method (CPM) network, along which any delay will cause a delay in the completion of the project.

Data   In an MIS or data processing context: unprocessed information; the input to an information-processing system.

Data analysis   The use of a terminal or other on-line input/output device to perform mathematical or statistical analyses of data stored in a data base or master file.

Data base   Collectively, all data files in an organization; the collection of data records in a data base management system.

Data base administrator (DBA)   The individual in an MIS office responsible for establishing data policy and maintaining the security and integrity of the data base.

Data base management system (DBMS) A software or software/ hardware combination that maintains data in direct access storage devices and makes them available to application programs or management queries.

Data description language (DDL) The data base management system language used to describe the *schema* of the data base.

Data element The smallest unit of data that can stand alone and convey information.

Data file A collection of related data records.

Data management routines (DMR) The portion of data base management system software, comparable to the operating system of a computer, that establishes interface with the storage devices in which the data base is maintained.

Data manipulation language (DML) The data base management system language used to define records and to call them out of the data base for processing by an application program.

Data processing The manipulation of data by a computer to support the recordkeeping and report generation activities in an organization.

Data record A collection of related data elements.

Data set The term, in the System 2000 data base management system, to describe a logical collection of data elements analogous to a record.

Debugging The process of finding and correcting errors in a computer program.

Decision support system A specialized form of MIS devoted exclusively to the support of decision making at upper levels of management.

Decision tree A branching diagram of the payoffs and probabilities in a decision situation. Decision trees are particularly useful to analyze multistage decisions.

Design In the decision-making process: suggesting and evaluating alternative solutions to a problem.

Detail reports Reports that include information on all transactions within the subject matter covered by the report.

Device media control language (DMCL) A specialized language used to assign physical storage space to data in a data base.

Direct access storage device (DASD) A storage device, such as a disk drive, in which any storage location can be accessed directly, without regard to physical sequence.

Distributed system A system of electronically linked computers. A *star* system uses a large, central computer while a *ring* system consists only of distributed computers.

Element In set terminology: the fundamental unit of a set. In the System 2000 data base management system terminology: a component, comparable to a data element, that has a value and conveys information.

Exception reports   Reports that give only information that falls within certain management-defined parameters.

Expected value   A weighted average; the sum of the products of alternative payoffs weighted by the probability of outcomes; the generally accepted decision criterion under risk.

Feasibility study   A study to determine if a major endeavor, such as developing a new MIS, is economically, technically, and behaviorably feasible.

Feedback   Output of a system that is used to keep the system under control.

FORTRAN   *For*mula *Trans*lation, an application programming language particularly well suited to mathematical applications.

Functional subsystem   In an MIS: the collection of application programs, procedures, information flows, and decision processes to support a specific organizational function, such as production.

Gantt chart   A project management technique in which activities are represented as horizontal lines on a graph which has its horizontal axis labeled in units of time.

Hardware   The physical components of a computer, such as input devices, the central processing unit (CPU), and output devices.

Hashing   The use of an algorithm for converting the value of a data element into a random storage location. Also called "key transformation."

Heuristic programming   The simulation of human judgment with a computer program.

Holism   To view as a whole instead of a collection of parts. Systems are said to be holistic. (Also spelled wholism.)

Host language (DBMS)   A data base management system in which the data manipulation language (DML) statements are incorporated into a standard application programming language.

Iconic Model   A physical model that *looks* like the real-world object it represents.

Immediate conversion   A technique in which the new system replaces the old system in one sweeping change without phasing or parallel operations.

Information analyst   A systems analyst who helps functional users identify information needs and use the MIS to satisfy those needs.

Inquiry processing   The use of a terminal or other on-line input/output device to obtain limited information from a data base or master file.

Intelligence   In the decision-making process: the identification of a problem and the collection of input data essential to the solution of the problem.

Inverted tree   A revised tree data structure in which data are placed at different levels to create a desired subschema or simply to show an alternative representation of the data hierarchy.

Key element   An element, usually numerical, in a data record that uniquely identifies the record and facilitates access to it.

Linear programming   An optimizing technique of management science used when a decision situation can be described with linear equations.

Logic error   A programming error that violates no programming rules but causes incorrect or inappropriate output.

Logical entry   The term, in the System 2000 data base management system, to define a hierarchy of data sets.

Machine language   A binary code of 1's and 0's represented by the presence or absence of an electronic pulse.

Macro flowchart   A general flowchart showing the relationships between users and program modules of an MIS. The basis for micro flowcharting. Also called a **Systems flowchart.**

Magnetic ink character recognition (MICR)   A system, used almost exclusively by the banking industry on checks, to read and write stylized characters printed in magnetic ink.

Mainframe   A large computer capable of handling many peripherals and/or satellite computers.

Maintenance programmer   A special category of application programmer whose job it is to make corrections or other changes to application software.

Management audit   A postinstallation check to determine whether or not an MIS is satisfying the information needs of management.

Management information system (MIS)   An organized set of processes that provides information to managers to support the operations and decision making within an organization.

Master file   The basic reference collection of records for a specific application.

Mathematical model   A symbolic model that uses mathematical expressions to describe a real-world object or situation.

Maximax   A decision-making strategy under uncertainty in which an optimistic attitude prevails; to pick the alternative with the greatest *maximum* payoff.

Maximin   A decision-making strategy under uncertainty in which a pessimistic attitude prevails; to pick the alternative with the greatest *minimum* payoff.

Microcomputer   A very small (hand-held or desk-top) computer. Sometimes called a "personal computer."

Micro flowchart   A very detailed flowchart in which each symbol represents a single input, output, or process. The output of systems analysis upon which programming is based. Also called a **Programming flowchart.**

Microprogramming   The technique of substituting coded instructions (software) for electronic circuitry (hardware).

Milestone chart   A project management technique in which key events (milestones) are listed with their expected completion dates.

Minicomputer   A small-to-intermediate sized computer, often with capabilities that exceed those of all but the largest computers of ten years ago.

Model   An abstraction of reality used when the real-world situation represented is too complex, too costly, or too time-consuming for experimentation.

Model bank   The collection, in an on-line storage device, of the application programs and mathematical models used in an MIS.

Modem   An acronym for *mo*dulator-*dem*odulator, a data communications device that converts digital data into an analog, such as a modulated sound signal, and back again.

Multiprocessing   A timesharing technique in which two or more programs are executed simultaneously. Multiprocessing is a hardware feature.

Multiprogramming   A timesharing technique in which programs are executed while the CPU is idle with respect to other programs. Multiprogramming is achieved through systems software.

Node   In drawing decision trees, network diagrams, or data structures: a circle from which branches or arcs emanate. In network diagrams: an event.

Nonprogrammable decision   A decision that, because of the nonquantitative nature of the input data or the requirement for subjective evaluation cannot be made computationally. Also called an **Unstructured decision.**

Off-line   Not in direct electronic linkage with the CPU. Off-line storage must be brought on-line by an operator before it can be accessed by an application program.

On-line   In direct electronic linkage with the CPU. On-line storage can be accessed by application programs without operator assistance.

Operational activity   The applications of MIS, such as programmable decision making, ordinarily associated with first-line management.

Operational audit   A postinstallation check to determine whether or not an MIS is performing to the standards against which it was designed.

Optimize   To select the best possible alternative in a decision-making situation; to **maximize** (profits, income, etc.) or to **minimize** (cost, time, etc.).

Parallel conversion   A technique in which the old or manual system continues to operate for a few cycles as a check on the accuracy of the new system.

Parity   An extra bit added to the binary representation of a character as a check against loss of a bit during transmission. In *even parity*, a bit is added to make the total number of bits in the character even. Similarly, parity can be odd.

Performance evaluation and review technique (PERT)   A network analysis technique used in project management. PERT is particularly helpful in complex, long-range projects such as MIS development.

Performance monitor   A means, either using software or hardware, of measuring the efficiency of a computer in processing the application programs of an MIS.

Phase-in conversion   A technique in which one program or application at a time is introduced until the old or manual system is eventually replaced with the new system.

Pilot conversion   A technique in which the new system is implemented in a limited fashion—in one plant or in one product line—until it can be determined that the system works and can be implemented organization-wide.

Plex data structure   A hierarchical representation of the logical relationships between data in which higher levels may have many branches to lower levels and any lower level may be related to more than one higher level.

Pointer   A data element inserted in a record to show the storage location of the next record to be processed.

Programmable decision   A decision that can be reached by following certain rules that lead to unambiguous results; routine decisions involving quantitative inputs and computational processes. Also called a **Structured decision.**

Programming flowchart   See **Micro flowchart.**

Query language (QL)   The data base management system language employed by users at terminals to make inquiries or perform data analyses on data in the data base.

Random file   A file in which records are stored in random locations selected by a hashing or key transformation process.

Real-time processing   The updating of a master file or data base with transaction data in time for feedback to influence the outcome of the transaction; extremely rapid transactional processing.

Reasonableness check   Limits on numerical data, such as pay or an order quantity, beyond which the data will be rejected from processing.

Regression analysis   A statistical prediction technique based on the values of variables related to the predicted variable.

Relational data base   A flat, two-dimensional, tabular representation of the logical relationships between data in a data base.

Repeating group The term, in the System 2000 data base management system, to identify a number of similar data sets.

Risk A decision-making environment in which the outcomes of future events are not known, but probabilities can be assigned to those outcomes.

Satisfice To select the first alternative that meets predefined criteria; the decision-making process associated with administrative behavior.

Scheduled reports Reports that are produced at regular intervals—daily, weekly, etc.

Schema An overall description of the relationship between data elements in a data base; the data base administrator's view of data.

Self-contained (DBMS) A data base management system in which a unique language is used for application programming and as a data manipulation language (DML) and/or data description language.

Sequential access storage device (SASD) A storage device, such as a tape drive, in which each record must be read in the physical sequence in which it is stored in order to be accessed by an application program.

Sequential file A file in which records are stored in alphabetical or numerical sequence.

Serial file A file in which records, usually transactions, are stored in the order in which they occurred or were recorded.

Simulation To mimic or imitate a process. When random numbers are used to assign values to process variables, the technique is called *Monte Carlo* simulation.

Software The symbolic component of a computer system, to include the operating system, the data base management system, compilers, and application programs.

Special reports Reports for which application software does not exist when the report is requested and must be specially prepared before the report can be produced.

Strategic activity The applications of MIS, such as generating summary reports and simulation of long-range financial plans, ordinarily associated with top management.

Structured decision See **Programmable decision.**

Structured programming An approach to writing application programs according to a specified format or structure to facilitate program maintenance.

Subschema The relationship among data elements in a data base required for a specific application program; the user's view of data.

Subsystem A part of a system that is itself a system; the hierarchical level of systems below the one under consideration. A production information system is a subsystem of an MIS.

Summary reports   Reports that use summary measures, such as the mean, the range, or the standard deviation, to describe data in less volume than detail reports.

Supercomputer   A very large computer, frequently one-of-a-kind, marked by extraordinary processing speeds and storage capacities.

Suprasystem   A system made up of other systems; the hierarchical level of systems above the one under consideration. An MIS is a system in the suprasystem of the organization.

System   A set of interrelated parts that work together to accomplish some goal or objective.

Systems analysis   The analytical process of determining information needs in an organization and describing an information system to satisfy those needs.

Systems designer   A systems analyst who describes, with flowcharts and other techniques, the programs that will produce information needed by managers.

Systems flowchart   See **Macro flowchart.**

Systems programmer   One who prepares, frequently in machine language, operating systems, compilers, data base management systems, and other systems software.

Synergism   The systems attribute of the sum being *more* than the total of its parts.

Synonym   A record that, as a result of hashing or key transformation, is assigned to a storage location already occupied by another record.

Syntax error   A programming error that violates one or more rules of the programming language and may prevent the program from being executed.

Tactical activity   The applications of MIS, such as generating exception reports and using management science models, ordinarily associated with a middle management.

Terminal   An on-line input and/or output device, usually with keyboard entry and cathode ray tube (CRT) or typewriter output; a flowcharting symbol for the beginning or end of a program sequence.

Timesharing   The use of a computer system by several users simultaneously.

Totals check   A verification technique that compares total or net changes after processing to the total or net changes represented by transactions before processing.

Transaction file   A collection of transactions (additions, deletions, or changes) for the purpose of updating a master file.

Transaction processing   The preparation, editing, sorting, classifying, storing, retrieving, and limited calculating of data for recordkeeping, report generation, and input to managerial activities.

Transactional processing   The updating of a master file or data base with transaction data as the transactions occur.

Tree data structure   A hierarchical representation of the logical relationships between data in which higher levels may have many branches to lower levels but each lower level is related to only one higher level.

Trend analysis   A statistical prediction technique based on past performance of the predicted variable.

Uncertainty   A decision-making environment in which the outcomes of future events are not known nor can probabilities be assigned to outcomes.

Unscheduled reports   Reports that can be produced with existing application programs but are not unless specifically requested. Also called *demand* or *on-call* reports.

Unstructured decision   See **Nonprogrammable decision.**

Verification   The process by which data are checked for accuracy; in card input, the keying of data into a *verifier* for comparison to data already punched into the card.

Index

Index

A

Accounts payable, 241–42
Accounts receivable, 241
Administrative behavior, 82–84
Arithmetic and logic unit (ALU), 23
Audits, 163–64
  financial, 163
  management, 163
  operational, 163
  trail, 240

B

Bayes' theorem, 93n
Bit, 22
Budget, 237–38
Byte, 22

C

Card
  Hollerith, 28
  reader, 28, 33t
  system, 52–53
Central processing unit (CPU), 21
Conference on data systems languages (CODASYL), 195
Computers
  classification, 43, 44t
  generations of, 118–20, 131n
  hardware, 21–38
  host, 37
  language, 39–41
    assembler, 39
    BASIC, 40
    COBOL, 40, 49, 190
    FORTRAN, 40
    GPSS, 41

Computers (*cont.*)
  problem-oriented, 41
  procedure-oriented, 41
  RPG, 41
  translator, 40
  mainframe, 44*t*, 45
  memory. *See* Storage
  micro-, 44*t*, 45
  mini-, 44*t*, 45
  in MIS, 15
  operators, 125
  programs. *See* Software
  satellite, 38
  social issues, 95
  super-, 44*t*, 45
Control
  in management, 100, 107, 210
  in MIS, 13, 139–41, 160–64
Controller, 24
Coordinating
  in management, 100
  reports, 107
Core memory, 22
Cost accounting, 238
Cost/benefit analysis, 162
Critical path method (CPM),
  140–41

D

Data
  actual, 210–11
  element, 147
  external, 210–11, 220
  file, 47
  hierarchy, 47
  internal, 210–11
  processing. *See* Data processing
  record, 47
  security, 173, 204
  standard, 210–11, 220
Data analysis, 110–12, 201, 220
Data base, 172–73, 191, 199, 202,
  204, 218–19

Data base administrator (DBA),
  124, 127, 188, 204
Data base management systems
  (DBMS), 18, 108, 172, 174,
  185–205
Data base task group (DBTG),
  195
Data description language (DDL),
  188–189
Data management routines
  (DMR), 186
Data manipulation language
  (DML), 189–90
Data processing, 46–62
  and MIS, 16, 61
Data structures, 191–94
  plex, 193–94
  relational, 194
  tree, 191–92
Decisions
  under certainty, 76–84
  compromise, 65
  computational, 64
  environment of, 64–66
  financial, 81–82
  inspirational, 65
  judgmental, 64–65
  nonprogrammable, 219
  phases of, 210–15
    choice, 214–15
    design, 213–14
    intelligence, 210–12
  programmable, 218–19
  under risk, 71–76
  strategies, 66–84
  structured, 208–209
  trees, 72–76
  under uncertainty, 66–70
  unstructured, 90, 208–10
Decision support systems, 180
Device media control language
  (DMCL), 186
Disk
  drive, 26, 30, 33*t*, 58–60
  floppy, 27, 111

pack, 26
system, 55–56

E

Economic order quantity (EOQ),
  80, 213
Entropy, 12
Errors, 152–53, 159–60
  detection, 159–60
  logic, 152–53
  syntax, 153–54
Estimates, 85–86
  interval, 85
  point, 85
Expected value, 71–72

F

Feasibility (of MIS), 135–137
  behavioral, 136–37
  economic, 136
  studies, 135–37
  technical, 136
Feedback, 13
File
  card, 52–53
  design, 150
  disk, 55
  master, 48, 53–61
  random, 49, 55, 59
  sequential, 49, 53–54, 56–59
  serial, 51
  tape, 52–53
  transaction, 48, 53–61
Finance subsystem (of MIS),
  237–43
Financial accounting, 240
Firmware, 24
Flowcharts, 146
  programming, 146
  system, 146
Funds management, 239

G

Gantt chart, 139

H

Hashing, 49
Holism, 10

I

Inquiry processing, 108–10
Inventory analysis, 79–80

K

Key transformation, 49
Keypunch machine, 28

L

Labor relations, 243–44
Light pen, 35
Linear programming, 76–78, 214

M

Magnetic ink, 32, 33t
Management
  cycle, 100, 103
  hierarchy, 101–102
  information systems. See Man-
    agement information systems
  and MIS, 18
  process, 98–100, 102, 133
Management information systems
  (MIS)
  committee, 124
  conversion, 155–57
    immediate, 156–57

MIS (*cont.*)
    parallel, 155–56
    phase-in, 156
    pilot, 156
    planning, 157
  and data processing, 16, 61
  and decision making, 93
  defined, 9
  design, 142–51
    and analysis, 145–51
    bottom-up, 142–43
    eclectic, 144–45
    file, 150
    input, 149
    logical system, 146–50
    modular, 143–44
    output, 146–47
    physical system, 150–51
    process, 149–50
    top-down, 142
    total system, 143
  development, 141–51
  director, 124
  impact on management,
    112–16
  and management, 18
  management implications, 97
  master plan, 137–41
  model of, 169–84
  objectives, 135
  office, 120–23
  and organizations, 130
  personnel, 123–26
  responsibility for, 117
  role in management, 104–12
  security, 157–60
Marketing research, 233
Marketing subsystem (of MIS),
    231–37
Mark-sense reader, 32, 33*t*
Material requirements planning
    (MRP), 226–27
Maximax strategy, 67–68
Maximin strategy, 68

Microprogramming, 24
Milestone schedule, 139, 140*t*
Models
  analog, 170
  bank, 111, 172, 175, 218, 235
  descriptive, 92
  deterministic, 80, 90
  dynamic, 90
  iconic, 169
  mathematical, 170
  MIS, 170–83
  optimization, 77
  selection, 213
  static, 90
  strategic, 214
  symbolic, 170–71
  verbal, 171
Modem, 37
Monitors, 164
  hardware, 164
  performance, 164
  software, 164
Multiprocessing, 38

O

Operational level (of MIS),
    177–78, 212, 218–19
Opportunity loss, 69–70
Optical scanner, 32, 33*t*
Organization
  and MIS, 130
  of MIS office, 121–23
  theory, 99
Organizing
  in management process, 99

P

Payoff table, 67–68, 68*t*
Payroll, 245–46
Performance, monitors, 164

Personnel subsystem (of MIS), 243–46
Planning
  in management process, 98
  for MIS, 133–41
Pointer, 57, 192–93
Postinstallation review, 162–63
Present value, 82
  net present value, 82
Printer, 34, 36*t*
  character, 34, 36*t*
  impact, 34, 36*t*
  nonimpact, 34, 36*t*
Probability, 71–75
  conditional, 74
  revised, 74
  simple, 73–74
Process generator, 90
Processing
  data. *See* Data processing
  dimensions, 175
  modes
    batch, 56–58
    real-time, 60–61
    transaction, 176–77, 212, 216–18
    transactional, 58–60
Production subsystem (of MIS), 225–31
Program evaluation and review technique (PERT), 139–41
Programs
  application, 39
  heuristic, 65
  See also Computers; Software
Programmers, 125, 139
  application, 125
  systems, 125
Progress review, 160–61

Q

Quality control, 231
Query language, 190–91

R

Register, 23
Regression analysis, 88–89
  multiple, 89
  regression line, 89
  simple, 89
Reports
  control, 107
  coordinating, 107
  detail, 106, 223
  exception, 106, 219
  scheduled, 104
  special, 105–106
  summary, 106, 219
  unscheduled, 105
Request for proposal (RFP), 151

S

Schema, 188
Simulation, 90–92
  Monte Carlo, 91
Site preparation, 152
Software, 39–45
  application, 39
  system, 41
    control programs, 41
    service programs, 41
Staffing
  in management process, 99
Strategic level (of MIS), 179–80, 220–21
Storage
  devices
    direct access, 26, 58, 108
    off-line, 24
    on-line, 24
    sequential access, 24
    virtual, 42
Subschema, 188–89
Subsystem, 12, 180, 223–45
Suprasystem, 12

Synergism, 11
Synonym, 50
System, 9–15
  distributed, 37–38
    star, 37, 128
    ring, 38, 127
  media-oriented, 51–56
    card, 52–53
    disk, 55–56
    tape, 53–54
  operating, 41
  view, 222
System 2000, 195–204
Systems analysis, 124
  personnel, 124–25

T

Tactical level (of MIS), 179,
  219–20
Tape
  Magnetic, 25, 29–30
    drive, 29–30, 33t

paper, 32, 33t
  punch, 32
  reader, 32
  system, 53–54
Terminal, 31, 33t, 108–109, 175,
  204
  cathode ray tube (CRT),
    34–35, 60
  intelligent, 31
  point-of-sale, 32, 58
  remote job entry, 32
Testing
  acceptance, 161
  and debugging, 152–53
  systems, 161
Theory X, 130
Theory Y, 130
Timesharing, 42, 54
Training, 153–55, 245
Trend analysis, 86–87, 111

V

Verifier, 28